1992 NEW YORK AREA GOLF GUIDE
A Guide to Facilities Open to the Public

The Golfers Advantage

A Powers Golf Guide
Briarcliff Press, Inc.

Every effort has been made to provide dependable data in this guide. The great majority of the information was supplied by the courses. However, the publisher does not warrant that the data contained herein is complete or accurate. Any rates, special offers, etc, are subject to change by the individual golf courses and are not guaranteed by Briarcliff Press, Inc. It is recommended that you call the course ahead of time, whether or not tee times are required, and that prices and directions be verified.

Cover Photo: Courtesy of Jacqueline Duvoisin/Sports Illustrated
Cover Design: Ron Meckler, Re:Design, NYC
              Cover electronically painted

ISBN 0-9631658-0-1

To contact us, call (800) 446-8884
or write to: **Powers Golf Guides**
              Briarcliff Press, Inc.
              PO Box 1961, NYC 10011

To order additional guides, send $12.95 plus $1.50 for shipping and handling.

$1.50 from the sale of each guide will be donated to Muscular Dystrophy.

YOU'RE INVITED TO PLAY OVER 500 ROUNDS OF GOLF FREE AT 350 MICHIGAN GOLF COURSES

Each year more golfers than ever are making Michigan their primary golf vacation destination. One reason is, wherever you play in Michigan, there's another course just over the next horizon and over 600 of the courses are open to the public, more than you'll find in any other state. And with a copy of the Michigan Golfers Map & Guide they can find out where they all are and will be able to get more distance from their golf vacation dollars.

The 1992 Michigan Golfers Map & Guide names and describes each public golf course in Michigan, S.W. Ontario and N.W. Ohio in detail; holes, par, yards, USGA Rating, green fees, club house and course information. The exact location of each course is also pinpointed on area maps.

Slice your green fees in half!

The Michigan Golfers Map & Guide also contains certificates allowing two golfers to play over 500 rounds of golf for the price of one at over 350 golf facilities throughout Michigan, S.W. Ontario and N.W. Ohio. For the past ten years golfers have come to rely on it as their primary source of information and have discovered it literally pays for itself over and over again.

For a copy of the 1992 Michigan Golfers Map & Guide mail $15.95 (Mich. Res. add 4% sales tax) plus $2 shipping to RSG Publishing, Inc., P.O. Box 612, Plymouth, MI 48170.

Credit card orders can call
_1-800-223-5877._

Directions to an Endless Golf Adventure in the Great Lakes Region

Throughout the Great Lakes region there's an open tee time waiting for you everyday at over 2000 public golf courses and if your a member of a private golf club you also have an opportunity to play at hundreds of private courses.

Five regional editions of the "Golfers Travel Guides" name every public and private golf course, provides their address (including directions), phone number, holes, par, yardage and USGA rating. Estimated green fees, power cart rates, special discounts, plus course and club house amenities of public and resort courses are also featured.

The **"Michigan Golfers Travel Guide"** lists over 750 golf courses, the **Ohio** edition over 700 courses, the **Indiana** edition 400 courses including 250 courses in N.E. Illinois, the **Illinois** edition 600 courses including 85 courses in N.W. Indiana and the **Wisconsin / Minnesota** edition lists over 750 courses.

Order any one of the five editions at $6.95; (additional copies $5.95 each) plus a total of $2 for shipping and handling (MI Res. add 4% sales tax). Send check to RSG Publishing, Inc., P.O. Box 612, Plymouth MI 48170.

*Credit Card Orders call **1-800-223-5877.***

Table Of Contents

Dedicated to Roy Rasmussen

The best way to improve your game is to get on the right course!

It's really in no ones interest to perpetuate the notion that there aren't enough courses for the burgeoning ranks of golfers in this country. Yet, we don't know any public course golfer who feels there is an adequate number of courses or tee times within a reasonable distance from their home.

The 1992 New York Area Golf Guide is designed to dispel that notion and to give every golfer a range of choices that appeals to their level of play and desire for challenge, regardless of where they live. There is every type of facility imaginable within an area stretching from Connecticut to Southern New Jersey and from the tip of Long Island to the Poconos.

And to make it even more appealing, there are 97 rounds of free golf, plus other incentives, available to you through this guide.

In using the guide, there are several things to keep in mind. First, things change! Despite our efforts to ensure our data's accuracy, some prices, tee time rules, and other regulations may differ slightly by the opening of the 1992 season. You are urged to call ahead, especially if you are using a coupon.

Second, all the coupons come with stipulations, so please read them carefully. Having a coupon does not entitle the bearer to benefits and courtesies not granted to any other player. You'll still need to reserve tee times. If you follow the stipulations in each coupon, it is likely that these courses and many more will invite you for a free round or two in 1993.

Third, for the benefit of the courses and the growth of this program, the coupons must be validated in the book. There is no guarantee they will be honored if they are torn out. So keep this guide with your clubs.

Don't let anyone tell you it's tough to play out there. There is a lot of golf available to the public in this region. Enjoy it and we'll look forward to seeing you again next year!

The Publishers

NOTES ON USING THE GUIDE:

• Directions were provided by the courses, but they may not be from your particular vantage point. It will be helpful to carry a map.

• The yardage of the courses is listed from the back tees, in most cases the blues. Make adjustments for play from the white or red tees.

• The operating times listed are for mid-season. Adjustments should be made for seasonal variations.

• In cases where different fee schedules apply, those listed are for non-residents or non-members during mid-season.

• Rates are subject to change. Many of the rates listed here were those effective in 1991. Expect modest increases at most courses. Many of the Connecticut course prices are without the addition of the sales tax.

Connecticut

Connecticut

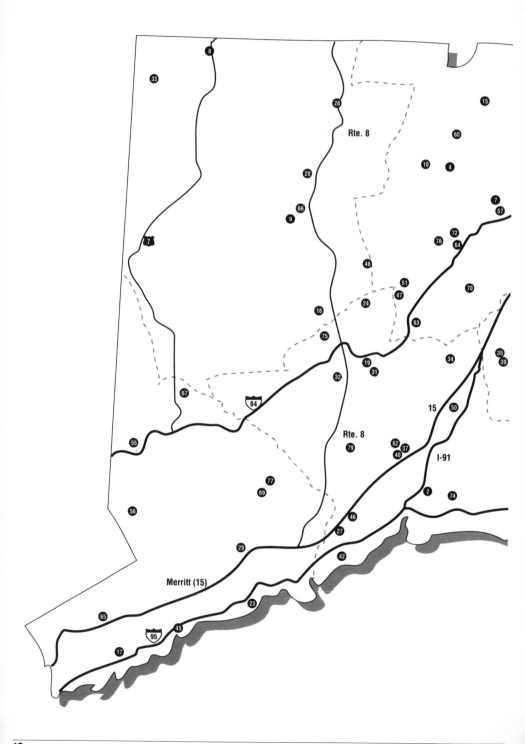

Connecticut

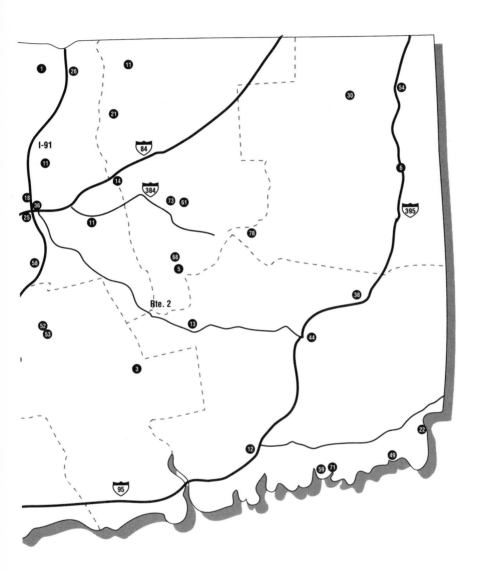

Airways Golf Course

1070 S. Grand, Suffield CT — Tee Times: (203)668-4973

Directions: North of Hartford on I-91 to Exit 40. Go West on Rte 20 to the town of East Granby. Go right at the 4th light (East St.), and the course is 1.5 mi. on right.

Facility Type: Public

Coupon page 53

Club Pro: Wayne Leal
Discounts: Seniors
Tee Times: Yes, Thursday for the following week.

Features: Lessons, Pro Shop - Limited, Bar, Snack Bar, Clubhouse

Description: A flat course and an easy walk for seniors.

Holes	Par	Yards Back Tees	Rating	Slope
18	70	5659	65.7	105

	9 Holes	18 Holes	Hours Mid Season
Weekday:	$8.75	$17.00	Dawn to Dusk
Weekend:	$9.50	$18.00	Dawn to Dusk
Cart Fees:	$10.00	$20.00	

Mandatory Cart Rental: No
Club Rental: Yes

Alling Memorial Golf Course

35 Eastern Street, New Haven CT — Info: (203)787-8014   Tee Times: (203)787-8013

Directions: I-91 to Exit 8, Rte 80 East to the 2nd light, Eastern Street. Take a right and course is 1/2 mi. on left.

Facility Type: Public

Coupon page 53

Club Pro: John Wilson
Discounts: Seniors, Juniors
Tee Times: Yes, weekends only, 3 days prior after 12 PM

Features: Lessons, Showers/Lockers, Practice Area, Pro Shop - Complete, Restaurant, Bar, Clubhouse, Banquet Facilities

Description: This a Robert Pride design. The course is picturesque with rolling hills, open fairways but small greens and some water hazards. It is a good play for all handicap levels.

Holes	Par	Yards Back Tees	Rating	Slope
18	72	6241	69.5	123

	9 Holes	18 Holes	Hours Mid Season
Weekday:	$12.00	$23.00	6 am - Dusk
Weekend:	—	$24.00	6 am - Dusk
Cart Fees:	$11.00	$19.00	

Mandatory Cart Rental: No
Club Rental: Yes

Notes: Lower rates for New Haven residents. Weekends and holidays for non-residents only after 3 PM. No 9 hole rate on weekends or holidays.

Banner Lodge Country Club   CT 3

10 Moodus Rd, Moodus CT — Tee Times: (203)873-9075

Directions: Ct Rte 9 to Exit 7 (Rte 82) to Rte 154 North. Turn left. At the first light take a right onto Rte 82 again. Go over the swing bridge and left onto Rte 149. Go 5 mi. to Moodus Rd at the top of the hill and take a left. Go 3/4 mi. to Banner Rd left. The course is on the right.

Facility Type: Public

Club Pro: John Holst
Discounts: None
Tee Times: Yes, Tuesday before for weekends/holidays,

Features: Lessons, Driving Range, Practice Area, Pro Shop - Complete, Restaurant, Bar, Snack Bar

Description: This is a challenging course, but the average golfer can still score and enjoy playing on it. The course is hilly with small greens that are in excellent shape. Water comes into play on 6 holes.

Holes	Par	Yards Back Tees	Rating	Slope
18	72	6000	69.8	118

	9 Holes	18 Holes	Hours Mid Season
Weekday:	$8.50	$16.00	7 am - Dusk
Weekend:	$10.00	$18.00	6 am - Dusk
Cart Fees:	$9.00	$18.00	

Mandatory Cart Rental: No
Club Rental: Yes

Notes: Memberships are avilable for 1992. Weekday special - 2 people, 18 holes with cart, $40 before 1 pm.

Bel Compo Golf Club   CT 4

65 Nod Road, Avon CT — Tee Times: (203)678-1358

Directions: I-84 to Exit 39 (Rte 10 North). Go 5 mi. to the intersection of Rte 44. Go through the intersection and Rte 10 becomes Nod Road. The course 1/4 mi. on left.

Facility Type: Public

Club Pro: Skip Rotondo
Discounts: Seniors
Tee Times: Yes, Prior Thursday at 8 AM for weekends/holidays,

Features: Lessons, Driving Range, Practice Area, Pro Shop - Complete, Restaurant, Bar, Snack Bar

Description: The Farmington River runs through this course. The front 9 is tight and wooded, and the back 9 more open. The signature hole is your finisher, in more ways than one. It's a 434 yard par 4. The 2nd shot has to carry a large pond that surrounds the green on the front. The 2-tiered green is also guarded by a bunker on the left.

Holes	Par	Yards Back Tees	Rating	Slope
18	72	7028	73.4	131

	9 Holes	18 Holes	Hours Mid Season
Weekday:	$10.00	$19.00	7:00 am - 7:00 pm
Weekend:	$14.00	$23.50	6:00 am - 7:00 pm
Cart Fees:	$11.00	$22.00	

Mandatory Cart Rental: No
Club Rental: Yes

Blackledge Country Club   CT 5

180 West Street, Hebron CT — Tee Times: (203)228-0250

Directions: Rte 2 East to Exit 12. Go left off the ramp. The second left is West St. to the course. Rte 2 West to Exit 13. Go right to Rte 66, left onto Rte 85, which becomes Rte 94. Turn left onto West St. and go 1 mi. to the course.

Facility Type: Public

Club Pro: Tony Roberto
Discounts: Seniors, Juniors, Twilight
Tee Times: Yes, Monday for following weekend for play after 11.

Features: Lessons, Showers/Lockers, Driving Range, Practice Area, Pro Shop - Complete, Restaurant, Bar, Snack Bar, Banquet Facilities, Clubhouse

Description: The course features aerated greens and watered fairways. Much improvement has gone into this Geoffrey Cornish design recently. Black-ledge has been one of Golf Digest's choices for "Places to Play" for the last two years.

Holes	Par	Yards Back Tees	Rating	Slope
18	72	6853	72.3	123

	9 Holes	18 Holes	Hours Mid Season
Weekday:	$10.00	$20.00	7:00 am - 7:00 pm
Weekend:	$11.00	$22.00	6:00 am - 7:00 pm
Cart Fees:	$9.00	$18.00	

Mandatory Cart Rental: No
Club Rental: Yes

Notes: Golf Shop Operations magazine has selected the pro shop as one of the top 20 at public courses in the country several years running.

Brooklyn Country Club   CT 6

170 South St, Danielson CT — (203)779-2400

Directions: I-395 to Exit 91 (Rte 6 West). Go 1 mile to the rotary and follow signs to Brooklyn/Hartford/Rte 6 West. Turn left at the sign for Brooklyn CC opposite Markley Motors. Go 8/10 mi. to South Street and take a left to course.

Facility Type: Public

Club Pro: Ray Carignan
Discounts: None
Tee Times: No

Coupon page 53

Features: Lessons, Driving Range, Pro Shop - Limited, Bar, Snack Bar

Description: This is a picturesque and wooded course with rolling fairways. The greens are in excellent condition. #9 is a 150 yard par 4 carry over water to a small and slanted green.

Holes	Par	Yards Back Tees	Rating	Slope
9	35	2880	—	—

	9 Holes	18 Holes	Hours Mid Season
Weekday:	$8.00	$14.00	7:00 am - Dusk
Weekend:	$9.00	$16.00	6:00 am - Dusk
Cart Fees:	$9.00	$18.00	

Mandatory Cart Rental: No
Club Rental: Yes

Notes: Memberships are available. Call for weekday specials during the fall.

Buena Vista Golf Course

CT 7

37 Buena Vista Rd., West Hartford CT — **Info:** (203)521-7359

Directions: Going either direction on I-84, take Exit 43. Make a left at the end of the ramp onto Park Rd. Go through 3 traffic lights and take the first left onto Buena Vista Rd. Look for course signs on the left.

Facility Type: Public

Club Pro: None
Discounts: None
Tee Times: No

Features: Practice Area

Description: This is a short course. It's good for beginners and seniors with some relatively challenging holes.

Holes	Par	Yards Back Tees	Rating	Slope
9	31	1832	—	—

	9 Holes	18 Holes	Hours Mid Season
Weekday:	$6.50	—	7:00 am - Dusk
Weekend:	$7.50	—	7:00 am - Dusk
Cart Fees:	—	—	

Mandatory Cart Rental: No
Club Rental: No

Notes: Residents pay $4 weekday, $5 weekends.

Canaan Country Club

CT 8

South Canaan Rd., Canaan CT — **Tee Times:** (203)824-7683

Directions: In Canaan on Rte 7 watch for the course sign on the left going north and on the right going south.

Facility Type: Public

Club Pro: None
Discounts: Seniors
Tee Times: Yes

Features: Snack Bar, Restaurant, Pro Shop - Complete, Driving Range, Lessons, Practice Area

Description: This is a fairly flat course and a good walk.

Holes	Par	Yards Back Tees	Rating	Slope
9	35	2793	67.0	113

	9 Holes	18 Holes	Hours Mid Season
Weekday:	$10.00	$20.00	7:00 am - 7:00 pm
Weekend:	$10.00	$20.00	7:00 am - 7:00 pm
Cart Fees:	$10.00	$10.00	

Mandatory Cart Rental: No
Club Rental: No

Notes: The personel at this course would not provide us with any information, but in the interest of completeness, we have assembled our own data. We hope it is accurate.

Candlewood Valley CC

401 Danbury Rd., New Milford CT —   Tee Times: (203)354-9359

Directions: Rte 7 to the New Milford Exit. Go toward New Milford, and the course is approximately 4 mi. on left.

Holes	Par	Yards Back Tees	Rating	Slope
18	70	5596	67.0	113

Facility Type: Public

	9 Holes	18 Holes	Hours Mid Season
Weekday:	—	$18.00	7:00 am - 7:00 pm
Weekend:	—	$23.00	6:30 am - 7:00 pm
Cart Fees:	$13.00	$22.00	

Club Pro: Mike Papp
Discounts: Seniors, Twilight
Tee Times: Yes, weekends/holidays only, Thurs 7:30 am before

Mandatory Cart Rental: No
Club Rental: No

Features: Lessons, Showers/Lockers, Practice Area, Pro Shop - Complete, Restaurant, Bar, VISA/MC

Description: This is a flat and well-maintained course, good for seniors. Renovations are expected for '93 that will add yardage.

Canton Golf Course

Canton CT —   Tee Times: (203)693-8305

Directions: The course is on Rte 44, 12 mi. west of Hartford.

Holes	Par	Yards Back Tees	Rating	Slope
9	36	6136	68	117

Facility Type: Public

	9 Holes	18 Holes	Hours Mid Season
Weekday:	$8.50	$16.00	Dawn - Dusk
Weekend:	$9.50	$18.00	Dawn - Dusk
Cart Fees:	$11.00	$22.00	

Club Pro: Walter Lowell
Discounts: Seniors
Tee Times: Yes, Weekends/holidays, 1 day before.

Mandatory Cart Rental: No
Club Rental: Yes

Features: Lessons, Practice Area, Snack Bar, Pro Shop - Complete

Description: This course was built by James Lowell 60 years ago and is still in the family. It is well maintained, with wide fairways and challenging greens. Lessons are taught by Walter Lowell, who was voted "PGA Pro of the Year" in 1978.

Cedar Knob Golf Course

Billings Rd, Somers CT 06071 — Tee Times: (203)749-3550

Directions: I-91 North of Hartford to Exit 47. Take Rte 190 East toward Somers. Go right on Rte 83 and 1 mi. to Billings Rd. Take a right to the course.

Facility Type: Public

Club Pro: John Holst
Discounts: None
Tee Times: Yes, weekends/holidays, 1 week ahead.

Features: Lessons, Driving Range, Practice Area, Pro Shop - Complete, Restaurant, Bar, Snack Bar, Banquet Facilities, Lodging Nearby

Description: A Geoffrey Cornish design, it has large greens and is well-bunkered.

Holes	Par	Yards Back Tees	Rating	Slope
18	72	6735	72.3	119

	9 Holes	18 Holes	Hours Mid Season
Weekday:	$8.50	$16.00	7:00 am - Dusk
Weekend:	$10.00	$18.00	5:30 am - Dusk
Cart Fees:	$9.00	$18.00	

Mandatory Cart Rental: No
Club Rental: Yes

Cedar Ridge Golf Course

18 Drabick Rd, East Lyme CT — (203)739-8439

Directions: I -95 to Exit 74. Take Rte 161 North 1 mi. to Drabick Rd. Turn and the course is on the left.

Facility Type: Executive

Club Pro: Ernie Rose
Discounts: Seniors
Tee Times: No

Features: Lessons, Practice Area, Snack Bar

Description: This is an executive Par 3, however the course plays a lot like regulation with rolling hills and water. It is more challenging than it sounds.

Holes	Par	Yards Back Tees	Rating	Slope
18	54	3200	—	—

	9 Holes	18 Holes	Hours Mid Season
Weekday:	$9.00	$11.00	7:00 am - Dusk
Weekend:	—	$14.00	7:00 am - Dusk
Cart Fees:	—	—	
Club Rental:	Yes		

Notes: No 9 hole play on weekends. No carts.

Chanticlair Golf Course

CT 13

288 Old Hebron Rd, Colchester CT — Tee Times: (203)537-3223

Directions: Rte 2 East to exit 17. Go left off the ramp to the State Police barracks and left on Old Hebron Rd to the course.

Facility Type: Public

Club Pro: None
Discounts: None
Tee Times: Yes, 5 days ahead

Features: Lessons, Practice Area, Pro Shop - Complete, Bar, Snack Bar

Description: This is an easy walking course and a good challenge. An example is the 4th hole, a 138 yd shot to an island green.

Holes	Par	Yards Back Tees	Rating	Slope
9dt	70	5983	69.8	117

	9 Holes	18 Holes	Hours Mid Season
Weekday:	$7.50	$13.00	7:00 am - Dusk
Weekend:	$8.50	$15.00	5:30 am - Dusk
Cart Fees:	$9.00	$18.00	

Mandatory Cart Rental: No
Club Rental: Yes

Notes: 10-play ticket discounts are available. There are accommodations for groups up to 75 during warm weather.

Connecticut Golfland

CT 14

Vernon CT — (203)643-2654

Directions: East on I-84 to Exit 63. Go left onto Rte 83. The course 1 mi. on the left. Going West on I-84 take Exit 64. Make 2 right turns onto Rte 83 and the course 1 mi. on the right.

Facility Type: Pitch & Putt

Club Pro: None
Discounts: Seniors
Tee Times: No

Features: Lessons, Restaurant, Snack Bar

Description: There is miniature golf on the premise and a go cart track.

Holes	Par	Yards Back Tees	Rating	Slope
18	56	980	—	—

	9 Holes	18 Holes	Hours Mid Season
Weekday:	$4.50	—	9:00 am - 9:00 pm
Weekend:	$5.00	—	9:00 am - 9:00 pm
Cart Fees:	—	—	
Club Rental:			

Notes: Clubs are furnished with price.

Copper Hill Country Club — CT 15

145 Newgate Rd, E. Grandby CT — Tee Times: (203)653-6191

Directions: I-91 to Exit 40 North of Hartford. Take Rte 20 West and turn right on Newgate Rd. Take a left at the stop just past the prison. The course is on the right at the bottom of the hill.

Facility Type: Public

Club Pro: Vic Svenberg
Discounts: Seniors, Juniors
Tee Times: Yes, recommended for any day May through Sept.

Features: Lessons, Practice Area, Pro Shop - Complete, Restaurant, Bar, Snack Bar, Clubhouse, Banquet Facilities, Lodging Nearby

Description: The course is slightly rolling with several challenging and narrow fairways. It's a scenic course with mountains all around.

Holes	Par	Yards Back Tees	Rating	Slope
9	36	2886	69.0	116

	9 Holes	18 Holes	Hours Mid Season
Weekday:	$7.00	$13.00	6:30 am - 7:00 pm
Weekend:	$8.00	$16.00	6:30 am - 7:00 pm
Cart Fees:	$9.00	$17.00	

Mandatory Cart Rental: No
Club Rental: Yes

Crestbrook Park Golf Course — CT 16

834 Northfield Rd, Watertown CT — Tee Times: (203)945-3054

Directions: Rte 8 to Exit 37. Go West 1 mi. to Buckingham Rd. Take a right and go to the stop at Northfield Rd. Take a right and the course is on the right.

Facility Type: Public

Club Pro: Ken Gemmell
Discounts: Seniors, Juniors
Tee Times: Yes, weekends/holidays, 2 days prior.

Features: Lessons, Driving Range, Pro Shop - Complete, Restaurant, Bar, Snack Bar

Description: This course is long and difficult. Greens are undulating

Holes	Par	Yards Back Tees	Rating	Slope
18	71	6906	73.8	132

	9 Holes	18 Holes	Hours Mid Season
Weekday:	$10.00	$18.00	7:30 am - Dusk*
Weekend:	$11.00	$20.00	6:30 am - Dusk
Cart Fees:	$11.00	$21.00	

Mandatory Cart Rental: No
Club Rental: Yes

Notes: *On Mondays the course opens at 10 am.

E. Gaynor Brennan Golf Course CT 17

Stamford CT — Tee Times: (203)324-4185

Directions: I-95 to Exit 6. Go North on West Ave to the end. Take a left onto West Broad St. and go 1/2 mi. to the course.

Facility Type: Public

Club Pro: Charles Pugliese Jr.
Discounts: Seniors, Juniors
Tee Times: Yes, beginning on Tuesday for any day.

Features: Lessons, Practice Area, Pro Shop - Complete, Restaurant, Bar, Snack Bar

Description: This course is somewhat hilly with well-maintained greens.

Holes	Par	Yards Back Tees	Rating	Slope
18	71	5868	67.6	122

	9 Holes	18 Holes	Hours Mid Season
Weekday:	$12.00	$18.00	Dawn - Dusk
Weekend:	—	$20.00	Dawn - Dusk
Cart Fees:	$15.00	$20.00	

Mandatory Cart Rental: No
Club Rental: Yes

Notes: There are reduced rates for residents of Stamford.

East Hartford Golf Course CT 18

130 Longhill St, E Hartford CT — Tee Times: (203)528-5082

Directions: I-84 to Exit 60. Take Rte 44 North to E Hartford. Go 1/2 mi. to Longhill St, and take a right. The course is 1/2 mi. on the right.

Facility Type: Public

Club Pro: Richard Thivia
Discounts: Seniors, Juniors
Tee Times: Yes, one week in advance for weekends

Features: Lessons, Showers/Lockers, Practice Area, Pro Shop - Complete, Restaurant, Bar, Banquet Facilities, Clubhouse

Description: This is a flat and wide open course that plays longer than it reads and will test the better golfer. The greens are difficult to judge. A brook touches 7 holes.

Holes	Par	Yards Back Tees	Rating	Slope
18	71	6076	68.6	114

	9 Holes	18 Holes	Hours Mid Season
Weekday:	$9.00	$18.00	7:00 am - Dusk
Weekend:	$10.00	$20.00	6:00 am - Dusk
Cart Fees:	$9.00	$18.00	

Mandatory Cart Rental: No
Club Rental: No

Notes: Reduced rates for residents.

East Mountain Golf Course   CT 19

171 E. Mountain Rd, Waterbury CT — **Tee Times:** (203)753-1425

Directions: I-84 East of Waterbury, take Exit 23 (Hamilton Ave.). Take Rte 69 South for 3 mi. to East Mountain Rd. Take a right, and the course is on the left.

Facility Type: Public

Club Pro: None
Discounts: Juniors, Seniors
Tee Times: Yes, weekends/holidays, 2 days prior

Features: Showers/Lockers, Driving Range, Practice Area, Pro Shop - Limited, Snack Bar

Description: This is an old and very straightforward course built in the 1930's by the WPA. It's good for seniors.

Holes	Par	Yards Back Tees	Rating	Slope
18	68	5927	67	118

	9 Holes	18 Holes	Hours Mid Season
Weekday:	$9.50	$15.50	6:30 am - Dusk
Weekend:	$12.00	$18.00	6:30 am - Dusk
Cart Fees:	$10.00	$17.00	

Mandatory Cart Rental: No
Club Rental: No

Notes: There are programs for seniors from Waterbury and towns surrounding. There is a junior program weekdays before 11. Reduced green fees for Waterbury residents.

Eastwood Country Club   CT 20

1301 Torringford West St, Torrington CT — (203)489-2630

Directions: Rte 8 to Exit 45 (Kennedy Dr). Go East uphill to a 4-way stop. Take a left onto Torringford St. and the course is 1/2 mi. on the left.

Facility Type: Public

Club Pro: None
Discounts: Seniors
Tee Times: No

Features: Showers/Lockers, Practice Area, Pro Shop - Limited, Restaurant, Bar, Banquet Facilities

Description: This is a moderately difficult course with rolling hills and several narrow fairways.

Holes	Par	Yards Back Tees	Rating	Slope
9	36	2933	66.5	111

	9 Holes	18 Holes	Hours Mid Season
Weekday:	$10.00	$15.00	Dawn - Dusk
Weekend:	$12.00	$17.00	Dawn - Dusk
Cart Fees:	$5.50	$11.00	

Mandatory Cart Rental: No
Club Rental: Yes

Notes: Cart fees are per person. Senior discount for weekdays.

Ellington Golf Center

CT 21

125 West Rd, Ellington CT — (203)872-7471

Directions: I-84 East of Hartford to Exit 64-65. Take Rte 83 North. The course is 5 miles on right.

Holes	Par	Yards Back Tees	Rating	Slope
9	27	858	—	—

Facility Type: Pitch & Putt

Club Pro: Jim Kroll

Discounts: Seniors, Juniors

Tee Times: No

	9 Holes	18 Holes	Hours Mid Season
Weekday:	$6.00	—	8:00 am - 10:00 pm
Weekend:	$6.50	—	8:00 am - 10:00 pm
Cart Fees:	—	—	
Club Rental:			

Features: Lessons, Driving Range, Practice Area, Pro Shop - Complete, Restaurant, Bar, Snack Bar

Notes: Clubs are included. There is a complete driving range with buckets available. Open all year.

Description: This is a good starter and practice course, complete with traps. There is a junior program all summer long.

Elmridge Golf Course

CT 22

Elmridge Rd, Pawcatuck CT — **Tee Times:** (203)599-2248

Directions: I-95 to Exit 92. Take Elmridge South to course 1/2 mi. on the right.

Holes	Par	Yards Back Tees	Rating	Slope
18	71	6501	71.2	121

Facility Type: Public

Club Pro: Tom Jones

Discounts: None

Tee Times: Yes, Monday prior for weekend/holidays, Friday for following Mon through Friday.

	9 Holes	18 Holes	Hours Mid Season
Weekday:	$12.50	$19.00	6:30 am - Dusk
Weekend:	—	$21.00	5:00 am - Dusk
Cart Fees:	$12.00	$20.00	

Mandatory Cart Rental: No

Club Rental: Yes

Features: Lessons, Driving Range, Practice Area, Pro Shop - Complete, Restaurant, Bar, Banquet Facilities, Lodging Nearby, VISA/MC, American Express

Description: This is a flat and relatively fair course. The fairways are watered. The signature is #15, a 201 yard par 3. It's uphill to an elevated green with a huge bunker front and right. The green is considerably sloped.

Fairchild Wheeler Golf Course CT 23

2390 Easton Turnpike, Fairfield CT — (203)372-6265

Directions: Merritt Pkwy to the Park Ave Exit in Bridgeport. Go East 1/2 mi. to the course.

Facility Type: Public

Club Pro: Dave McGoldrick
Discounts: None
Tee Times: No, ticket information is on (203)372-6265.

Features: Lessons, Showers/Lockers, Driving Range, Practice Area, Pro Shop - Complete, Restaurant, Bar, Snack Bar, Banquet Facilities

Description: This course is a little hilly. The back nine of the black course is a good par 35. Refurbishing is planned for 1992.

Holes	Par	Yards Back Tees	Rating	Slope
18	72	6402	70.0	124
18	71	6382	69.7	122

	9 Holes	18 Holes	Hours Mid Season
Weekday:	$11.00	$15.00	7:00 am - Dusk
Weekend:	$13.00	$19.00	6:00 am - Dusk
Cart Fees:	$12.00	$19.00	

Mandatory Cart Rental: No
Club Rental: Yes

Notes: Reduced rate for residents.

Farmingbury Hill Country Club CT 24

141 East St, Wolcott CT (203)879-9380

Directions: I-84 to the Exit for Rte 322. (West of Hartford - the truck stop exit). Go North on 322 up a steep hill. Take a right at the top of the hill (still 322) and the course is on the right.

Facility Type: Public

Club Pro: Frank Guerrera
Discounts: Seniors, Juniors
Tee Times: No

Features: Lessons, Showers/Lockers, Pro Shop - Complete, Restaurant, Bar, Snack Bar, Banquet Facilities

Description: There are actually more holes with several double tees. The course is a good test with narrow fairways, small greens and some hills.

Holes	Par	Yards Back Tees	Rating	Slope
9	36	3169	68.4	119

	9 Holes	18 Holes	Hours Mid Season
Weekday:	$8.50	$16.00	7:00 am - 7:00 pm
Weekend:	$8.50	$16.00	6:00 am - 7:00 pm
Cart Fees:	$11.00	$22.00	

Mandatory Cart Rental: No
Club Rental: No

Goodwin Golf Course

1130 Maple Ave, Hartford CT — Tee Times: (203)525-3601

Directions: Going North on I-91, take Exit 27 (Airport Rd). Take a left off the exit and left again at the first stop. Go 1 mile to Maple Ave, and take a left to the course.

Facility Type: Public

Coupon page 54

Club Pro: Kevin Tierney
Discounts: Juniors, Twilight, Seniors
Tee Times: Yes, weekends/holidays - 1 week in advance

Features: Lessons, Driving Range, Practice Area, Pro Shop - Complete, Bar, VISA/MC, Clubhouse, Snack Bar, Lodging Nearby

Description: The 9 hole is a good beginner course, flat and open. The 18 hole is in great shape. Water comes into play several times. The course is a good contrast between open and tight holes. The finishing stretch is the best, especially the 18th. It's a par 4, 456 yard shot to an elevated and contoured green. The fairway is tree-lined and narrow.

Holes	Par	Yards Back Tees	Rating	Slope
9	35	2544	—	—
18	70	5879	67.8	108

	9 Holes	18 Holes	Hours Mid Season
Weekday:	$9.00	$15.00	6:00 am - Dusk
Weekend:	$11.00	$17.00	5:30 am - Dusk
Cart Fees:	$10.00	$17.00	

Mandatory Cart Rental: No
Club Rental: Yes

Notes: Reduced green fees for Hartford residents.

Grassmere Country Club

130 Town Farm Rd, Enfield CT — Tee Times: (203)749-7740

Directions: Going North on I-91 north of Hartford take Exit 46. At the end of the exit ramp take a right. Take another right at the third light. This is Post Office Rd, which becomes Town Farm Rd. The course is approximately 1 mi. on right.

Facility Type: Public

Coupon page 54

Club Pro: None
Discounts: Seniors
Tee Times: Yes, 2 days prior for any day.

Features: Practice Area, Pro Shop - Limited, Restaurant, Bar, Snack Bar, Banquet Facilities, Clubhouse

Description: This course mixes everything, including sand and water, for a good challenge. It's a good walking course, as well.

Holes	Par	Yards Back Tees	Rating	Slope
9	35	3065	34.5	111

	9 Holes	18 Holes	Hours Mid Season
Weekday:	$8.50	$16.00	6:00 am - Dusk
Weekend:	$10.00	$17.50	6:00 am - Dusk
Cart Fees:	$8.00	$16.00	

Mandatory Cart Rental: No
Club Rental: Yes

Notes: The above are 1992 rates. Jr and Sr rates apply during the week.

Grassy Hill Country Club

441 Clark Lane, Orange CT — Tee Times: (203)795-1422

Directions: Take the Merritt Pkwy to Exit 56 (Rte 121). Go East on 121. The course is 1.5 mi. on right.

Facility Type: Public

Club Pro: Pete Pulaski
Discounts: Seniors, Twilight
Tee Times: Yes, Thursday 7 am for weekends/holidays.

Features: Lessons, Showers/Lockers, Driving Range, Practice Area, Pro Shop - Complete, Restaurant, Bar, Snack Bar, Banquet Facilities, VISA/MC

Description: This is a well maintained course with watered fairways. It is hilly and challenging. The 610 yd, par 5, 5th is the signatuture hole.

Holes	Par	Yards Back Tees	Rating	Slope
18	70	6325	69.8	122

	9 Holes	18 Holes	Hours Mid Season
Weekday:	$12.00	$20.00	6:00 am - 7:30 pm
Weekend:	$14.00	$23.00	5:30 am - 7:30 pm
Cart Fees:	—	$12.00	

Mandatory Cart Rental: No
Club Rental: Yes

Notes: Cart rental fees listed are per person. The facility includes a complete driving range.

Greenwoods Country Club

Winsted CT — Tee Times: (203)379-8302

Directions: Rte 8 to Exit 46. Go East off the exit and up the hill for about 1/2 mile. Take a left on Rte 183 and the course is 1/2 mi. on the left.

Facility Type: Semi-private

Club Pro: David Dell
Discounts: None
Tee Times: Yes, for non-members, 1 week prior for weekends and holidays

Features: Lessons, Showers/Lockers, Driving Range, Practice Area, Pro Shop - Complete, Clubhouse, Restaurant, Bar, Snack Bar, VISA/MC

Description: This short and narrow course is tree-lined with a lot of out-of-bounds. There is some water coming into play and an average number of bunkers. The greens are in excellent shape and the course is well-maintained. One hole is a par 4 going out and a par 5 coming back. That explains the par 71

Holes	Par	Yards Back Tees	Rating	Slope
9dt	71	5886	68.4	117

	9 Holes	18 Holes	Hours Mid Season
Weekday:	$14.00	$25.50	8:00 am - Dusk
Weekend:	$16.00	$30.00	3:00 pm - Dusk
Cart Fees:	$14.00	$24.00	

Mandatory Cart Rental: No
Club Rental: Yes

Notes: Weekend play until 3 is reserved for non-members.

H Smith Richardson GC

CT 29

2425 Moorehouse Hwy, Fairfield CT — Tee Times: (203)255-6094

Directions: Merritt Parkway North to Exit 45 (Black Rock Trnpke). Go back under the Merritt and take the first right. 2nd left is Moorehouse, to course.

Facility Type: Public

Club Pro: Michael Homa
Discounts: None
Tee Times: Yes, (Non-residents must get time in person.) Call Wed. for Sat. and Thurs. for Sun. at 9 am for residents only.

Features: Lessons, Showers/Lockers, Driving Range, Practice Area, Pro Shop - Complete, Restaurant, Bar, Snack Bar, Banquet Facilities, Clubhouse

Description: A Golf Digest pick for "Places to Play" in both '90 and '91, it's a good mix of trees, sand, water, and hills. Tees are very good, fairways are narrow, and greens are average in size. Improvements are expected for '92. The facility includes a complete driving range.

Holes	Par	Yards Back Tees	Rating	Slope
18	72	6676	70.5	124

	9 Holes	18 Holes	Hours Mid Season
Weekday:	$14.50	$19.00	7:00 am - Dusk
Weekend:	$15.00	$22.50	6:00 am - Dusk
Cart Fees:	—	$17.00	

Mandatory Cart Rental: No
Club Rental: Yes

Notes: 9 hole play only after 5.

Harrisville Golf Course

CT 30

125 Harrisville Rd, Woodstock CT — (203)928-6098

Directions: I-395 to Rte 44 West, or I-84 to 74 East to 44 East. From 44 go north on 169 into Woodstock. Take the 2nd right, Harrisville Rd. Go through a 4-way stop (Harrisville Rd), and the course is on the right..

Facility Type: Public

Club Pro: None
Discounts: None
Tee Times: No

Features: Lessons, Practice Area, Pro Shop - Limited

Description: This course has a rolling terrain. #5 and, especially, the 610 yd par 5 #6 holes have challenged many good golfers.

Holes	Par	Yards Back Tees	Rating	Slope
9	35	2964	—	—

	9 Holes	18 Holes	Hours Mid Season
Weekday:	$8.50	$13.00	8:00 am - Dusk
Weekend:	$12.00	$17.00	7:00 am - Dusk
Cart Fees:	$8.00	$16.00	

Mandatory Cart Rental: No
Club Rental: Yes

Notes: Call for details on the 10 am to 3 pm weekday special.

Highland Greens Golf Course　　CT 31

Prospect CT — (203)758-4022

Directions: I-84 going East, take Exit 23 onto Rte 69 South. Take 69 into the town of Prospect and turn left on Rte 68. Go 2 mi. and turn right on Cooke Rd. The course is 1.5 mi. Going West on 84, take the 2nd Chesire Exit, Rte 70. Go toward Chesire and take a right at 68. The 4th left is Cooke Rd. to the course.

Holes	Par	Yards Back Tees	Rating	Slope
9	27	1398	—	—

	9 Holes	18 Holes	Hours Mid Season
Weekday:	$6.00	—	7:00 am - 10:00 pm
Weekend:	$6.50	—	7:00 am - 10:00 pm
Cart Fees:	—	—	
Club Rental:			

Facility Type: Executive

Club Pro: None
Discounts: Seniors
Tee Times: No

Features: Lessons, Pro Shop - Limited, Snack Bar

Description: This is the only lighted Par 3 in CT. Price goes up $1 after 7.

Hop Brook Country Club　　CT 32

615 N Church St, Naugatuck CT —　Tee Times: (203)729-8013

Directions: Rte 8 to Exit 26 (63 North) or I-84 to Exit 17 (63 South) Course is on Rte 63.

Holes	Par	Yards Back Tees	Rating	Slope
9	36	2887	67.8	109

Facility Type: Public

Coupon page 54

Club Pro: None
Discounts: Seniors
Tee Times: Yes, weekends/holidays - 2 days prior

	9 Holes	18 Holes	Hours Mid Season
Weekday:	$11.00	$17.00	Dawn - Dusk
Weekend:	$13.00	$17.00	Dawn - Dusk
Cart Fees:	$8.00	$15.00	

Mandatory Cart Rental: No
Club Rental: Yes

Features: Lessons, Practice Area, Pro Shop - Limited, Restaurant, Bar, Snack Bar, Banquet Facilities, American Express

Description: This is a short and fairly level course.

Hotchkiss School Golf Course   CT 33

Rte 112, Lakeville CT — (203)435-9033

Directions: Rte 44 West from Rte 7 in CT or East from Rte 22 in NY to Rte 112. South 1/8 mi. to course.

Facility Type: Semi-private

Club Pro: Joe Rueger
Discounts: None
Tee Times: No

Features: Lessons, Practice Area, Pro Shop - Complete

Description: This was designed by Seth Raynor who designed the Yale University Course. It is hilly, wooded and well maintained.

Holes	Par	Yards Back Tees	Rating	Slope
9	35	3118	69.2	111

	9 Holes	18 Holes	Hours Mid Season
Weekday:	$9.00	$15.00	8:00 am - 6:00 pm
Weekend:	$10.00	$20.00	11:00 am - 6:00 pm
Cart Fees:	$9.00	$18.00	

Mandatory Cart Rental: No
Club Rental: Yes

Hunter Memorial Golf Club   CT 34

685 Westfield Rd, Meriden CT —   Tee Times: (203)634-3366

Directions: I-91 North to Exit 16. Straight off exit 1.5 mi. to course. Southbound on I-91 to Exit 19. Right at stop, next stop right again to course.

Facility Type: Public

Club Pro: Paul Brown
Discounts: None
Tee Times: Yes, 3 days ahead for weekends/holidays

Features: Lessons, Showers/Lockers, Driving Range, Practice Area, Pro Shop - Complete, Restaurant, Bar, Snack Bar, Banquet Facilities, Clubhouse

Description: This is a well maintained course with a lot of variation. It sports the oldest oak tree in Connecticut.

Holes	Par	Yards Back Tees	Rating	Slope
18	71	6593	71.0	128

	9 Holes	18 Holes	Hours Mid Season
Weekday:	$11.00	$18.00	7:00 am - 7:00 pm
Weekend:	$13.00	$20.00	6:00 am - 7:00 pm
Cart Fees:	$10.50	$18.50	

Mandatory Cart Rental: No
Club Rental: Yes

Notes: The driving range is for irons only. Buckets are available.

Indian Springs Golf Club
CT 35

Mack Rd, Middlefield CT — **Tee Times:** (203)349-8109

Directions: I-91 to Exit 18 (Rte 66 East). Go 2 mi. to Rte 147 and take a right. 1.5 mi. to course sign on the left.

Facility Type: Public

Club Pro: Rich Broderick
Discounts: Seniors
Tee Times: Yes, 4 days prior for weekends/holidays

Features: Lessons, Driving Range, Pro Shop - Limited, Clubhouse, Restaurant, Bar

Description: this is an excellent course for variety and to practice position shots. It's an older course with small greens and hills.

Holes	Par	Yards Back Tees	Rating	Slope
9	36	3100	69.7	116

	9 Holes	18 Holes	Hours Mid Season
Weekday:	$10.00	$18.00	Dawn - Dusk
Weekend:	$12.00	$22.00	Dawn - Dusk
Cart Fees:	$10.00	$20.00	

Mandatory Cart Rental: No
Club Rental: Yes

Notes: Senior discount only for season ticket holders

Keney Golf Course
CT 36

Barbour St Extension, Hartford CT — **Tee Times:** (203)525-3656

Directions: I-91 North of Hartford to Exit 34. Go left off the exit. Take a left at the light. Go right at the 5th light (Tower). Take a right at the 2nd light (Barbour) and the course is on the right-hand side.

Facility Type: Public

Club Pro: Robert Powell
Discounts: Seniors
Tee Times: Yes, 10 days in adva

Coupon page 55

Features: Lessons, Showers/Lockers, Practice Area, Pro Shop - Complete, Snack Bar, Banquet Facilities, VISA/MC, Clubhouse

Description: This is an old style course built in 1927. It's carved out of the woods and is hilly. This is a well-maintained and over-all attractive golf facility. The 5th hole is a favorite and the toughest. It's a 406 yard par 4. The 2nd shot is over a ravine to an elevated green

Holes	Par	Yards Back Tees	Rating	Slope
18	70	5969	68.2	118

	9 Holes	18 Holes	Hours Mid Season
Weekday:	$8.00	$14.00	7:00 am - Dusk
Weekend:	$9.00	$17.00	Dawn - Dusk
Cart Fees:	$12.00	$18.00	

Mandatory Cart Rental: No
Club Rental: Yes

Notes: Reduced fees for Hartford residents.

Laurel View Country Club

310 West Shepard Ave, Hamden CT — Tee Times: (203)281-0670

Directions: Merritt Parkway (Rte 15) to the Wilbur Cross Parkway. Take Exit 60. Make a right off the exit to Dixwell Ave and follow the signs for the "public golf course."

Facility Type: Public

Club Pro: David McQuade
Discounts: Seniors, Juniors
Tee Times: Yes, 3 days prior for weekends/holidays

Features: Lessons, Showers/Lockers, Driving Range, Practice Area, Pro Shop - Complete, Restaurant, Bar, Banquet Facilities, Snack Bar

Description: This is a demanding Geoffrey Cornish design. It has a long front 9 and a tight back 9. It is the site of the Ben Hogan Open qualifier, and claims to be one of the toughest courses in New England.

Holes	Par	Yards Back Tees	Rating	Slope
18	72	6889	70.8	130

	9 Holes	18 Holes	Hours Mid Season
Weekday:	$12.00	$18.00	7:30 am - Dusk
Weekend:	$14.00	$21.00	6:00 am - Dusk
Cart Fees:	—	$18.00	

Mandatory Cart Rental: No
Club Rental: Yes

Lisbon Country Club

78 Kendall Rd, Lisbon CT — (203)376-4325

Directions: I-395 North to Exit 83 A. Go left off the ramp to Kendall Rd. The course is on the left. I-395 going South to Exit 84 N. Take a right onto Rte 12 and a left at the 1st light onto Rte 138. Go to the 1st stop and take a left onto Rte 169, and a right onto Kendall Rd. The course is on the right.

Facility Type: Public

Club Pro: Cathy Williams
Discounts: Seniors, Juniors
Tee Times: No

Coupon page 55

Features: Lessons, Practice Area, Pro Shop - Limited, Snack Bar

Description: This a picturesque course with six natural water hazards. It reads short, but offers a good challenge. It is certainly not a walkover. In fact, it is a good course for the duffer or the pro.

Holes	Par	Yards Back Tees	Rating	Slope
9	33	2350	65.5	102

	9 Holes	18 Holes	Hours Mid Season
Weekday:	$8.00	$12.00	7:30 am - Dusk
Weekend:	$9.00	$13.00	6:30 am - Dusk
Cart Fees:	$8.00	$16.00	

Mandatory Cart Rental: No
Club Rental: Yes

Notes: This is a very friendly family owned and operated course. Seasonal passes and family memberships are available. Sr, jr and ladies discounts are on season tickets only. The course only closes officially for the 1st two weeks in March. Otherwise, it is open, weather permitting.

Lyman Meadow Golf Club

Rte 157, Middlefield CT 06455 — **Tee Times:** (203)349-8055

Directions: I-91 to Exit 15 (Rte 68). Go East on 68 to Rte 157. Take a left and the course is 1 mi. on the right.

Facility Type: Semi-private

Club Pro: Dick Bierkan
Discounts: Seniors
Tee Times: Yes, Friday for following week, Monday for weekend.

Features: Lessons, Showers/Lockers, Driving Range, Practice Area, Pro Shop - Complete, Restaurant, Bar, Snack Bar, Clubhouse, VISA/MC

Description: This is a Robert Trent Jones course and a Golf Digest pick for both 1990 and 1991 for "Places to Play". The front 9 is dry and partially wooded. The back 9 is flatter and has water on most of it. The 12th hole is an interesting par 5 dogleg left. This is a highly-rated course.

Holes	Par	Yards Back Tees	Rating	Slope
18	72	7011	73.5	129

	9 Holes	18 Holes	Hours Mid Season
Weekday:	$9.50	$18.00	7:00 am - 7:00 pm
Weekend:	$12.00	$23.00	6:00 am - 7:00 pm
Cart Fees:	$10.00	$20.00	

Mandatory Cart Rental: No
Club Rental: No

Meadowbrook Country Club

2761 Dixwell Ave, Hamden CT — (203)281-4847

Directions: Take the Wilbur Cross Pkwy (Rte 15) to Exit 60. Go North on Dixwell toward Hamden approximately 1 mile to the course.

Facility Type: Public

Club Pro: None
Discounts: Seniors, Juniors
Tee Times: No

Features: Driving Range, Practice Area, Pro Shop - Limited, Snack Bar

Description: This is a relatively flat course, and good for seniors, but it offers a challenge for the average golfer. It has 2 par 3's, 1 par 5 and the rest 4's. The fairways are fairly open. This course maintains 6 of the original holes of an 18 hole course that once hosted the CT Pro Golf Association Tournaments.

Holes	Par	Yards Back Tees	Rating	Slope
9	35	2721	—	—

	9 Holes	18 Holes	Hours Mid Season
Weekday:	$7.00	$10.00	7:00 am - 7:00 pm
Weekend:	$8.00	$12.00	7:00 am - 7:00 pm
Cart Fees:	$9.00	$18.00	

Mandatory Cart Rental: No
Club Rental: Yes

Notes: Memberships available.

Millbrook Golf Course

CT 41

147 Pidgeon Hill Rd, Windsor CT — Tee Times: (203)688-2575

Directions: I-91 North of Hartford. Northbound take Exit 38 and a left at the bottom of the ramp. The course sign is 1 mi. on the right. (Pidgeon Hill Rd)

Holes	Par	Yards Back Tees	Rating	Slope
18	71	6427	71	125

Facility Type: Public

Club Pro: None
Discounts: Seniors, Juniors, Twilight
Tee Times: Yes, call ahead for weekends/holidays

Features: Practice Area, Pro Shop - Limited, Restaurant

Description: The course is hilly and features a number of water hazards. This is a well maintained facility.

	9 Holes	18 Holes	Hours Mid Season
Weekday:	$10.75	$16.00	6:00 am - Dusk
Weekend:	$12.75	$19.25	6:00 am - Dusk
Cart Fees:	$9.00	$18.00	

Mandatory Cart Rental: No
Club Rental: Yes

Notes: Cart fees are slightly higher on weekends.

Millstone Country Club

CT 42

348 Herbert St, Milford CT —(203)874-5900

Directions: East on I-95 to Exit 37 (High St.). Go left off the ramp and the road becomes Wheeler Farm Rd. Go West on Wheeler Farm under the Merritt Pkwy to Herbert St., the 1st street past the Merritt, and take a left. The course 1/2 mi. on Herbert. From the Merritt, exit on Wheeler Farm (Exit 55).

Holes	Par	Yards Back Tees	Rating	Slope
9	36	2910	—	—

	9 Holes	18 Holes	Hours Mid Season
Weekday:	$8.00	$8.00	7:00 am - Dusk
Weekend:	$10.00	$10.00	6:00 am - Dusk
Cart Fees:	$15.00	$15.00	

Mandatory Cart Rental: No
Club Rental: Yes

Facility Type: Public

Club Pro: None
Discounts: Seniors
Tee Times: No

Features: Lessons, Practice Area, Snack Bar, Pro Shop - Limited

Description: The course is pretty flat with some water, and not too difficult. It's a good walking course, even for the octogenarian. The greens are in excellent shape.

Minnechaug Golf Course

16 Fairway Crossing, Glastonbury CT — Tee Times: (203)643-9914

Directions: I-84 East of Hartford to 384. Take Exit 3 off 384. Go left at the light (Main St) after the off ramp. This becomes Manchester Rd or Rte 83. The course is 1/4 mi. past Manchester Country Club on the right.

Facility Type: Public

Club Pro: Chet Dunlop
Discounts: Seniors
Tee Times: Yes, 2 days ahead for weekdays, Tues prior for weekends/holidays

Features: Lessons, Practice Area, Pro Shop - Complete, Snack Bar, Banquet Facilities, VISA/MC

Description: This is a tight and challenging course with an island green on the #8 par 3.

Holes	Par	Yards Back Tees	Rating	Slope
9	35	3255	70.4	122

	9 Holes	18 Holes	Hours Mid Season
Weekday:	$9.00	$18.00	6:30 am - Dusk
Weekend:	$10.00	$20.00	6:00 am - Dusk
Cart Fees:	$10.00	$20.00	

Mandatory Cart Rental: No
Club Rental: Yes

Notes: This course is set up for and welcomes tournaments.

Norwich Golf Course

685 New London Trnpke, Norwich CT — Tee Times: (203)889-6973

Directions: I-395 to Exit 80 East onto Rte 82 heading East. Take a right at the 5th light, New London Turnpike, and the course 1 mile on the right.

Facility Type: Public

Club Pro: John Paesani
Discounts: Twilight
Tee Times: Yes, 3 days prior for weekends/holidays, morning of for weekday.

Features: Lessons, Practice Area, Pro Shop - Complete, Restaurant, Bar, Snack Bar, Banquet Facilities, Showers/Lockers, Clubhouse, Lodging Nearby

Description: Norwich is a Donald Ross design and was a Golf Digest pick for "Places to Play" in '90 and '91. The course is short, yet challenging. The emphasis is on careful iron shots to score well. There is some water, and it is hilly.

Holes	Par	Yards Back Tees	Rating	Slope
18	71	6221	69.4	119

	9 Holes	18 Holes	Hours Mid Season
Weekday:	—	$16.00	7:00 am - Dusk
Weekend:	—	$19.00	6:30 am - Dusk
Cart Fees:	—	$18.00	

Mandatory Cart Rental: No
Club Rental: Yes

Notes: Twilight begins at 5 midseason.

Oak Hills Golf Course

165 Fillow St, Norwalk CT — Info: (203)853-8400   Tee Times: (203)838-1015

Directions: I-95 to Exit 13. Take a right off the exit. Go to the 2nd light and take a left onto Richards Ave. Go to the end and take a sharp right onto Fillow St. The course is on the right.

Facility Type: Public

Club Pro: Vincent Grillo
Discounts: None
Tee Times: Yes, not on phone, weekends by lottery for residents only, weekdays 1 week prior in person

Features: Lessons, Practice Area, Pro Shop - Complete, Snack Bar

Description: This is an Alfred Tull design. It's a hilly and very scenic course that goes from tight on the 1st 7 holes to open on the next 5 and back to tight. Water comes into play on 6 holes. The par 4 460 yard 9th hole is the signature.

Holes	Par	Yards Back Tees	Rating	Slope
18	71	6382	70.5	125

	9 Holes	18 Holes	Hours Mid Season
Weekday:	—	$20.00	6:30 am - 7:00 pm
Weekend:	—	$22.00	6:00 am - 7:00 pm
Cart Fees:	—	$20.00	

Mandatory Cart Rental: No
Club Rental: Yes

Notes: 9 holes are playable only after 5:30 on weekdays.

Orange Hills Country Club

489 Racebrook Rd, Orange CT —   Tee Times: (203)795-4161

Directions: I-95 to Exit 41 (Marsh Hill Rd). Left off exit going north, right going south. Right at bottom of hill onto Post Rd. 1st light is Racebrook Rd (114). Take a left and course is on the right.

Facility Type: Public

Coupon page 55

Club Pro: Art Decko
Discounts: None
Tee Times: Yes, Wed. 6 pm for weekends, 2-3 days prior for weekdays.

Features: Lessons, Showers/Lockers, Practice Area, Pro Shop - Limited, Bar, Snack Bar, VISA/MC

Description: This is the only course in CT and one of 50 in the country to win the Public Golf Achievement Award from National Golf Foundation in 1990. The course is carved out of the woods with some water hazards. It is a challenging course with a tight and hilly back 9. The par 185 #13 carries over water and though the woods.

Holes	Par	Yards Back Tees	Rating	Slope
18	71	6389	71	122

	9 Holes	18 Holes	Hours Mid Season
Weekday:	$10.00	$16.00	6:30 am - Dusk
Weekend:	$13.00	$24.00	Dawn - Dusk
Cart Fees:	$11.00	$22.00	

Mandatory Cart Rental: No
Club Rental: No

Pattonbrook Country Club
CT 47

201 Pattonwood Dr, Southington CT — Tee Times: (203)747-9466

Directions: I-84 to Exit 32. Going East take a left off the exit. Go 100 yds and take another left at Bickford's Pancake House onto Laning St.. Follow signs to course. Going West take a right off the same exit, go back under 84 and take a left at Bickford's onto Laning. Follow the signs.

Facility Type: Public

Coupon page 56

Club Pro: None
Discounts: Seniors
Tee Times: Yes, call Wednesday for weekends.

Features: Showers/Lockers, Practice Area, Pro Shop - Complete, Clubhouse, Snack Bar, Bar

Description: This is a typical New England course - short and hilly. Trouble lurks with a good number of hazards. The front is wooded and narrow, the back is longer and open. The greens are small, fast and in great shape. #17 par 4 is 400 yds with water all down the left and water in front of the green.

Holes	Par	Yards Back Tees	Rating	Slope
18	60	4335	60.6	97

	9 Holes	18 Holes	Hours Mid Season
Weekday:	$8.50	$14.00	7:00 am - Dusk
Weekend:	$9.50	$16.00	7:00 am - Dusk
Cart Fees:	$12.00	$20.00	

Mandatory Cart Rental: No
Club Rental: Yes

Pequabuck Golf Club
CT 48

Pequabuck CT — (203)583-7307

Directions: Rte 6 to Bushnel Rd (only one way). Go 1/4 mi. to School Street and turn left to the course. Pequabuck is right next to Bristol.

Facility Type: Semi-private

Club Pro: Chris Tremblay
Discounts: None
Tee Times: No, open to public before 2pm weekdays and after 2 weekends if time available.

Features: Lessons, Driving Range, Practice Area, Pro Shop - Complete, Snack Bar, Clubhouse

Description: Once known as the best kept secret in the area, this course has excellent drainage and is always in good shape. It has a tight and short back 9.

Holes	Par	Yards Back Tees	Rating	Slope
18	69	6015	69.1	122

	9 Holes	18 Holes	Hours Mid Season
Weekday:	$15.00	$28.00	7:30 am - Dusk
Weekend:	$15.00	$28.00	6:30 am - Dusk
Cart Fees:	$11.00	$20.00	

Mandatory Cart Rental: No
Club Rental: No

Pequot Golf Club   CT 49

127 Wheeler Rd, Stonington CT — Tee Times: (203)535-1898

Directions: I-95 to Exit 91 (right off exit going North, left going South). Take Pequot Trail, and turn right onto Wheeler Rd. The course is on the left.

Facility Type: Public

Club Pro: None
Discounts: Seniors, Twilight
Tee Times: Yes, 1 week ahead for any day

Features: Lessons, Practice Area, Pro Shop - Complete, Restaurant, Bar, Snack Bar, Clubhouse

Description: Careful shots are necessary on this course, because it is tight with trees.

Holes	Par	Yards Back Tees	Rating	Slope
18	70	5903	67.2	108

	9 Holes	18 Holes	Hours Mid Season
Weekday:	$12.00	$16.00	6:00 am - Dusk
Weekend:	—	$20.00	5:00 am - Dusk
Cart Fees:	$12.00	$22.00	

Mandatory Cart Rental: No
Club Rental: Yes

Pilgrim's Harbor Golf Club   CT 50

Harrison Rd, Wallingford CT — Tee Times: (203)269-6023

Directions: I-91 to Exit 14. Going North on 91 take a right off the exit to Woodhouse Rd (Rte 150). Take the next right onto Harrison and 1/2 mi. to the course. Going South on 91, go right off exit and immediately left on South Airline Rd. Go left at the next light (Woodhouse -150) and right onto Harrison to the course.

Facility Type: Semi-private

Coupon page 56

Club Pro: None
Discounts: None
Tee Times: Yes, Wednesday for the weekends and holidays

Features: Practice Area, Pro Shop - Limited, Snack Bar, Banquet Facilities

Description: A Robert Trent Jones course, this is considered the second toughest in the state of CT by the CT Golf Association. The course is hilly and the greens are well kept and fast. The signature is #4, a par 4, 405 yard severe dogleg left. A brook lies left and right and the landing area is fully tree lined. The green is small and slopes away to the back.

Holes	Par	Yards Back Tees	Rating	Slope
9	36	3337	72.6	127

	9 Holes	18 Holes	Hours Mid Season
Weekday:	$9.00	$15.00	7:00 am - 7:00 pm
Weekend:	$12.00	$21.00	6:00 am - 8:00 pm
Cart Fees:	$13.00	$25.00	

Mandatory Cart Rental: No
Club Rental: Yes

Notes: Memberships are available.

Pine Valley Golf Course

CT 51

300 Welch Rd, Southington CT — **Tee Times:** (203)628-0879

Directions: I-84 to Exit 31. Go North on Rte 229 to Welch Rd and take a left to the course.

Holes	Par	Yards Back Tees	Rating	Slope
18	71	6325	70.3	122

Facility Type: Public

	9 Holes	18 Holes	Hours Mid Season
Weekday:	$9.50	$18.00	8:00 am - 6:30 pm
Weekend:	$13.50	$22.00	7:00 am - 6:00 pm
Cart Fees:	$10.50	$21.00	

Club Pro: Jack McConachie
Discounts: None
Tee Times: Yes, Wed. at 6 pm for weekends/holidays or prepay 4 days prior for weekdays.

Mandatory Cart Rental: No
Club Rental: No

Features: Lessons, Showers/Lockers, Practice Area, Pro Shop - Complete, Snack Bar, Clubhouse, Restaurant, Bar, Banquet Facilities, Lodging Nearby

Description: This is a particularly well-maintained and manicured course. The drainage is good so it is usually the first course in the area to allow carts in the Spring. In the Fall the leaves are continually blown off the course. The front 9 is a hilly terrain, the back nine more level. Water comes into play on three holes. Accuracy is required on this course.

Portland Golf Club West

CT 52

105 Gospel Lane, Portland CT — **Tee Times:** (203)342-4043

Directions: From Hartford on Rte 2, go to Rte 17 South and approximately 9 miles to the course. From the Merritt Parkway, take Rte 66 East to Middletown. Cross the Middletown/Portland Bridge and take a right to continue on Rte 66. Go 2.5 miles and take a left onto Rte 17 North to the course.

Holes	Par	Yards Back Tees	Rating	Slope
18	60	4000	60.4	84

	9 Holes	18 Holes	Hours Mid Season
Weekday:	$9.00	$17.00	7:00 am - Dusk
Weekend:	$10.50	$19.00	6:00 am - Dusk
Cart Fees:	$8.50	$16.00	

Facility Type: Public

Mandatory Cart Rental: No
Club Rental: Yes

Club Pro: Gerald D'amora
Discounts: Seniors, Juniors
Tee Times: Yes, 1 week for weekends/holidays

Features: Lessons, Driving Range, Practice Area, Pro Shop - Complete, Restaurant, Bar, Banquet Facilities, Clubhouse

Description: Although short, this is a challenging course. It's a true test for the experienced player, but a good place to begin, as well. Al Zikorus designed the course. It has a lot of water and bunkers, and the greens are medium to small in size.

Portland Golf Course
CT 53

169 Bartlett St, Portland CT — **Tee Times:** (203)342-2833

Directions: From Hartford on Rte 2 go to Rte 17 South and 9 mi. to Bartlett St. Take aleft to the course. From the Merritt Pkwy, take Rte 66 East to Middletown. Cross the Middletown/Portland Bridge. Take a right to continue on Rte 66. Go 2.5 mi. and take a left onto Rte 17 North. Take the 2nd right, Bartlett St., to the course.

Facility Type: Public

Coupon page 56

Club Pro: Mark Sloan
Discounts: Seniors, Juniors
Tee Times: Yes, Call 1 week in advance for weekend, and call ahead for weekdays.

Features: Lessons, Showers/Lockers, Practice Area, Pro Shop - Complete, Clubhouse, Restaurant, Bar, Snack Bar, Banquet Facilities, Lodging Nearby

Description: This course was designed by Geoffrey Cornish. It has a rolling terrain with some water holes. Several shots are blind. The course drains well and is always in good condition. It is known for its high level of maintenance. It's a good course for any level of player.

Holes	Par	Yards Back Tees	Rating	Slope
18	71	6213	70.8	124

	9 Holes	18 Holes	Hours Mid Season
Weekday:	$10.00	$19.00	7:00 am - Dusk
Weekend:	$12.00	$22.00	6:00 am - Dusk
Cart Fees:	$10.00	$19.00	

Mandatory Cart Rental: No
Club Rental: Yes

Notes: Driving range is at Portland West. There are expansion plans for an additional 9 holes to open Fall of 92 or Spring of 93. The name will be Quarry Ridge and it will be designed by Al Zikorus.

Raceway Golf Club
CT 54

Thompson CT — **Tee Times:** (203)923-9591

Directions: I-395 to Exit 99 and follow signs to Thompson Speedway.

Facility Type: Semi-private

Coupon page 57

Club Pro: Jack Kelly
Discounts: None
Tee Times: Yes, 1 week prior

Features: Lessons, Showers/Lockers, Driving Range, Practice Area, Pro Shop - Complete, Clubhouse, Restaurant, Bar, Snack Bar

Description: This is a fairly flat and easy walking course with water on several holes.

Holes	Par	Yards Back Tees	Rating	Slope
18	72	6600	68.0	119

	9 Holes	18 Holes	Hours Mid Season
Weekday:	—	$15.00	6:30 am - Dusk
Weekend:	—	$18.00	6:00 am - Dusk
Cart Fees:	—	$18.00	

Mandatory Cart Rental: No
Club Rental: Yes

Richter Park Golf Course

100 Aunt Hack Rd, Danbury CT — **Tee Times:** (203)792-2550

Directions: Going East on I-84, take Exit 2. Go left off the ramp and right at 2nd light (Rte 6). Go through the light to Aunt Hack Rd and take a left to the course. Going West on I-84 take Exit 2B, and go right off the ramp. Take a right at the 1st light (Mill Plain Rd -Rte 6) and left on Aunt Hack to the course.

Holes	Par	Yards Back Tees	Rating	Slope
18	72	6741	73	130

	9 Holes	18 Holes	Hours Mid Season
Weekday:	—	$40.00	9:00 am - 3:00 pm*
Weekend:	—	$40.00	2:00 pm - Dusk*
Cart Fees:	$13.00	$22.00	

Facility Type: Public

Mandatory Cart Rental: No
Club Rental: Yes

Club Pro: Bob Rogers
Discounts: None
Tee Times: Yes, Thursday at 9 am for weekends/holidays

Notes: * The above operating times are for non-residents. Residents of Danbury pay reduced green fees.

Features: Lessons, Showers/Lockers, Practice Area, Pro Shop - Complete

Description: This course was designed by Edward Ryder. It was chosen by Golf Digest for "Places to Play" in '90 and'91. It is in good shape and it plays hard for the average golfer or the unsuspecting. It's scenic and wooded. The fairways are narrow, and water comes into play on 16 holes.

Ridgefield Golf Club

545 Ridgebury Rd, Ridgefiled CT — **Tee Times:** (203)748-7008

Directions: I-84 to Exit 1, Saw Mill Rd South 2.5 mi. to a stop. Go through the stop. The road becomes Ridgebury Rd. and the course is on the right.

Holes	Par	Yards Back Tees	Rating	Slope
18	70	6380	70	122

	9 Holes	18 Holes	Hours Mid Season
Weekday:	—	$22.00	8:00 am - Dusk
Weekend:	—	$27.00	6:30 am - Dusk
Cart Fees:	$10.00	$20.00	

Facility Type: Public

Club Pro: Vince Adams
Discounts: Seniors, Juniors
Tee Times: Yes, Thurs. 9 am for weekends/holidays

Mandatory Cart Rental: No
Club Rental: Yes

Features: Lessons, Showers/Lockers, Driving Range, Practice Area, Pro Shop - Complete, Restaurant, Bar, Snack Bar

Notes: Tuesday Ladies in the morning. Reduced rates for residents of Ridgefield.

Description: This course has a sporting front nine and a tight, long, woody and difficult back 9. It's in great condition for a municipal course. It features a floating bridge.

Rockledge Country Club   CT 57

289 S Main St, West Hartford CT — Info: (203)521-3156   Tee Times: (203)521-6284

Directions: I-84 to Exit 41. Go North on S. Main Street. The course is on the left 1/4 mi.

Facility Type: Public

Club Pro: Richard Crowe
Discounts: Seniors
Tee Times: Yes, 3 days for weekends/holidays, 1 day for weekdays

Features: Lessons, Showers/Lockers, Driving Range, Practice Area, Pro Shop - Complete, Restaurant, Bar, Snack Bar, Clubhouse, Lodging Nearby

Description: This course is in excellent shape. A new par 3 #16 goes over water. The course rolls a little and is considered a fair test for the average golfer. This course has a lot of history. Tommy Armour was the pro here, along with Julius Boros.

Holes	Par	Yards Back Tees	Rating	Slope
18	72	6500	70.0	123

	9 Holes	18 Holes	Hours Mid Season
Weekday:	$10.50	$18.00	7:00 am - Dusk
Weekend:	$12.00	$22.00	7:00 am - Dusk
Cart Fees:	$9.00	$17.00	

Mandatory Cart Rental: No
Club Rental: Yes

Rolling Greens Golf Club   CT 58

600 Cold Spring Rd, Rocky Hill CT —   Tee Times: (203)257-9775

Directions: I-91 to Exit 23 (Rocky Hill). Going North take a left off the exit and go 1/4 mi. to Rte 3. Take a left and then a right onto Cold Spring to the course. Going South, take a right off the exit to Rte 3 and left to Cold Spring.

Facility Type: Public

Coupon page 57

Club Pro: Joe De Candia
Discounts: Seniors, Juniors
Tee Times: Yes, 3 days prior for weekends/holidays

Features: Lessons, Showers/Lockers, Practice Area, Pro Shop - Complete, Restaurant, Bar, VISA/MC

Description: A Geoffrey Cornish design, this is a championship layout and considered one of the top 9 hole courses in the state. It is rolling and tight - a target course. It has bent grass greens and is well maintained.

Holes	Par	Yards Back Tees	Rating	Slope
9	35	3250	72	131

	9 Holes	18 Holes	Hours Mid Season
Weekday:	$9.00	$15.00	7:00 am - Dusk
Weekend:	$10.00	$20.00	7:00 am - Dusk
Cart Fees:	$11.00	$22.00	

Mandatory Cart Rental: No
Club Rental: Yes

Shennecossett Golf Club

Plant St, Groton CT — **Tee Times:** (203)445-0262

Directions: I-95 to Exit 87. Take 349 South. Go to the 2nd light and make a right. At the 1st light go left to the course.

Facility Type: Semi-private

Club Pro: Phil Jones
Discounts: Seniors
Tee Times: Yes, Tues for Sat, Wed for Sun

Features: Lessons, Showers/Lockers, Practice Area, Pro Shop - Complete, Clubhouse, Restaurant, Bar, Banquet Facilities, Lodging Nearby

Description: Donald Ross design. A links-type course, it was completed in the early 1900's and was an exclusive private club. It is a Golf Digest selection for "Places to Play" for both '90 and '91.

Holes	Par	Yards Back Tees	Rating	Slope
18	72	6491	71.1	122

	9 Holes	18 Holes	Hours Mid Season
Weekday:	$9.75	$15.00	6:30 am - Dusk
Weekend:	$12.00	$18.25	6:00 am - Dusk
Cart Fees:	—	$20.00	

Mandatory Cart Rental: No
Club Rental: Yes

Notes: 9 holes only after 3. The senior discount is only on the cart before 9 and only on weekdays.

Simsbury Farms Golf Course

West Simsbury CT — **Tee Times:** (203)658-6246

Directions: I-84 to Exit 39. Take Farmington Ave West to Rte 10 North into Simsbury. Go left on Strattonbrook Rd in town and 4 mi. to the course.

Facility Type: Public

Club Pro: Dick Casavant
Discounts: None
Tee Times: Yes, 2 days prior at 10 am for any day.

Features: Lessons, Driving Range, Practice Area, Pro Shop - Complete, Snack Bar, Clubhouse

Description: This is another well-maintained Geoffrey Cornish course. It features rolling hills, tree-lined fairways carved out of an orchard, and some water. The fairways are narrow, but plenty of short rough lines them.

Holes	Par	Yards Back Tees	Rating	Slope
18	72	6400	71.0	124

	9 Holes	18 Holes	Hours Mid Season
Weekday:	$9.00	$18.00	7:30 am - Dusk
Weekend:	$11.00	$22.00	7:00 am - Dusk
Cart Fees:	$11.00	$22.00	

Mandatory Cart Rental: No
Club Rental: Yes

Notes: Showers but no lockers.

Skungamaug River Golf Club
CT 61

Folly Lane, Coventry CT — Tee Times: (203)742-9348

Directions: I-84 to Exit 68. Take Rte 195 South to the 1st light (Goose Lane). Turn right and follow the yellow arrows to the course, approximately 2.5 mi.

Facility Type: Semi-private

Club Pro: Lou Galasso
Discounts: Seniors
Tee Times: Yes, Monday for following weekend

Features: Lessons, Driving Range, Practice Area, Pro Shop - Complete, Clubhouse, Restaurant, Bar, Snack Bar, Banquet Facilities

Description: This is a heavily wooded and narrow course. the greens are undulating. A stream plays into several holes. There is an obvious emphasis on accuracy.

Coupon page 57

Holes	Par	Yards Back Tees	Rating	Slope
18	70	6085	68.8	131

	9 Holes	18 Holes	Hours Mid Season
Weekday:	$9.50	$19.00	7:00 am - Dusk
Weekend:	$11.00	$21.00	5:30 am - Dusk
Cart Fees:	$9.00	$18.00	

Mandatory Cart Rental: No
Club Rental: Yes

Notes: The above are 1992 prices.

Sleeping Giant Golf Course
CT 62

Hamden CT — (203)281-9456

Directions: I-91 to Exit 10 (Hamden/Chesire). Go right off the exit going either North or South to Rte 10. The course is 2.5 mi. on the right.

Facility Type: Public

Club Pro: Lee Carter
Discounts: Seniors
Tee Times: No

Features: Lessons, Pro Shop - Complete, Restaurant, Bar, Banquet Facilities

Description: This course faces Sleeping Giant Mountain. It rolls gently. It's fairly open and a river runs through #5 and #6.

Holes	Par	Yards Back Tees	Rating	Slope
9	35	2821	—	—

	9 Holes	18 Holes	Hours Mid Season
Weekday:	$9.00	$14.00	7:00 am - Dusk
Weekend:	$11.00	$17.00	6:00 am - Dusk
Cart Fees:	—	—	
Club Rental:	Yes		

Southington Country Club
CT 63

Savage St, Southington CT — **Tee Times:** (203)628-7032

Directions: I-84 to Queen St. Exit. South on Rte 10 through Southington to left on Rte 120 (Meriden Ave). 1st light (Savage) turn right and course is 1.5 mi. on right.

Holes	Par	Yards Back Tees	Rating	Slope
18	72	5675	67.0	113

	9 Holes	18 Holes	Hours Mid Season
Weekday:	$9.00	$16.50	7:00 am - Dusk
Weekend:	$12.00	$20.00	7:00 am - Dusk
Cart Fees:	$11.00	$20.00	

Facility Type: Public

Club Pro: Walt Richter
Discounts: Seniors
Tee Times: Yes, after 10 am on Monday for following weekend/holiday

Mandatory Cart Rental: No
Club Rental: No

Features: Practice Area, Pro Shop - Complete, Snack Bar, Clubhouse

Description: This is a good course for beginners. The greens are beautiful. It's a fairly flat course with a few hills on the front 9.

Stanley Municipal Golf Course
CT 64

245 Hartford Rd, New Britain CT — **Info:** (203)827-8144   **Tee Times:** (203)827-1362

Directions: I-84 to Exit 40 (New Britain) West of Hartford. Going West, take a left off the ramp and the 1st right. Go 1/2 mi. to the course. Going East on 84, take a right off the ramp and go past Town Farms Mall. The course is on the left.

Holes	Par	Yards Back Tees	Rating	Slope
9	35	3016	34.6	—
18	72	6464	70.8	122

	9 Holes	18 Holes	Hours Mid Season
Weekday:	$9.50	$16.00	7:00 am - Dusk
Weekend:	$11.00	$19.50	6:00 am - Dusk
Cart Fees:	$10.30	$17.60	

Facility Type: Public

Club Pro: Ted Pisk
Discounts: None
Tee Times: Yes, 3 days prior for weekends starting at 6:30 am

Mandatory Cart Rental: No
Club Rental: Yes

Notes: Reduced fees for residents.

Features: Lessons, Showers/Lockers, Practice Area, Pro Shop - Complete, Restaurant, Bar, Snack Bar, Clubhouse, Banquet Facilities

Sterling Farms Golf Club
CT 65
1349 Newfield Ave, Stamford CT — (203)329-8171

Directions: Merritt Pkwy to Exit 35 (Highridge Rd). Take a right off the exit from either direction onto High Ridge Rd. Go to Vine and take a left. At the end of Vine at the light, take another left to the course.

Facility Type: Public

Club Pro: Tom Lupinacci
Discounts: Seniors, Juniors
Tee Times: No, no reservations during the week. Residents of Stamford have first shot at weekend times through lottery.

Features: Lessons, Practice Area, Pro Shop - Complete, Driving Range, Restaurant, Bar, Snack Bar, Banquet Facilities

Description: The course is in tremendous condition with new bunkers. It is moderately hilly and has water on 4 holes. A Geoffrey Cornish design, it is acclaimed as one of the better public courses in New England.

Holes	Par	Yards Back Tees	Rating	Slope
18	72	6401	71.1	127

	9 Holes	18 Holes	Hours Mid Season
Weekday:	—	$22.00	6:30 am -7:00 pm
Weekend:	—	$29.00	12:00 pm - 7:00 pm*
Cart Fees:	—	$10.00	

Mandatory Cart Rental: No
Club Rental: Yes

Notes: * Weekend time is for non-residents.

Stonybrook Golf Course
CT 66
263 Milton Rd, Litchfield CT — **Tee Times:** (203)567-9977

Directions: On Rte 8 take the Exit for Litchfield/Harwinton. Take Rte 118 toward Litchfield. Go left on Rte 202. Take a right at 4th stop light (Milton Rd) and go 1.5 mi. to course on left.

Facility Type: Public

Club Pro: Rich Bredice
Discounts: None
Tee Times: Yes, 1 week for weekends

Features: Lessons, Showers/Lockers, Practice Area, Pro Shop - Complete, Snack Bar, Clubhouse, VISA/MC, Bar, Banquet Facilities, Lodging Nearby

Description: A well maintained course with no carts on fairways. It's a little hilly with water on several holes. It's a good challenge.

Holes	Par	Yards Back Tees	Rating	Slope
9	34	2714	67.6	118

	9 Holes	18 Holes	Hours Mid Season
Weekday:	$10.00	$18.00	6:00 am - Dusk
Weekend:	$14.00	$25.00	6:00 am - Dusk
Cart Fees:	$11.00	$22.00	

Mandatory Cart Rental: No
Club Rental: Yes

Sunset Hill Golf Course CT 67

13 Sunset Hill Rd, Brookfield CT — (203)775-9959

Directions: Take I-84 to Exit 9 and turn onto Rte 25 North. Go 2.5 mi. and make a left onto Sunset Hill. The course is 1/4 mile on the left.

Facility Type: Public

Club Pro: None
Discounts: Seniors
Tee Times: No

Features: Lessons, Practice Area, Pro Shop - Limited, Bar, Snack Bar

Description: Gene Sarazan design this course, and the pro Ken Green learned his golf here. The greens are especially good.

Holes	Par	Yards Back Tees	Rating	Slope
9	35	2626	66	110

	9 Holes	18 Holes	Hours Mid Season
Weekday:	$13.00	—	8:00 am - Dusk
Weekend:	$18.00	—	7:00 am - Dusk
Cart Fees:	$20.00	—	

Mandatory Cart Rental: No
Club Rental: Yes

Notes: Greens fees are for all day play. Cart rental is not however.

Tallwood Country Club CT 68

91 North St, Hebron CT — Info: (203)646-3437   Tee Times: (203)646-1151

Directions: I-84 East of Hartford take 384 to Exit 5. Go right onto Rte 85 South and the course is 6 mi. on the right.

Facility Type: Public

Club Pro: John Nowobilski
Discounts: Seniors
Tee Times: Yes, Monday morning for weekends

Features: Lessons, Showers/Lockers, Driving Range, Practice Area, Pro Shop - Complete, Clubhouse, Restaurant, Bar

Description: This course is scenic and relatively flat. Water comes into play on 6 of the back 9 holes. This is nothing the average golfer can't handle.

Holes	Par	Yards Back Tees	Rating	Slope
18	72	6364	70.6	119

	9 Holes	18 Holes	Hours Mid Season
Weekday:	$9.00	$18.00	6:30 am - Dusk
Weekend:	$10.00	$20.00	Dawn - Dusk
Cart Fees:	—	$18.00	

Mandatory Cart Rental: No
Club Rental: Yes

Tashua Knolls Golf Club

40 Tashua Knolls Lane, Trumbull CT — Info: (203)261-5989 Tee Times: (203)261-6245

Directions: Merritt Pkwy (15) to Exit 49 (Rte 25). Go North on 25 to the end. Go through the light to the 2nd left (Tashua Rd). The course is on the left at the top of the hill.

Facility Type: Public

Club Pro: Walter Bogues
Discounts: Seniors, Juniors
Tee Times: Yes, 1 day for weekdays, Wednesday morning for weekends. Foursome only on the phone and only for 18 holes.

Features: Lessons, Showers/Lockers, Driving Range, Practice Area, Pro Shop - Complete, Clubhouse, Restaurant, Bar, Banquet Facilities

Holes	Par	Yards Back Tees	Rating	Slope
18	72	6502	69.8	125

	9 Holes	18 Holes	Hours Mid Season
Weekday:	$11.00	$16.00	7:00 am - 7:00 pm*
Weekend:	$12.50	$20.00	7:00 am - 7:00 pm
Cart Fees:	$12.00	$20.00	

Mandatory Cart Rental: No
Club Rental: No

Notes: Monday hours are 12 pm to 7 pm.

Description: This is another Al Zikorus design - a good solid and challenging layout, but not unfair. Some water, hills and sharp doglegs offer a good mix. The 506 yd par 5 #14 is the signature. The shot is from an elevated tee to a dogleg left to right. It plays between two ponds. First-timers comment on the beauty of this course. It was a Golf Digest selection for "Places to Play" in '90

Timberlin Golf Club

330 Southington Rd, Kensington CT — Tee Times: (203)828-3228

Directions: I-84 to the exit for Rte 72. Go East on 72 to Rte 71 South. Travel approximately 5 miles to Southington Rd and take a right. The course is 1 mile.

Facility Type: Public

Club Pro: Lindsey Hansen
Discounts: None
Tee Times: Yes, 2 days prior at 7 am for any day.

Features: Lessons, Showers/Lockers, Driving Range, Practice Area, Pro Shop - Complete, Clubhouse, Restaurant, Bar, Snack Bar

Holes	Par	Yards Back Tees	Rating	Slope
18	72	6800	72.0	127

	9 Holes	18 Holes	Hours Mid Season
Weekday:	$11.00	$17.00	7:00 am - Dusk
Weekend:	$12.00	$21.00	7:00 am - Dusk
Cart Fees:	$10.00	$18.00	

Mandatory Cart Rental: No
Club Rental: Yes

Description: This is an Al Zikorus course design that is long and rolling with a reasonable amount of water. The 12th hole, a 175 yd par 3 across a pond is a favorite. This was one of Golf Digest's "Places to Play" in 1991.

Trumbull Golf Course CT 71

119 Highrock Rd, Groton CT — (203)445-7991

Directions: I-95 to Exit 87. Follow signs to Groton/New London Airport. The course is just before airport.

Facility Type: Executive

Club Pro: Art DeWolf
Discounts: Seniors
Tee Times: No

Features: Lessons, Driving Range, Practice Area, Pro Shop - Limited, Clubhouse

Description: This is a great course for seniors and beginners. It is straightforward and in good shape.

Holes	Par	Yards Back Tees	Rating	Slope
18	54	2666	—	—

	9 Holes	18 Holes	Hours Mid Season
Weekday:	—	$10.00	6:00 am - Dusk
Weekend:	—	$12.00	6:00 am - Dusk
Cart Fees:	—	$18.00	

Mandatory Cart Rental: No
Club Rental: Yes

Tunxis Plantation Country Club CT 72

87 Town Farm Road, Farmington CT — **Tee Times:** (203)677-1367

Directions: I-84 to Exit 39. Go West over Farmington River. Take the first right onto Town Farm Road, and the course 2 mi. on left.

Facility Type: Public

Club Pro: Lou Pandolfi
Discounts: Seniors, Juniors
Tee Times: Yes, Tuesday prior for weekends/holidays

Features: Lessons, Showers/Lockers, Driving Range, Practice Area, Pro Shop - Complete, Clubhouse, Restaurant, Bar, Snack Bar, Banquet Facilities, American Express, VISA/MC

Description: Al Zikorus designed the first 18, the Red & Green course. It is flat, narrow and heavily treed. The Farmington River comes into play as do several ponds. The second 18, the White course, is flat but open with more water. There are 5 island greens. Tunxis is a '90 and '91 selection of Golf Digest for "Places to Play".

Holes	Par	Yards Back Tees	Rating	Slope
18	72	6647	71.5	125
18	72	6638	71.3	123

	9 Holes	18 Holes	Hours Mid Season
Weekday:	$10.00	$18.00	7:00 am - Dusk
Weekend:	$13.00	$22.00	6:00 am - Dusk
Cart Fees:	$11.00	$22.00	

Mandatory Cart Rental: No
Club Rental: Yes

Twin Hills Country Club

Rte 31, Coventry CT — (203)742-9705

Directions: I-84 to Exit 67. Take Rte 31 south. The course is 5 mi. on the right.

Facility Type: Public

Club Pro: None
Discounts: Seniors
Tee Times: No

Coupon page 58

Features: Practice Area, Clubhouse, Snack Bar, Pro Shop - Limited

Description: This is a good course for beginners. There's a little water to make it interesting, but it's not overly challenging.

Holes	Par	Yards Back Tees	Rating	Slope
18	71	6194	69.7	118

	9 Holes	18 Holes	Hours Mid Season
Weekday:	$8.50	$17.00	6:00 am - Dusk
Weekend:	$ 10.00	$19.00	6:00 am - Dusk
Cart Fees:	$9.00	$18.00	

Mandatory Cart Rental: No
Club Rental: Yes

Notes: Senior discount weekdays until 4.

Twin Lakes Golf Course

Branford — (203)488-8778

Directions: I-91 North to Exit 8. Take Rte 80 East toward North Branford about 5 mi. Go right on Twin Lakes Rd (1st light after quarry) to the course.

Facility Type: Executive

Club Pro: None
Discounts: Seniors
Tee Times: No

Description: Good practice for putting and short irons.

Holes	Par	Yards Back Tees	Rating	Slope
9	27	860	—	—

	9 Holes	18 Holes	Hours Mid Season
Weekday:	$5.00	$7.50	8:00 am - 8:00 pm
Weekend:	$6.00	$9.00	8:00 am - 8:00 pm
Cart Fees:	—	—	
Club Rental: Yes			

Western Hills Golf Course   CT 75

Park Road, Waterbury CT —   Tee Times (203)756-1211

Directions: East on I-84 to Exit 17. Take Rte 63 North. Make a right at the 3rd light (Park Rd). Go 1/4 mi. to Clough Rd, and turn left to the course.

Holes	Par	Yards Back Tees	Rating	Slope
18	72	6427	69.6	125

Facility Type: Public

Club Pro: Ralph Tremaglio

Discounts: Seniors

Tee Times: Yes, Thurs. for Sat. and Fri. for Sun. after 9 am on the phone, or after 7 am in person.

	9 Holes	18 Holes	Hours Mid Season
Weekday:	$9.50	$15.50	7:00 am - Dusk
Weekend:	$12.00	$18.00	7:00 am - Dusk
Cart Fees:	$10.00	$17.00	

Mandatory Cart Rental: No

Club Rental: Yes

Features: Lessons, Showers/Lockers, Practice Area, Pro Shop - Complete, Clubhouse, Restaurant, Bar, Snack Bar, Banquet Facilities

Notes: Senior discounts for Waterbury residents and surrounding towns. Junior program weekdays before 11 am. Reduced fees for Waterbury residents. There is an indoor lesson facility here.

Description: This is a fairly hilly course with not too much sand or water, but many different lies will test the average golfer.

Westwoods Golf Course   CT 76

Rte 177, Farmington CT —   Tee Times: (203)677-9192

Directions: I-84 to the Bristol Exit. Take Rte 6 West to the 5th light, Rte 177. Take a right and the course is 1/2 mi. on the left.

Holes	Par	Yards Back Tees	Rating	Slope
18	61	4407	60.1	87

Facility Type: Public

Club Pro: Jim Tennant

Discounts: Seniors

Tee Times: Yes, 1 week prior for weekends /holidays

	9 Holes	18 Holes	Hours Mid Season
Weekday:	$8.00	$14.00	7:00 am - Dusk
Weekend:	$10.50	$17.00	7:00 am - Dusk
Cart Fees:	$10.00	$18.00	

Mandatory Cart Rental: No

Club Rental: Yes

Features: Lessons, Driving Range, Practice Area, Pro Shop - Complete, Clubhouse, Restaurant, Bar

Description: This is a Geoffrey Cornish design. It's a well-maintained and watered course. It is flat and short, but challenging.

Whitney Farms Golf Course
CT 77
175 Shelton Rd, Monroe CT — Tee Times: (203)268-0707

Directions: Merritt Pkwy to Exit 49 N. Take a right at the 1st stop (Rte111). Go approximately 4 mi. to Rte 110, and take a right. The course is 1 mi. on the left.

Facility Type: Public

Club Pro: Paul McGuire
Discounts: None
Tee Times: Yes, 1 week prior for weekends

Features: Lessons, Showers/Lockers, Driving Range, Practice Area, Pro Shop - Complete, Clubhouse, Restaurant, Bar, Snack Bar, American Express, VISA/MC, Banquet Facilities

Description: This well maintained and modern course was a Golf Digest selection for "Places to Play" in both '91 and '91. It's playable and enjoyable for all levels of golfers. The terrain is rolling and very scenic, with some water and average-size greens. The 15th, a 175 yd par 3 is a favorite with an elevated tee and a shot across water.

Holes	Par	Yards Back Tees	Rating	Slope
18	72	6628	72.4	130

	9 Holes	18 Holes	Hours Mid Season
Weekday:	$15.00	$30.00	7:30 am - 6:00 pm
Weekend:	$17.50	$35.00	6:00 am - 6:00 pm
Cart Fees:	—	—	

Mandatory Cart Rental: Yes
Club Rental: Yes

Notes: Carts are included in green fees.

Willimantic Country Club
CT 78
184 Club Rd, Willimantic CT — (203)456-1971

Directions: East on 384 to Rte 6 East. This becomes Rte 6 Extension. Take it to the end and turn left onto Rte 66. The club is 1/4 mi. on the left.

Facility Type: Semi-private

Club Pro: John Boucher
Discounts: None
Tee Times: No

Features: Lessons, Showers/Lockers, Practice Area, Pro Shop - Complete, Clubhouse, Restaurant, Bar, Banquet Facilities

Description: The course is in great shape with watered fairways. The front 9 is older, hilly and open. The back is flat and tight. The greens are relatively small. The favorite is #17, a 430 yd par 4. It's a long shot to a small and hidden green.

Holes	Par	Yards Back Tees	Rating	Slope
18	71	6222	69.7	118

	9 Holes	18 Holes	Hours Mid Season
Weekday:	—	$25.00	See notes
Weekend:	—	—	
Cart Fees:	—	$10.00	

Mandatory Cart Rental: No
Club Rental: Yes

Notes: Weekdays before 3 pm. Fri. before 12 pm. Weekend play is not available for non-members.

Woodhaven Country Club
CT 79
275 Miller Rd, Bethany CT — Tee Times: (203)393-3230

Directions: Rte 15 (Wilbur Cross) to Exit 59 (Rte 69). Take Rte 69 West a very short distance to the first left, Lucy Street, and then a right onto Rte 63. Go 4 mi. on Rte 63 and take a left on Rte 67. 2.5 mi. on the right is Bear Hill Rd and the sign for course.

Facility Type: Public

Club Pro: None
Discounts: Seniors
Tee Times: Yes, 1 week for weekends

Features: Lessons, Practice Area, Pro Shop - Complete, Clubhouse, Snack Bar

Description: Al Zikorus designed this course. It is very well maintained. Fairways are tree-lined and the greens are challenging. It's scenic and a good course for walking.

Holes	Par	Yards Back Tees	Rating	Slope
9	36	3387	72.7	128

	9 Holes	18 Holes	Hours Mid Season
Weekday:	$9.00	$17.00	7:00 am - Dusk
Weekend:	$12.00	$23.00	6:00 am - Dusk
Cart Fees:	$11.00	$22.00	

Mandatory Cart Rental: No
Club Rental: Yes

Woodstock Golf Course
CT 80
Roseland Park Road, Woodstock, CT — (203)928-9991

Directions: I-395 to Exit 97. Go West on 171 approximately 3 mi. to the 1st right past the Woodstock Fair. Take a right onto Roseland and the course is 1 mi. on the left.

Facility Type: Executive

Club Pro: Dan Harder
Discounts: Seniors, Juniors
Tee Times: No

Features: Lessons, Driving Range, Pro Shop - Limited, Snack Bar

Description: The challenge on this semi-hilly course is the greens. It's a fun course and good practice for your putting.

Holes	Par	Yards Back Tees	Rating	Slope
9	33	2070	—	—

	9 Holes	18 Holes	Hours Mid Season
Weekday:	$7.00	$11.00	7:00 am - Dusk
Weekend:	$8.00	$12.00	6:00 am - Dusk
Cart Fees:	—	—	

Mandatory Cart Rental: No
Club Rental:

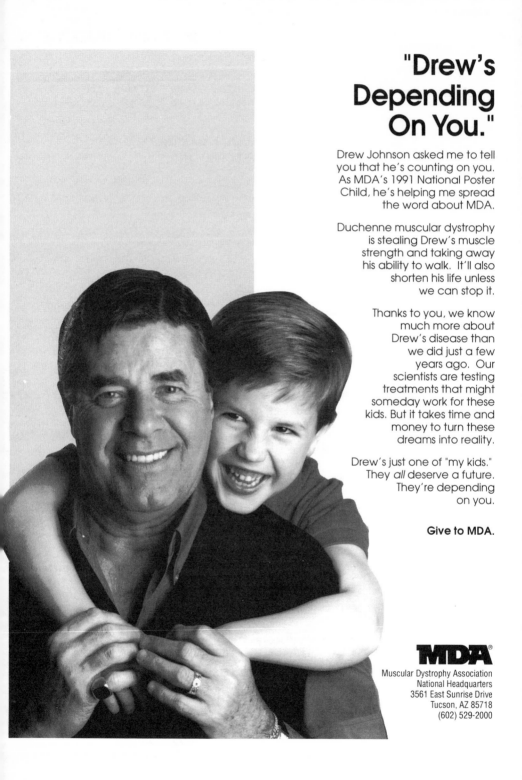

"Drew's Depending On You."

Drew Johnson asked me to tell you that he's counting on you. As MDA's 1991 National Poster Child, he's helping me spread the word about MDA.

Duchenne muscular dystrophy is stealing Drew's muscle strength and taking away his ability to walk. It'll also shorten his life unless we can stop it.

Thanks to you, we know much more about Drew's disease than we did just a few years ago. Our scientists are testing treatments that might someday work for these kids. But it takes time and money to turn these dreams into reality.

Drew's just one of "my kids." They *all* deserve a future. They're depending on you.

Give to MDA.

MDA®

Muscular Dystrophy Association
National Headquarters
3561 East Sunrise Drive
Tucson, AZ 85718
(602) 529-2000

CT 1   **Hartford**

AIRWAYS GOLF COURSE
1070 S Grand, Suffield, CT
(203)688-4773

Come enjoy 18 holes of challenging golf at scenic Airways. Restaurant. Lounge. Memberships available.

You are invited to play a COMPLIMENTARY 9 or 18 hole round of golf when accompanied with one fully paid round at the regular rate one time during the 1992 season.

Valid Mon thru Fri (except holidays) only from 11:00 am to 7:00 pm.

Must call ahead for assured tee times.

❏ Validation

PLEASE READ VALIDATION RESTRICTIONS CAREFULLY.

CT 2   **New Haven**

ALLING MEMORIAL GOLF COURSE
35 Eastern St, New Haven, CT
(203)787-8013

Come enjoy a fine municipal 18 hole golf course. Great layout. 35 gas carts. Golf professional. Restaurant. Lounge.

You are invited to play a COMPLIMENTARY 9 or 18 hole round of golf when accompanied with a fully paid round of equal value one time during the 1992 season.

Valid anytime Mon thru Fri (except holidays)

Call ahead for assured tee times.

POWER CART RENTAL IS REQUIRED

❏ Validation

OFFER IS NOT VALID IF DETACHED FROM BOOK.

CT 6   **Windham**

BROOKLYN COUNTRY CLUB
170 South St, Danielson, CT
(203)779-2400

You are invited to play a COMPLIMENTARY 9 or 18 hole round of golf when accompanied with a fully paid round of equal value one time during the 1992 season.

Valid Mon thru Fri (except holidays) only from 7:00 am to 4:00 pm

Call ahead for tee times.

POWER CART RENTAL IS REQUIRED

❏ Validation

You are invited to play a COMPLI-MENTARY 9 or 18 hole round of golf when accompanied with a fully paid round of equal value two times during the 1992 season.

Valid anytime Mon thru Fri (except holidays) only. Must call ahead for assured tee times.

POWER CART RENTAL IS RE-QUIRED

☐ 1st Time Validation

☐ 2nd Time Validation

CT 25   Hartford

GOODWIN GOLF COURSE
1130 Maple Ave, Hartford CT, 06114
(203)525-3601

There's a lot of golf here for every level of player - an 18 hole course and a 9 hole executive. Open all year.

OFFER IS NOT VALID IF DETACHED FROM BOOK.

You are invited to play a COMPLI-MENTARY 9 or 18 hole round of golf when accompanied with a fully paid round of equal value one time during the 1992 season.

Valid anytime after Sept 4, 1992.

Call ahead for tee times.

POWER CART RENTAL IS RE-QUIRED.

☐ Validation

CT 26   Hartford

GRASSMERE COUNTRY CLUB
130 Town Farm Rd, Enfield CT
(203)749-7740

COUPONS ARE NOT VALID FOR LEAGUE PLAY, SPECIAL EVENTS, OR OUTINGS.

You are invited to play a COMPLI-MENTARY 9 or 18 hole round of golf when accompanied with a fully paid round of equal value one time during the 1992 season.

Valid anytime.

Call ahead for assured tee times.

POWER CART RENTAL IS RE-QUIRED

☐ Validation

CT 32   New Haven

HOP BROOK GOLF COURSE
615 N Church St, Naugatuck CT
(203)729-8013

CT 36 **Hartford**

KENEY GOLF COURSE

Barbour St Extension, Hartford, CT
(203)525-3656

Come enjoy challenging golf at a course built in the 1920's. American Golf Corporation has returned this course to its once-beautiful condition. A variety of tournament and banquet packages available.

You are invited to play a COMPLIMENTARY 9 or 18 hole round of golf when accompanied with a fully paid round of equal value one time during the 1992 season.

Valid Mon thru Fri (except holidays) from 8:00 am to 2:00 pm and weekends and holidays after 2:00 pm.

Call ahead for tee times.

POWER CART RENTAL IS REQUIRED

❏ Validation

PLEASE READ VALIDATION RESTRICTIONS CAREFULLY.

CT 38 **New London**

LISBON COUNTRY CLUB

78 Kendall Rd, Lisbon, CT
(203)376-4325

Come play challenging and enjoyable golf in a friendly atmosphere.

You are invited to play a COMPLIMENTARY 9 or 18 hole round of golf when accompanied with a fully paid round of equal value one time during the 1992 season.

Valid Mon thru Fri (except holidays) from 9:00 am to 4:00 pm and weekends and holidays after 1 pm.

Call ahead for tee times.

POWER CART RENTAL IS REQUIRED.

❏ Validation

OFFER IS NOT VALID IF DETACHED FROM BOOK.

CT 46 **New Haven**

ORANGE HILLS COUNTRY CLUB

489 Racebrook Rd, Orange CT
(203)795-4161

Only course in CT to receive the 1990 National Golf Foundation Public Course Achievement Award. Come enjoy this challenging and hilly course carved out of the woods.

You are invited to play a COMPLIMENTARY 9 or 18 hole round of golf when accompanied with a fully paid round of equal value one time during the 1992 season.

Valid from March 31 to May 15 and from Sept 14 to Dec 1 Mon thru Fri (except holidays) from 7:00 am to 12:30 pm.

Call ahead for tee times.

POWER CART RENTAL IS REQUIRED.

❏ Validation

You are invited to play a COMPLI-MENTARY 9 or 18 hole round of golf when accompanied with a fully paid round of equal value one time during the 1992 season.

Valid Mon thru Fri (except holidays) only from 7:00 am to 12:00 pm.

Call ahead for tee times.

POWER CART RENTAL IS RE-QUIRED

☐ Validation

CT 47   **Hartford**

PATTONBROOK COUNTRY CLUB
201 Pattonwood Dr, Southington, CT
(203)747-9466

Play 18 holes on our scenic layout, featuring small, fast greens and tight fairways to challenge your golf skills. Outings and full and out-of-state memberships.

OFFER IS NOT VALID IF DETACHED FROM BOOK.

You are invited to play a COMPLI-MENTARY 9 or 18 hole round of golf when accompanied with a fully paid round of equal value 2 times during the 1992 season. Valid only in the months of March and April and from Oct 1 to close of the season on Mon thru Fri (except holidays) only until 12:00 noon.
Call ahead for tee times.

POWER CART RENTAL IS RE-QUIRED

☐ 1st Time Validation

☐ 2nd Time Validation

CT 50   **New Haven**

PILGRIM'S HARBOR GOLF CLUB
Harrison Rd, Wallingford, CT
(203)269-6023

Come enjoy this challenging and manicured course. The greens are fast and mowed to 1/2 inch. Season passes are available

COUPONS ARE NOT VALID FOR LEAGUE PLAY, SPECIAL EVENTS, OR OUTINGS.

You are invited to play a COMPLI-MENTARY 9 or 18 hole round of golf when accompanied with a fully paid round of equal value one time during the 1992 season.

Valid Mon thru Fri (except holidays) only from 7:00 am to dusk.

Call ahead for tee times.

POWER CART RENTAL IS RE-QUIRED

☐ Validation

CT 52   **Middlesex**

PORTLAND GOLF CLUB WEST
105 Gospel Lane, Portland CT
(203)342-4043

Come play our challenging 18 hole par 60 and a driving range. Rated #1 par 60 in CT. It's a true test for the low handicapper and compatible with the beginner, as well.

CT 54   **Windham**

RACEWAY GOLF COURSE
East Thompson Road, Thompson, CT
(203)923-9591

Come enjoy 18 holes at a fun course.

You are invited to play a COMPLI-MENTARY 9 or 18 hole round of golf when accompanied with a fully paid round of equal value two times during the 1992 season.

Valid Mon thru Fri (except holidays) only after 12:00 noon.

Must call ahead for tee times.

POWER CART RENTAL IS RE-QUIRED

☐ 1st Time Validation

☐ 2nd Time Validation

PLEASE READ VALIDATION RESTRICTIONS CAREFULLY.

CT 58   **Hartford**

ROLLING GREENS GOLF CLUB
600 Cold Spring Rd, Rocky Hill CT
(203)257-9775

You are invited to play a COMPLI-MENTARY 9 hole round of golf when accompanied with a fully paid round of equal value one time during the 1992 season.

Valid Mon thru Fri (except holidays) only from 8:00 am to 3:00 pm

Call ahead for assured tee times

POWER CART RENTAL IS RE-QUIRED.

☐ Validation

OFFER IS NOT VALID IF DETACHED FROM BOOK.

CT 61   **Tolland**

SKUNKAMAUG RIVER GOLF CLUB
Folly Lane, Coventry CT
(203)742-9348

Nestled in the woods, our shortish but tight 18 holes offer every golfer a challenge. No back and forth fairways here.

You are invited to play a COMPLI-MENTARY 9 or 18 hole round of golf when accompanied witha fully paid round of equal value one time during the 1992 season.

Valid Mon thru Fri (except holidays) from 8:00 am to 1:00 pm.

Call ahead for tee times.

POWER CART RENTAL IS RE-QUIRED

☐ Validation

You are invited to play a COMPLI-MENTARY 9 or 18 hole round of golf when accompanied by a fully paid round of equal value one time during the 1992 season.

Valid Mon thru Fri (except holidays) from 9:00 am to 3:00 pm.

Call ahead for tee times.

POWER CART RENTAL IS RE-QUIRED.

☐ Validation

CT 73

Tolland

TWIN HILLS COUNTRY CLUB
Rte 31, Coventry CT
(203)742-9705

Play an 18 hole round of golf in the rolling hills of Connecticut. Pro shop. Restaurant.

OFFER IS NOT VALID IF DETACHED FROM BOOK.

New Jersey

Northern New Jersey

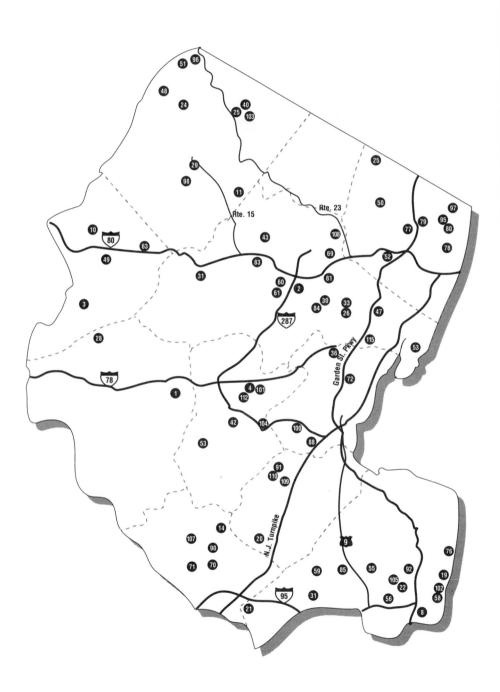

Southern New Jersey

New Jersey County Systems

Many of the counties in New Jersey have or are in the process of establishing programs to benefit their resident golfers with lower green fees and systems for reserving tee times. Since some of these systems are not exclusive to county residents, it pays to understand how they work. Proof of residence may include a current drivers license, a tax bill, a lease agreement, an electric bill, or a phone bill.

BERGEN COUNTY: Overpeck, Rockleigh, Darlington, Orchard Hills
In order to receive a discount, a photo ID must be obtained with proof of residency and $20 at one of the courses, good for the calendar year.

ESSEX COUNTY: Hendricks Field, Weequaick, Francis Byrne
To be able to reserve in person on Thursday for weekend play and receive county discounts, a photo ID can be obtained with proof of residency at 160 Fairview Avenue in Cedar Grove for $25, valid for the calendar year.

MERCER COUNTY: Mercer Oaks, Princeton, Mountain View
Mercer Oaks has instituted a reservation system for weekends for county residents. It has not been applied to Princeton or Mountain View. Proof of residency must be presented to any of the three courses for an ID costing $15, entitling residents to use the reservation system at Mercer Oaks and receive discounts at all three courses.

MIDDLESEX COUNTY: Tamarack
There are no tee times, but residents can receive a discount by showing ID obtained at the pro shop with proof of residency and paying $15 for the year.

MONMOUTH COUNTY: Hominy Hill, Howell Park, Pinebrook, Shark River
Residents can reserve 7 days prior on a phone system. To be put into the computer for 12 months they must present two (2) proofs of residency to any of the 4 pro shops and pay $12. Non-residents may purchase a card for $24, which allows them to call 5 days prior. A percentage of the tee times will be kept open for non-residents.

MORRIS COUNTY: Pinch Brook, Flanders Valley, Sunset Valley
Residents and non-residents may be put into the reservation system for tee times. Residents must present proof of residency at any one of the pro shops for a photo ID costing $25, good for the calendar year. A charge of $2 for residents and $4 for non-residents will be added to green fees for reserving tee times.

OCEAN COUNTY: Forge Pond, Ocean County at Atlantis
Residents may purchase ID at the courses for $10 for the calendar year by showing two (2) proofs of residency, entitling them to reduced green fees.

PASSAIC COUNTY: Passaic
County residents may purchase an ID at the course for $25 good for the calendar year to receive discounted green fees.

SOMERSET COUNTY: Green Knoll, Quail Brook, Spooky Brook, Warren Brook
Residents may obtain an application for the system at any of the pro shops, which they must mail with proof of residency and $25 to obtain an ID. Non-residents may be placed into the system for $50. Non-subscribers to the system may call the day before to reserve for a $6 additional charge.

UNION COUNTY: Galloping Hill, Oak Ridge, Ash Brook
County residents must present a drivers licence or other proof of residency at any of the three courses and pay $25 for an ID.

Al Bohems Golf Center

130 Rte 22, Whitehouse Station NJ — (908)534-4748

Directions: Rte 78 to the Whitehouse-Oldwick Exit. Take 523 South to Rte 22. Go right on 22. Going West on Rte22, the course is on the right 1 mi.

Facility Type: Pitch & Putt

Club Pro: None
Discounts: None
Tee Times:

Features: Lessons, Driving Range, Pro Shop - Limited, VISA/MC

Description: A complete driving range is on the facility, as well as miniature golf.

Holes	Par	Yards Back Tees	Rating	Slope
9	27	635	—	—

	9 Holes	18 Holes	Hours Mid Season
Weekday:	$5.00	—	8:00 am - 10:30 pm
Weekend:	$5.00	—	8:00 am - 10:30 pm
Cart Fees:	—	—	
Club Rental:			

Anchor Golfland

21 Rte 10, Whippany NJ — (201)887-0898

Directions: On Rte 10, 3 miles East of Rte 287 before the light at Sandoz.

Facility Type: Pitch & Putt

Club Pro: Roger Stone
Discounts: Seniors
Tee Times: No

Features: Lessons, Driving Range, Pro Shop - Complete, Snack Bar

Description: A complete facility with driving range. "Everything for your swing".

Holes	Par	Yards Back Tees	Rating	Slope
18	54	—	—	—

	9 Holes	18 Holes	Hours Mid Season
Weekday:	$5.00	$8.00	9:00 am - 10:00 pm
Weekend:	$5.00	$8.00	9:00 am - 10:00 pm
Cart Fees:	—	—	
Club Rental:			

Apple Mountain Golf & CC NJ 3

Belvedere NJ — Info: (908)453-3023   Tee Times: (800)PLA-Golf

Directions: Rte 78 to Rte 31 North. Go 7 traffic lights, approximately 17 mi. and take left on Wall St. in the town of Oxford. Road becomes 624 West. Course is 2.5 mi. on left.

Facility Type: Public

Coupon page 123

Club Pro: Bob Dacey
Discounts: Seniors, Twilight
Tee Times: Yes, 2 weeks ahead

Features: Lessons, Showers/Lockers, Practice Area, Pro Shop - Complete, Clubhouse, Restaurant, Bar, Snack Bar, Banquet Facilities, VISA/MC

Description: A pretty course, especially in Sept, with a view of Del Water gap. Course is cut out of an apple orchard. Elevated tees and greens. Undulating greens. The 17th is a favorite - 651 yd par 5 dogleg left on the side of a mountain with woods on both sides.

Holes	Par	Yards Back Tees	Rating	Slope
18	71	6500	71.8	122

	9 Holes	18 Holes	Hours Mid Season
Weekday:	$9.50	$14.00	7:00 am - Dusk
Weekend:	—	$ 35.00	6:00 am - Dusk
Cart Fees:	—	$20.00	

Mandatory Cart Rental: See notes.
Club Rental: Yes

Notes: Residents of New Jersey and 215 area code call 1 800 PLA GOLF. 9 hole on weekday only after 3. Weekends - $35 includes cart before 3 pm. Rocking Ridge DR 1/4 away.

Ash Brook Golf Course NJ 4

1210 Raritan Rd, Scotch Plains NJ — (908)756-0414

Directions: Rte 22 West (Exit 140A off Grdn St Pkwy) to Terrill Rd in Scotch Plains. (You can only exit 1 way). Go approx 3 miles to end and turn right onto Raritan Rd. Go up hill to course on left.

Facility Type: Public

Club Pro: None
Discounts: Seniors, Juniors
Tee Times: No

Features: Showers/Lockers, Practice Area, Snack Bar, Clubhouse

Description: A good mix of holes, water on several. Course is of average difficulty. The course is relatively flat. Forcasting opening of proshop for '92

Holes	Par	Yards Back Tees	Rating	Slope
18	72	6916	73.4	121

	9 Holes	18 Holes	Hours Mid Season
Weekday:	—	$16.00	7:00 am - 8:00 pm
Weekend:	—	$20.00	6:00 am - 8:00 pm
Cart Fees:	$12.00	$18.50	

Mandatory Cart Rental: No
Club Rental: No

Notes: Reduced fees for Union county residents with county cards. Greens fees for out of state players are $35 on weekdays and $50 on weekends. Jr discount only for county residents and sr discounts only for Union county residents and counties with reciprocal plans.

Avalon Country Club

1510 Rte 9 North, Cape May Court House NJ — Tee Times: (609)465-Golf

Directions: Garden State Parkway to Exit 13. Take a right off the exit and go 1/2 mi. to Rte 9 and take a left. The course is 1 mi. on the left.

Holes	Par	Yards Back Tees	Rating	Slope
18	72	6517	70.3	122

Facility Type: Semi-private

	9 Holes	18 Holes	Hours Mid Season
Weekday:	—	—	Dawn - Dusk
Weekend:	—	—	Dawn - Dusk
Cart Fees:	—	—	

Club Pro: Ted Wenner
Discounts: None
Tee Times: Yes, 1 week ahead for any day

Mandatory Cart Rental: See notes.
Club Rental: Yes

Features: Lessons, Showers/Lockers, Practice Area, Pro Shop - Complete, Clubhouse, Restaurant, Bar, Snack Bar, Banquet Facilities, American Express, VISA/MC, Lodging Nearby

Notes: Walking allowed in off season only. Green fees vary according to the season. Prices vary greatly so call ahead for specifics.

Description: This is a flat, treed and scenic course. A favorite hole is # 5, a 590 yard par 5, slight dogleg left. Shoot through woods on the left and water and woods on the right to an elevated green. The architect was Bob Hendricks.

B L England Golf Course

Marmora NJ — Tee Times: (609)390-0472

Directions: Garden State Parkway North to Exit 25. Go left off the exit to Rte 9 and take a right. The course 1 mi. on the left. Going South on the Parkway, take exit 25. Go right off the exit to Rte 9 and right to the course.

Holes	Par	Yards Back Tees	Rating	Slope
9	34	2478	63.7	100

	9 Holes	18 Holes	Hours Mid Season
Weekday:	$18.00	$18.00	7:00 am - Dusk
Weekend:	$18.00	$18.00	6:30 am - Dusk
Cart Fees:	$8.00	$16.00	

Facility Type: Semi-private

Club Pro: Ralph Carson
Discounts: Seniors
Tee Times: Yes, 3 days ahead for any day.

Mandatory Cart Rental: No
Club Rental: Yes

Features: Lessons, Pro Shop - Complete, Snack Bar

Description: This course is in good condition. It's a fairly flat course that features trees, water on 4 holes, very good small greens and many doglegs. It demands accuracy.

Beckett Country Club

Swedesboro NJ — Tee Times: (609)467-4700

Directions: Rte 295 to Exit 10. At the top of the ramp going North take a right, going South take a left. Go 4 1/2 mi. and at the 3rd stop take a right onto Old Kings Highway. The course is 1.5 mi. on the right.

Facility Type: Public

Club Pro: Steve DeVito
Discounts: Twilight
Tee Times: Yes, for public (non members) Monday before for weekend/holidays.

Features: Lessons, Showers/Lockers, Driving Range, Practice Area, Pro Shop - Complete, Restaurant, Bar, Clubhouse, Banquet Facilities, Lodging Nearby

Description: This course offers a great deal of variety at a reasonable rate and it's in good condition. There are some very interesting holes. The most notable is the "blue monster" - the 5th hole. It's a 488 yd par 5 severe horseshoe-shaped dogleg. It is narrow and plays over water - a real conversation piece.

Holes	Par	Yards Back Tees	Rating	Slope
9	B 36	3166	—	—
9	R 36	3162	—	—
9	W 36	3159	—	—

	9 Holes	18 Holes	Hours Mid Season
Weekday:	—	$10.00	6:30 am - Dusk
Weekend:	—	$12.00	6:00 am - Dusk
Cart Fees:	—	$18.00	

Mandatory Cart Rental: No
Club Rental: Yes

Notes: Red to Blue is 69.0 and 114. Blue to White is 68.8 and 113. White to Red is 68.9 and 113.

Bel - Aire Golf Course

Highway 34, Allenwood NJ — (908)449-6024

Directions: Garden St Parkway to Exit 98 to Rte 34 South. The course is on the traffic circle. I-95 to Exit 35 to Rte 34. Again, South to the traffic circle.

Facility Type: Executive

Club Pro: Powers McLean
Discounts: Seniors
Tee Times: No

Coupon page 123

Features: Lessons, Practice Area, Pro Shop - Complete, Snack Bar, Driving Range

Description: Two good executive courses. The 18 hole is challenging enough to be real golf, with traps on every hole and water on four of them. It is much harder than it reads. You are challenged to shoot par the 1st time.

Holes	Par	Yards Back Tees	Rating	Slope
9	27	1600	—	—
18	60	3590	55.6	72

	9 Holes	18 Holes	Hours Mid Season
Weekday:	$7.00	$13.00	6:00 am - 6:00 pm
Weekend:	$7.50	$15.00	6:00 am - 6:00 pm
Cart Fees:	$13.00	$18.00	

Mandatory Cart Rental: No
Club Rental: Yes

Bey Lea Golf Course

1536 N. Bay Ave, Toms River NJ — Tee Times: (908)349-0566

Directions: Garden State Parkway South to Exit 82. Take Rte 37 East toward Seaside. The 2nd light is Hooper Ave (Rte 549). Jug handle North on 549. Go 6 lights and jug handle again to the course.

Facility Type: Public

Club Pro: None
Discounts: Seniors, Twilight
Tee Times: Yes, Weekends/holidays from Memorial Day to Labor Day. Call in the morning 3 days prior.

Features: Driving Range, Practice Area, Pro Shop - Limited, Restaurant, Bar, Snack Bar

Description: The course is relatively open and flat. The back 9 offers a little more challenge with water hazards.

Holes	Par	Yards Back Tees	Rating	Slope
18	72	6677	71.4	115

	9 Holes	18 Holes	Hours Mid Season
Weekday:	—	$18.00	7:00 am - Dusk
Weekend:	—	$20.00	6:00 am - Dusk
Cart Fees:	—	$22.00	

Mandatory Cart Rental: No
Club Rental: Yes

Notes: The course has a stand alone driving range.

Blair Acadamy Golf Course

Blairstown NJ — (908)362-6218

Directions: Rte 80 West to Rte 521 North (Blairstown/Hope Exit). Follow signs to the course in Blairstown.

Facility Type: Semi-private

Club Pro: None
Discounts: Twilight
Tee Times: No

Features: Practice Area, Pro Shop - Limited

Description: The course is hilly and tight with small greens. There are no carts so it is good exercise.

Holes	Par	Yards Back Tees	Rating	Slope
9	35	2975	—	—

	9 Holes	18 Holes	Hours Mid Season
Weekday:	—	$12.00	7:00 am - Dusk
Weekend:	—	$17.00	12:00 pm - Dusk
Cart Fees:	—	—	

Club Rental: Yes

Notes: Weekend mornings are reserved for member play. No carts.

Bowling Green Golf Course NJ 11

Schoolhouse Rd, Milton NJ — Tee Times: (201)697-8688

Directions: Rte 80 West to Exit 34B (15 North). Take 15 North to Berkshire Valley Rd Exit. Bear right off of the exit and go 8.6 mi. to the 1st light, Ridge Rd, and turn left. Go 1 mi. to the blinking yellow light (Schoolhouse Rd), and take a left. The course is 1 mi. on right.

Facility Type: Public

Club Pro: Tom Staples
Discounts: None
Tee Times: Yes, 2 days ahead for any day.

Coupon page 123

Features: Lessons, Showers/Lockers, Driving Range, Practice Area, Pro Shop - Complete, Clubhouse, Restaurant, Bar, Snack Bar

Holes	Par	Yards Back Tees	Rating	Slope
18	72	6789	72.9	131

	9 Holes	18 Holes	Hours Mid Season
Weekday:	$14.00	$21.00	7:00 am - Dusk
Weekend:	—	$33.00	6:30 am - Dusk
Cart Fees:	—	$25.00	

Mandatory Cart Rental: No
Club Rental: No

Description: This is one of the only Geoffrey Cornish designed courses in New Jersey. It is very challenging off the tee. Pine trees throughout the front nine offer beauty, while challenging the golfer to hit accurately. Water and trees come into play on the back nine often. Large undulating greens are well maintained. Management claims this course will "bring a good golfer to his/her knees".

Brigantine Golf Links NJ 12

Roosevelt Blvd & The Bay, Brigantine NJ — Tee Times: (609)266-1388

Directions: Garden State Parkway to the Atlantic City Exit 40 (Rte 30). Follow signs for Harrahs and Trump Castle. Go over the bridge separating the two to Brigantine Blvd. Go around the lighthouse traffic circle and after approximately 2 miles take a left on Roosevelt Ave to the course.

Facility Type: Public

Club Pro: None
Discounts: Twilight
Tee Times: Yes, 1 week ahead for any day.

Coupon page 124

Features: Practice Area, Pro Shop - Complete, Clubhouse, Snack Bar

Holes	Par	Yards Back Tees	Rating	° Slope
18	72	6700	71.3	117

	9 Holes	18 Holes	Hours Mid Season
Weekday:	—	$30.00	6:00 am - Dusk
Weekend:	—	$35.00	5:30 am - Dusk
Cart Fees:	—	—	

Mandatory Cart Rental: Yes
Club Rental: Yes

Notes: Cart is included in green fees.

Description: Built in 1926, this is one of the few true links courses in the country, and certainly in this area. It is long for this open a course, and the greens are in fantastic shape.

Buena Vista Country Club

Buena NJ — Tee Times: (609)697-3733

Directions: Garden State Parkway to the Atlantic City Expresswy West toward Phila to Exit 12 (322 -40). Take Rte 40 through Mays Landing. The course is 16 miles on the right. From Philadelphia take Exit 28 on the Atl Cty Exprsswy. Take 54 South to Rte 40. Make a left onto 40 going East. The course is 1.5 mi. on left.

Facility Type: Semi-private

Club Pro: Dennis Henderson
Discounts: Twilight
Tee Times: Yes, 6 days prior for non- members. Minimum of 3 people to reserve tee times

Features: Lessons, Showers/Lockers, Driving Range, Practice Area, Pro Shop - Complete, Clubhouse, Restaurant, Bar, Banquet Facilities

Holes	Par	Yards Back Tees	Rating	Slope
18	72	6869	73.5	131

	9 Holes	18 Holes	Hours Mid Season
Weekday:	—	$20.00	6:00 am - Dusk
Weekend:	—	$22.00	6:00 am - Dusk
Cart Fees:	—	$10.00	

Mandatory Cart Rental: See notes.
Club Rental: No

Notes: Carts are mandatory on weekends and holidays from June to October. The cart price above is per person.

Description: This is a flat and narrow course, heavily wooded and well-bunkered. The consensus hole is #10, a 502 yd par 5 that features a 200 yd long trap from the tee out. If you avoid that, there are 3 others and a dogleg on the way to a 2-bunkered green. There is also water on 5 holes. This course is in good shape.

Bunker Hill Golf Course   NJ 14

Bunker Hill Rd, Griggstown NJ — Tee Times: (908)359-6335

Directions: From Rte 1 in Monmouth Junction take New Rd West. The course is 5 mi. on right.

Facility Type: Public

Club Pro: Matt Evans
Discounts: Seniors
Tee Times: Yes, Monday before for weekends/holidays

Features: Lessons, Showers/Lockers, Pro Shop - Complete, Clubhouse, Snack Bar, VISA/MC

Description: This course is a good test for the average golfer. It is hilly and tight with small greens, so there is a premium on accurate shot placement. A creek comes into play on 5 holes.

Holes	Par	Yards Back Tees	Rating	Slope
18	72	6200	67.9	111

	9 Holes	18 Holes	Hours Mid Season
Weekday:	—	$13.50	Dawn - Dusk
Weekend:	—	$33.50	Dawn - Dusk
Cart Fees:	$12.00	$24.00	

Mandatory Cart Rental: See notes.
Club Rental: Yes

Notes: Cart price weekends included in green fees. Carts are mandatory untill 3 pm.

ay National Golf Club

e Times: (609)884-1563

State Parkway to Exit 4 A. Only
..t to 2nd light, Rte 9. Take left and
clu... s on left.

Facility Type: Semi-private

Club Pro: Russel Davis
Discounts: Twilight
Tee Times: Yes, up to 7 days in advance for non-members.

Features: Lessons, Driving Range, Practice Area, Pro Shop - Complete, Clubhouse, Snack Bar, VISA/MC, Lodging Nearby

Holes	Par	Yards Back Tees	Rating	Slope
18	71	6810	71.9	—

	9 Holes	18 Holes	Hours Mid Season
Weekday:	—	$48.00	Dawn - Dusk
Weekend:	—	$48.00	Dawn - Dusk
Cart Fees:	—	—	

Mandatory Cart Rental: See notes.
Club Rental: No

Notes: Cart fees are included and mandatory during season but on weekends only in the off season. Rates drop to $35 weekends and $28 weekdays off season. Open all year. Memberships are available.

Description: This course just opened in the Spring of '91. Improvements are being made continually. It's a links type course with North Carolina and Fla influences. It was designed by Carl Litten and Bob Mullock. The tees, fairways and greens are bent grass. With five sets of tees, you can make this course as difficult or as easy as you want. The signature hole is the prettiest, the #3 par 3, 200 yard shot from the black tees. It plays across a natural preserve.

Cedar Creek Golf Course

Bayville NJ — (908)269-4460

Directions: Garden St Parkway South to Exit 80. Take a left off the ramp onto Double Trouble Rd and go to the end. Take a left on Pinewall-Keswick Rd and the course is 1 mi. on the right.

Facility Type: Public

Club Pro: None
Discounts: Seniors, Juniors
Tee Times: No

Features: Practice Area, Pro Shop - Limited, Clubhouse, Restaurant, Bar, Banquet Facilities

Description: This is a scenic course carved out of the Pinelands. It's narrow and challenging. The front 9 is more links style. The back 9 features 3 lakes.

Holes	Par	Yards Back Tees	Rating	Slope
18	72	6647	71.8	115

	9 Holes	18 Holes	Hours Mid Season
Weekday:	—	$14.00	6:30 am - Dusk
Weekend:	—	$16.00	6:30 am - Dusk
Cart Fees:	—	$18.00	

Mandatory Cart Rental: No
Club Rental: Yes

Centerton Golf Club

Elmer NJ — **Tee Times:** (609)358-2220

Directions: Rte 55 South from Phila, take the Glassboro/Clayton/Centerton Exit. Take 553 South to the Centerton Inn. Go left on 540 and the course is 1/2 mi. on the left.

Facility Type: Public

Club Pro: Al Carman
Discounts: Twilight
Tee Times: Yes, 1 week prior for weekends/holidays and 1 day for weekdays.

Features: Lessons, Showers/Lockers, Driving Range, Practice Area, Pro Shop - Complete, Clubhouse, Restaurant, Bar, Banquet Facilities

Description: This is a gently rolling course with a variety of holes. Several holes have a "Scottish" attitude. Otherwise the course is nicely wooded. The 18th hole, a par 4, 450 yarder, is a favorite challenge.

Holes	Par	Yards Back Tees	Rating	Slope
18	71	6500	69.6	112

	9 Holes	18 Holes	Hours Mid Season
Weekday:	—	$13.75	7:00 am - Dusk
Weekend:	—	$15.75	6:00 am - Dusk
Cart Fees:	—	$16.50	

Mandatory Cart Rental: No
Club Rental: No

Notes: Twilight at 4 pm in midseason. Inquire about retiree weekday plan.

Cohanzick Country Club

Bridgeton/Fairton Rd, Fairton NJ — **Tee Times:** (609)455-2127

Directions: Rte 55 South from Phila to Exit 45 and take Rte 553 south. Follow the signs to the course on this road, approximately 12 - 15 miles. From the New Jersey Shore, come up Rte 49 West to Rte 553 and go South 12 - 15 miles to the course.

Facility Type: Public

Club Pro: John Stafford
Discounts: Twilight
Tee Times: Yes, Monday prior for weekends and holidays.

Features: Lessons, Showers/Lockers, Practice Area, Pro Shop - Complete, Restaurant, Bar, Banquet Facilities, Clubhouse, Lodging Nearby

Description: This is an intimidating course with hills and tight fairways. It is also deceiving. A good example is #17, a 406 yd par 4, a tight uphill shot to a 2-tiered trapped and mound-protected green. 4 par 3s are totally ravined.

Holes	Par	Yards Back Tees	Rating	Slope
18	71	6223	70.6	114

	9 Holes	18 Holes	Hours Mid Season
Weekday:	—	$10.00	7:00 am - Dusk
Weekend:	—	$12.00	6:00 am - Dusk
Cart Fees:	—	$18.00	

Mandatory Cart Rental: See notes.
Club Rental: Yes

Notes: Carts are mandatory on weekends from 6 am to noon.

Colonial Terrace Golf Club

1005 Wickapecko Dr , Wanamassa NJ — **Tee Times:** (908)775-3636

Directions: Garden St Parkway to Exit 102. Bear right off of the exit and go to the Asbury Park Traffic Circle. Go North on Rte 35 from the circle to the 2nd light, Sunset, and take a right. Take a right at the next light, Wickapecko, and the course is 1/2 mi. on the right.

Facility Type: Public

Club Pro: Lin Cesario
Discounts: Seniors
Tee Times: Yes, 1 week prior for weekends/holidays.

Features: Lessons, Practice Area, Pro Shop - Complete, Clubhouse, Snack Bar

Description: This is a good course for seniors and beginners. It is not too long and has wide fairways and a flat terrain. The greens are small and plush. This is also a good course for your irons game.

Holes	Par	Yards Back Tees	Rating	Slope
9	35	2724	—	—

	9 Holes	18 Holes	Hours Mid Season
Weekday:	—	$9.00	6:00 am - Dusk
Weekend:	—	$12.00	6:00 am - Dusk
Cart Fees:	—	$20.00	

Mandatory Cart Rental: No
Club Rental: Yes

Notes: Lin Cesario is one of the most respected teaching pros in the country. Senior rates weekdays only.

Cranbury Golf Club

49 Southfield Rd, Cranbury NJ — **Tee Times:** (609)799-0341

Directions: NJ Turnpike to Exit 8. Take 33 West into Heightstown and a left at the firehouse. Take the first right onto 571. Go over Rte 130 and after approximately 2 mi. take a left on Southfield across from the Sunoco Station. The course is 1 mi. on the right.

Facility Type: Semi-private

Club Pro: Dennis Bluett
Discounts: Twilight
Tee Times: Yes, 1 week ahead

Coupon page 124

Features: Lessons, Showers/Lockers, Driving Range, Pro Shop - Complete, Clubhouse, Restaurant, Bar, Snack Bar, Banquet Facilities, American Express, VISA/MC, Practice Area

Description: This is a challenging course for even the most experienced golfer. It is well bunkered with steep-faced traps. The course borders working farms and dense woods. #14 is the prettiest and the most challenging. It's a par 3, 211 yard approach over a pond with trees on both sides to a rolling green.

Holes	Par	Yards Back Tees	Rating	Slope
18	71	6319	69.0	114

	9 Holes	18 Holes	Hours Mid Season
Weekday:	$13.00	$18.00	7:00 am - Dusk
Weekend:	—	$25.00	10:00 am - Dusk
Cart Fees:	—	$24.00	

Mandatory Cart Rental: No
Club Rental: Yes

Notes: Memberships and golf outings are available. Weekends before 10 am are restricted for members.

Cream Ridge Golf Club

Cream Ridge NJ — Tee Times: (609)259-2849

Directions: NJ Turnpike to Exit 7A. Take 195 East to the Allentown Exit (Rte 7). This deadends at 539. Take a right and follow 539 to the course, 3 mi. on right.

Holes	Par	Yards Back Tees	Rating	Slope
18	71	6400	69.8	115

Facility Type: Semi-private

	9 Holes	18 Holes	Hours Mid Season
Weekday:	—	$18.00	6:30 am - 7 pm
Weekend:	—	$22.00	6:00 am - 6 pm
Cart Fees:	—	$26.00	

Club Pro: Bill Marine
Discounts: Seniors, Twilight
Tee Times: Yes, 1 week ahead for weekends/holidays

Mandatory Cart Rental: No
Club Rental: No

Features: Lessons, Showers/Lockers, Driving Range, Practice Area, Pro Shop - Complete, Snack Bar

Description: This cedar lined course is good for seniors, but still a challenge for the average golfer. Water comes into play on 11 holes.

Cruz Farm Country Club

55 Berdsal Rd, Farmingdale NJ — (908)938-3378

Directions: Garden State Parkway South to Exit 100 A. Go West on Highway 33 for 1 mi. to the Rte 34 Circle. Go South on 34 for to the 2nd light (Belmar Blvd) and take a right. Go 1 mi. and take a left onto Berdsal Rd to the course.

Holes	Par	Yards Back Tees	Rating	Slope
18	70	6200	—	—

Facility Type: Public

	9 Holes	18 Holes	Hours Mid Season
Weekday:	$8.00	$16.00	6:00 am - Dusk
Weekend:	$10.00	$20.00	6:00 am - Dusk
Cart Fees:	—	$24.00	

Club Pro: None
Discounts: Twilight
Tee Times: No

Mandatory Cart Rental: No
Club Rental: Yes

Features: Lessons, Showers/Lockers, Practice Area, Pro Shop - Limited, Snack Bar, American Express, VISA/MC

Description: This is a rolling and challenging course with a lot of water and sand. The fairways are fairly wide. This is a good straightforward playing course.

Crystal Springs Golf Club

123 Crystal Springs Rd, Hamburg NJ — Tee Times: (201)827-1444

Directions: Exit 53 off I-80. Take Rte 23 North through Franklin and just before Hamburg take a right onto Rte 517 North. The course is in new development 2 mi. on left.

Holes	Par	Yards Back Tees	Rating	Slope
18	72	6887	71.3	130

	9 Holes	18 Holes	Hours Mid Season
Weekday:	—	$40.00	7:00 am - Dusk
Weekend:	—	$55.00	6:30 am - Dusk
Cart Fees:	—	—	

Facility Type: Semi-private

Club Pro: David Glenz
Discounts: Twilight
Tee Times: Yes, 2 to 3 days ahead for any day.

Mandatory Cart Rental: Yes
Club Rental: No

Features: Lessons, Driving Range, Practice Area, Pro Shop - Complete, Clubhouse, Restaurant, Bar, Snack Bar, Banquet Facilities, American Express, VISA/MC, Lodging Nearby

Notes: Carts are included in greens fees.

Description: This is a relatively new course and is getting a lot of attention. It is a well maintained and unusual course, very Scottish in terrain. There are a lot of moundings and hills. Water comes into play on 4 holes. The greens are average to large. #10 is the signature hole. It's a par 3, 166 yard shot on an 80 ft drop on the site of an old quarry, over water to a butterfly shaped green. It's a tough and picturesque hole.

Culver Lake Golf Club

Branchville NJ — Tee Times: (201)948-5610

Directions: Rte 80 to Exit 35 (Sparta). Take 15 North to 206 North 5 mi. to East Shore of Culver Lake Rd. Take right and 1 mi. to course.

Holes	Par	Yards Back Tees	Rating	Slope
9dt	67	5224	—	—

	9 Holes	18 Holes	Hours Mid Season
Weekday:	$10.00	$15.00	7:00 am - Dusk
Weekend:	$13.00	$18.00	6:30 am - Dusk
Cart Fees:	$14.00	$20.00	

Facility Type: Public

Club Pro: None
Discounts: Twilight, Seniors
Tee Times: Yes, tee times available. A call ahead suggested.

Mandatory Cart Rental: No
Club Rental: Yes

Features: Showers/Lockers, Pro Shop - Limited, Restaurant, Bar

Description: A short course but requires thinking. Fairways are narrow and there is some sand. Double tees.

Darlington Golf Course

277 Campgaw Rd, Mahwah NJ — (201)327-8770

Directions: Rte 17 going North to Exit for Waldwick. Go back under 17 toward Waldwick. You are on Prospect St. Go to 1st light which is Franklin Turnpike. Make a right. Go to Ramsey, and make a left on Main Street. Make a right after the shopping center. Go 2 blocks to Darlington and make a left. Make a left on Seminary Lane. Left on Campgaw to the course about 1 mile.

Facility Type: Public

Club Pro: None
Discounts: Seniors, Juniors, Twilight
Tee Times: Yes, Must be made in person for Mon, Wed, Fri, Sat and Sun. Tues and Thurs open tee times. A telephone reservation system may be established in '92.

Features: Showers/Lockers, Practice Area, Clubhouse, Snack Bar, Driving Range, Pro Shop - Complete

Description: Well kept for a county course. You will lose your slices and hooks. Greens are large. The price is right for the amount of play.

Holes	Par	Yards Back Tees	Rating	Slope
18	71	6049	68.0	115

	9 Holes	18 Holes	Hours Mid Season
Weekday:	—	$18.00	7:00 am - Dusk
Weekend:	—	$24.00	6:30 am - Dusk
Cart Fees:	—	$20.00	

Mandatory Cart Rental: No
Club Rental: No

Notes: Residents pay $11 weekdays, $14 weekends for 18 holes. Out-of-state players pay $40 any day. Club rentals at Driving Range.

East Orange Golf Course

440 Parsonage Rd, Short Hills NJ — (201)379-6775

Directions: Rte 78 to Rte 24 West (stay right on 78 to get onto 24). Take Livingston Exit and go past Short Hills Mall, becomes Kennedy Blvd. 1st left is Parsonage Rd to course.

Facility Type: Public

Club Pro: None
Discounts: Twilight
Tee Times: No

Features: Showers/Lockers, Driving Range, Practice Area, Pro Shop - Limited, Clubhouse, Restaurant, Snack Bar

Description: This is a flat, easy walking course with no water and some sand traps.

Holes	Par	Yards Back Tees	Rating	Slope
18	72	6120	67.6	100

	9 Holes	18 Holes	Hours Mid Season
Weekday:	—	$20.00	6:00 am - Dusk
Weekend:	—	$25.00	6:00 am - Dusk
Cart Fees:	—	$16.00	

Mandatory Cart Rental: No
Club Rental: Yes

Notes: Non-members may play on weekends only after 12:30. Memberships are available. Twilight begins at 4 pm. The driving range is for short irons only. Purchase buckets.

Eastlyn Golf Course

4049 Italia Ave, Vineland NJ — (609)691-5558

Directions: Rte 55 South from Phila to Exit 26. Take a left off the exit and a quick right onto Lincoln Ave. Go thru the light to 3rd Street (Menantico) and take a right. Take the 1st right onto Italia and the course is 1m on the right.

Facility Type: Executive

Club Pro: Steve Holloway
Discounts: Twilight
Tee Times: No

Features: Lessons, Driving Range, Practice Area, Pro Shop - Complete, Snack Bar, VISA/MC

Description: This is a flat, relatively short executive-type course with some par 4s. The course is tight and wooded and a good challenge for an iron game, especially the 10th hole. There are lips on the sand traps. Water comes into play on 10 holes.

Holes	Par	Yards Back Tees	Rating	Slope
18	62	3600	—	—

	9 Holes	18 Holes	Hours Mid Season
Weekday:	—	$9.00	7:00 am - Dusk
Weekend:	—	$11.00	7:00 am - Dusk
Cart Fees:	—	$12.00	

Mandatory Cart Rental: No
Club Rental: Yes

Fairway Valley Golf Club

Minehill Rd, Washington NJ — (908)689-1530

Directions: Rte 80 West to the Budd Lake Exit. Go South on Rte 46 to Hackettstown. Take a right onto Rte 57 and go into the town of Washington. At the 2nd light take a right onto Belvedere Ave, which becomes Minehill Rd, and the course is directly on right.

Facility Type: Semi-private

Club Pro: None
Discounts: Seniors
Tee Times: No

Coupon page 124

Features: Pro Shop - Limited, Restaurant, Practice Area, Clubhouse, Banquet Facilities

Description: Nestled in the "Valley of the Hawk", this is a scenic course and a pleasure to walk. It is flat, surrounded by trees, and has two ponds. This course plays harder than it reads. Local knowledge makes the game more perfect. The signature is #5. It's a par 4, 420 yards. The tee shot is out of a shute 175 -180 yds to a tight fairway. The second shot is onto a postage stamp green.

Holes	Par	Yards Back Tees	Rating	Slope
9	35	3007	67.4	103

	9 Holes	18 Holes	Hours Mid Season
Weekday:	$10.00	$12.00	7:00 am - Dusk
Weekend:	$11.00	$13.00	6:00 am - Dusk
Cart Fees:	$8.00	$12.00	

Mandatory Cart Rental: No
Club Rental: No

Notes: Many improvements are in the works on this course. Seasonal memberships are available which will offer weekend tee times for members only.

Farmstead Golf & CC

Lafayette NJ — Tee Times: (201)383-1666

Directions: Rte 80 to Exit 34B (Rte 15 N) to the intersection of 15 and 94. Take a left at the intersection onto Rte 623. The course is 3.5 mi. on the left.

Holes	Par	Yards Back Tees	Rating	Slope
9	35	3310	71.2	120
9	36	3370	69.3	119
9	33	2851	68.9	117

Facility Type: Public

	9 Holes	18 Holes	Hours Mid Season
Weekday:	—	$18.00	7:00 am - Dusk
Weekend:	—	$24.00	6:00 am - Dusk
Cart Fees:	—	$22.00	

Club Pro: Scott Prudin
Discounts: Seniors, Twilight
Tee Times: Yes, 1 week prior for any day.

Mandatory Cart Rental: No
Club Rental: Yes

Features: Lessons, Showers/Lockers, Practice Area, Pro Shop - Complete, Clubhouse, Restaurant, Bar, Snack Bar, Banquet Facilities, American Express, VISA/MC

Description: This course was converted from an old dairy farm. It is scenic, always in top condition and harder than it reads. It features treed fairways and island holes. Lakeview 9 and Clubview 9 both feature par 3 island green holes.

Fernwood Country Club   NJ 30

Fernwood Ave, Roseland NJ — (201)226-3200

Directions: Go West on Rte 280 to Exit 5 B. The road dead ends at Eagle Rock Ave. Turn left and go 5 blocks through the town of Roseland to Fernwood Ave. Take a right to the course

Holes	Par	Yards Back Tees	Rating	Slope
9	27	1100	—	—

Facility Type: Executive

	9 Holes	18 Holes	Hours Mid Season
Weekday:	$5.00	$10.00	8:30 am - Dusk
Weekend:	$5.00	$10.00	8:30 am - Dusk
Cart Fees:	—	—	

Club Pro: None
Discounts: None
Tee Times: No

Mandatory Cart Rental:
Club Rental: Yes

Features: Showers/Lockers, Driving Range, Practice Area, Snack Bar

Notes: The driving range is a cage. No carts.

Description: This course is tree-lined. It was a private club for 30 years.

ers Valley Golf Course

Flanders, NJ — Info: (201)584-8964   Tee Times: (201)644-4022

o Exit 27 A. Take Rte 206 South
n Flanders Bartley Rd. Go 1 mi.
to Pleasant ... and the course is on the right.

Holes	Par	Yards Back Tees	Rating	Slope
18	72	6800	70.8	123
18	72	6800	71.1	122

Facility Type: Public

Club Pro: Bob Pomeroy
Discounts: None
Tee Times: Yes, starting in late '91 tee times will be taken. 7 days before for Morris Co. residents, 5 days for non-residents.

Features: Lessons, Showers/Lockers, Practice Area, Pro Shop - Complete, Snack Bar, Clubhouse

Description: A Golf Digest "Places to Play" selection for '90 and'91. Hal Purdy and Reese Jones were the designers. Blue/white is tree-lined and narrow and is consistantly rated one of the top 75 public courses in the US by Golf Digest. On the second 18, Red is flat and open and Gold is hilly and tree-lined with dog legs. Water comes into play throughout the course. This is a well-maintained course.

	9 Holes	18 Holes	Hours Mid Season
Weekday:	—	$15.00	7:00 am - Dusk
Weekend:	—	$22.00	7:00 am - Dusk
Cart Fees:	$14.00	$23.00	

Mandatory Cart Rental: No
Club Rental: Yes

Notes: Reduced rates for County residents. Out-of-state residents pay 25 weekdays and 35 weekends for 18. See details in County Systems at the beginning of this secton.

Forge Pond County Golf Course

301 Chambers Bridge Rd, Brick Township NJ —   Tee Times: (908)920-8899

Directions: Garden St Pkwy North to Exit 90. Right off exit to Chambers Bridge Rd. Course is 3/4 mile on left. Southbound on Pkwy to Exit 91. Bear right off exit on to Chambers Bridge and go 3 mi. to course on left.

Facility Type: Public

Club Pro: None
Discounts: Seniors
Tee Times: Yes, up to 7 days in advance.

Features: Practice Area, Pro Shop - Limited, Snack Bar

Description: This course is harder than it reads. It has 12 par 3's and 6 par 4's with tree-lined fairways most of the way. Water comes into play on several holes.

Holes	Par	Yards Back Tees	Rating	Slope
18	60	4000	59.4	98

	9 Holes	18 Holes	Hours Mid Season
Weekday:	—	$13.00	7:00 am - Dusk *
Weekend:	—	$16.00	7:00 am - Dusk
Cart Fees:	$9.00	$17.00	

Mandatory Cart Rental: No
Club Rental: Yes

Notes: *This course is closed on Thursdays. Ocean County residents purchase ID cards for $10 for reduced green fees ($8 weekdays, $10 weekends).

Francis Byrne Golf Course NJ 33

1100 Pleasant Valley Way, W Orange NJ — (201)736-2306

Directions: Rte 280 to Pleasant Valley Way (Exit 7). Go left off exit from either direction and course is 1/4 mi. on the left.

Facility Type: Public

Club Pro: None
Discounts: Seniors, Juniors
Tee Times: Yes, county ID holder can reserve in person for weekends.

Features: Practice Area, Pro Shop - Limited, Snack Bar

Description: This is a very hilly course that can be a little humbling on a windy day. There are no flat lies. It is a well-kept and well-trapped course with some variation, a little more difficult for the average golfer than might appear.

Holes	Par	Yards Back Tees	Rating	Slope
18	70	6338	70.1	127

	9 Holes	18 Holes	Hours Mid Season
Weekday:	—	$20.00	Dawn - Dusk
Weekend:	—	$24.00	Dawn - Dusk
Cart Fees:	$12.00	$24.00	

Mandatory Cart Rental: No
Club Rental: No

Notes: Reduced rates for registered county residents

Freeway Golf Course NJ 34

Sicklerville NJ — **Tee Times:** (609)227-1115

Directions: From Phila take last exit before the beginning of Atlantic City Expressway (Sign for Sicklerville). At the light take a right onto Sicklerville Rd. The course 2 miles.

Facility Type: Public

Club Pro: Bill Bishop
Discounts: Seniors, Twilight
Tee Times: Yes, Monday morning for following weekend.

Features: Lessons, Showers/Lockers, Driving Range, Practice Area, Pro Shop - Limited, Clubhouse, Restaurant, Bar, Lodging Nearby, VISA/MC

Description: This is a fair test for the average player, but don't get careless. Front 9 is wide open and the back 9 is shorter and narrow with trees. Water comes into play on 4 holes. The greens are large and gently rolling. A new greens keeper will bring a new attention to detail.

Holes	Par	Yards Back Tees	Rating	Slope
18	72	6536	73.6	111

	9 Holes	18 Holes	Hours Mid Season
Weekday:	$8.00	$13.00	6:00 am - Dusk
Weekend:	$10.00	$17.00	6:00 am - Dusk
Cart Fees:	—	$20.00	

Mandatory Cart Rental: No
Club Rental: No

Notes: Special on weekdays, $35 with cart for 2 for 18 holes. Cart fee for 2 people. Twilight at 4 during the season and 2 during the winter. Open all year round.

Frog Rock Golf & Country Club NJ 35

Rte30, White Horse Pike, Hammonton NJ — (609)561-5504

Directions: On Rte 30 in Hammonton. If you're coming from the Atlantic City Expressway, take Rte 54 North off Exit 28. Turn right on Rte 30 and the course is 3 miles.

Facility Type: Public

Club Pro: Billy Papa, Teaching pro
Discounts: None
Tee Times: No

Features: Lessons, Practice Area, Pro Shop - Complete, Clubhouse, Restaurant, Bar, Snack Bar, Banquet Facilities

Description: Richard Taylor designed this course, known in the area as a miniature Pine Valley. It's rolling, with tight fairways and water on 4 holes. The greens are tight and feature pen cross bent grass. Plans are on the drawing board for 9 more holes. Keep an eye out.

Holes	Par	Yards Back Tees	Rating	Slope
9	33	2400	—	—

	9 Holes	18 Holes	Hours Mid Season
Weekday:	$5.00	$10.00	Dawn - Dusk
Weekend:	$5.00	$10.00	Dawn - Dusk
Cart Fees:	$5.00	$10.00	

Mandatory Cart Rental: No
Club Rental: Yes

Notes: Regarding the above rates, the green fee is $5 for every 9 holes played.

Galloping Hill Golf Course NJ 36

Union NJ — (908)686-1556

Directions: Garden State Parkway to Exit 138. The course is just off exit to the West of the Parkway.

Facility Type: Public

Club Pro: Terry McCormack
Discounts: None
Tee Times: No

Features: Lessons, Showers/Lockers, Practice Area, Clubhouse, Snack Bar, Pro Shop - Complete

Description: A hilly course with some good variety. A creek cuts through 7 holes and there are bunkers.

Holes	Par	Yards Back Tees	Rating	Slope
9	36	2700	—	—
18	72	6700	71.3	122

	9 Holes	18 Holes	Hours Mid Season
Weekday:	—	$16.00	7:00 am - Dusk
Weekend:	—	$20.00	6:00 am - Dusk
Cart Fees:	$12.00	$18.50	

Mandatory Cart Rental: No
Club Rental: No

Notes: Resident fees are $8 weekdays, $10 weekends. Out-of-state fees are $35 and $50.

Gambler Ridge Golf Club

Burlington Path Rd, Cream Ridge NJ — **Tee Times:** (609)758-3588

Holes	Par	Yards Back Tees	Rating	Slope
18	71	6370	70	111

Directions: NJ Turnpike to Exit 7A. Take Rte 195 East to Exit 16. Take Rte 537 West past Great Adventurer Amusement Park to the 1st light. Go right onto 539. Go 2 mi. and take a right on Burlington Path Rd. The course 3/4 mi. on the right.

	9 Holes	18 Holes	Hours Mid Season
Weekday:	$10.50	$17.50	7:00 am - Dusk
Weekend:	—	$24.00	Dawn - Dusk
Cart Fees:	—	$26.00	

Facility Type: Public

Coupon page 125

Mandatory Cart Rental: No
Club Rental: Yes

Club Pro: Brian Jodoin
Discounts: Seniors, Twilight, Juniors
Tee Times: Yes, up to 7 days in advance for any day. NJ residents call (800) 624-0496

Notes: Weekdays 9 hole play only after 1 pm.

Features: Lessons, Driving Range, Practice Area, Pro Shop - Complete, Restaurant, Banquet Facilities, American Express, VISA/MC

Description: This is one of three courses in NJ to have bent grass greens and fairways. The fairways are open. #6 and #8 have double greens. The course is always well maintained. #12 is a favorite. You must play over 2 ponds on this 175 yard, par 3.

Golden Pheasant Golf Course

141 Country Club Dr, Medford NJ — **Tee Times:** (609)267-4276

Holes	Par	Yards Back Tees	Rating	Slope
18	72	6358	68.1	113

Directions: NJ Turnpike to Exit 5 (Mt Holly). Take Rte 541 South toward Mt Holly. Take the Mt Holly bypass to Rte 38 and turn left. Take a right at the 2nd light, Eayerstown Rd. Approx 4 miles the road dead ends. Take a sharp right and a quick left onto Country Club Drive. The course 1 mi. on the right.

	9 Holes	18 Holes	Hours Mid Season
Weekday:	—	$14.00	8:00 am - Dusk
Weekend:	—	$21.00	6:00 am - Dusk
Cart Fees:	—	$22.00	

Facility Type: Semi-private

Mandatory Cart Rental: No
Club Rental: No

Club Pro: None
Discounts: None
Tee Times: Yes, Monday for weekends/holidays

Features: Practice Area, Pro Shop - Limited, Restaurant, Snack Bar

Description: The course is scenic, hilly and in good condition. #8 is a 175 yd par 3. The tee is elevated, and a creek runs left and back of the green, with a trap in front.

Golf Farm

801 Haddonfield Berlin Rd, Vorhees NJ — (609)784-9791

Directions: 295 to Exit 32. Go East on Rte 561. Facility is 3 mi. on the left.

Facility Type: Pitch & Putt

Club Pro: None
Discounts: None
Tee Times: No

Features: Lessons, Driving Range, Practice Area

Description: Facility also has a complete driving range. Buckets $4.50 daytime and $5.00 weekends and nights. Home of Great Golf Learning Center lazer trainer. Miniature golf.

Holes	Par	Yards Back Tees	Rating	Slope
18	56	510	—	—

	9 Holes	18 Holes	Hours Mid Season
Weekday:	—	$4.50	8:00 am - 10:30 pm
Weekend:	—	$6.50	8:00 am - 10:30 pm
Cart Fees:	—	—	

Club Rental: No

Great Gorge's Country Club

Mcaffee NJ — **Tee Times:** (201)827-5757

Directions: Rte 80 to Exit 53. Take Rte 23 North to Hamburg. Go right onto 94N and 4 mi. to next light. Go through the light and the road becomes 517N. The entrance to the Seasons Resort & CC is 1/2 mi. on the right.

Facility Type: Resort

Club Pro: Tom Manziano
Discounts: Seniors, Twilight
Tee Times: Yes, 1 month

Coupon page 125

Features: Lessons, Showers/Lockers, Driving Range, Practice Area, Pro Shop - Complete, Clubhouse, Restaurant, Bar, Snack Bar, Banquet Facilities, Lodging Nearby, American Express, VISA/MC

Holes	Par	Yards Back Tees	Rating	Slope
9	L 36	3457	—	—
9	Q 35	3362	—	—
9	R 36	3345	—	—

	9 Holes	18 Holes	Hours Mid Season
Weekday:	$23.96	$47.91	7:15 am - 6:00 pm
Weekend:	—	$63.91	7:15 am - 6:00 pm
Cart Fees:	—	—	

Mandatory Cart Rental: Yes
Club Rental: Yes

Notes: Block rotations on weekend mornings for tee times. No 9 hole on weekends. Cart fees are included.

Description: The three 9's are Lakeside(1), Quarryside(2), and Railside(3). Lakeside plays its way through the most wooded area of the property, while offering numerous water hazards to avoid. Quarryside is our most unique 9, as it plays through various rock quarries. Railside offers the least amount of water hazards and trees, but sports treacherous sand bunkers and the most demanding putting surfaces. The architect was George Fazio. This was a pick for "Places to Play" by Golf Digest in '90 and '91. The course has hosted numerous tournaments in the past, including the NJ State Father/Son Championship, and the NJ PGA Nissan Classic.

Greate Bay Resort & CC NJ 41

901 Mays Landing Rd, Somers Point NJ — Tee Times: (609)927-1002

Directions: Garden St Parkway heading South to Exit 30. Go straight after the toll to the stop sign. Take a right onto Rte 9 South. Go just 1/4 mi. to Mays Landing Rd at the light. Take a left and proceed to the course.

Facility Type: Resort

Club Pro: Joe Lewis
Discounts: Twilight
Tee Times: Yes, up to3 days ahead for non-members.

Features: Lessons, Showers/Lockers, Driving Range, Practice Area, Pro Shop - Complete, Clubhouse, Restaurant, Bar, Snack Bar, Banquet Facilities, Lodging Nearby, American Express, VISA/MC

Description: This course was built in the 20's. It is near the water and generally flat but has a few rolls in the terrain. It is loaded with sand bunkers - 156 of them. The signature is #13, a 430 yd par 4. It's a dogleg left and over a pond to a 3-tiered green. The course has been the home of the Atlantic City Classic and a stop on the LPGA Tour for the last three years.

Holes	Par	Yards Back Tees	Rating	Slope
18	71	6750	72.3	130

	9 Holes	18 Holes	Hours Mid Season
Weekday:	—	$65.00	7:00 am - 7:00 pm
Weekend:	—	$65.00	7:00 am - 7:00 pm
Cart Fees:	—	—	

Mandatory Cart Rental: Yes
Club Rental: Yes

Notes: This is a semi-private facility. Carts are included in green fees. Call for discounts off season.

Green Knoll Golf Course NJ 42

587 Garretson Rd, Bridgewater NJ — Info: (908)722-1301   Tee Times: (908)560-1500

Directions: Rte 287 going South to Exit 13. Take 206 South. The first exit is a jug-handle to a light. Take a right onto Common Way and go to the end. Take a left onto Garretson Road and the 1st right after YMCA to the course.

Facility Type: Public

Club Pro: None
Discounts: None
Tee Times: Yes, County residents are placed in a system for reservations and can call 7 days prior. Non residents in the system can call 1 day prior for a $6 charge.

Features: Practice Area, Pro Shop - Complete, Snack Bar

Description: This is a well maintained course that offers a challenge for the average golfer. A fully-lit "Pitch & Putt" facility adjoins the course.

Holes	Par	Yards Back Tees	Rating	Slope
9	27	700	—	—
18	71	6584	70.9	117

	9 Holes	18 Holes	Hours Mid Season
Weekday:	—	$14.00	7:00 am - Dusk
Weekend:	—	$17.00	6:00 am - Dusk
Cart Fees:	$11.80	$18.20	

Mandatory Cart Rental: No
Club Rental: Yes

Notes: Residents pay $7 and $8.50 for green fees. Non-residents of Somerset County can be put into the reservation system for $50.

Green Pond Golf Course

NJ 43

765 Green Pond Rd, Rockaway NJ — (201)983-9494

Directions: Rte 80 to Exit 37. Take Green Pond Rd North 8 miles and the course is on left.

Facility Type: Public

Club Pro: None
Discounts: None
Tee Times: No

Features: Pro Shop - Limited, Snack Bar, Clubhouse, VISA/MC

Description: This is a walkable course. It's also narrow and demands accuracy. #9 features a pond.

Holes	Par	Yards Back Tees	Rating	Slope
9	35	2703	—	—

	9 Holes	18 Holes	Hours Mid Season
Weekday:	$14.00	$14.00	8:30 am - Dusk
Weekend:	$18.00	$18.00	6:30 am - Dusk
Cart Fees:	$12.00	$24.00	

Mandatory Cart Rental: No
Club Rental: Yes

Green Tree Country Club

NJ 44

Somers Point -Mays Landing Rd, Mays Landing NJ — **Tee Times:** (609)625-9131

Directions: Garden State Parkway North to Exit 29. Take a right at the light onto Rte 559. Go 10 mi. to Milepost 10, and the course is on the right. Going South on the Parkway take Exit 44 one way to Hamilton Mall. After the Mall, go through 2 lights to 322. Go a short distance to Rte 40. Take 40 to the 2nd left past Ceasars Restaurant at Mays Landing Village sign. Take this road to the end and left on to 559 approx 4 mi. to the course.

Facility Type: Public

Club Pro: Rob Gosman
Discounts: Seniors, Twilight
Tee Times: Yes, 5 days ahead for non members

Features: Lessons, Showers/Lockers, Driving Range, Practice Area, Pro Shop - Complete, Clubhouse, Restaurant, Bar, Snack Bar

Description: A relatively flat and short course makes it good for seniors. But it is surprisingly tough, even for good players because of narrow fairways, water on 15 holes, and small greens. A favorite is the 1st hole, a 401 yard par 4. It's a straight ahead drive with an approach shot over a pond to a 3-tiered green.

Holes	Par	Yards Back Tees	Rating	Slope
18	70	5700	66.6	110

	9 Holes	18 Holes	Hours Mid Season
Weekday:	$12.00	$16.00	6:00 am - 7:00 pm
Weekend:	$12.00	$16.00	6:00 am - 7:00 pm
Cart Fees:	$6.00	$9.00	

Mandatory Cart Rental: No
Club Rental: Yes

Notes: Memberships available.

Hamilton Trails Country Club · NJ 45

Ocean Hts Ave, Pleasantville NJ — (609)641-6824

Directions: Garden State Parkway to Exit 36. Take Tilton Rd West to the traffic circle and Rte 322. Approx 5.5 mi. to Hamilton Mall, U turn to Rte 40 West to Ceasars Restuarant on the right. Go 1500 ft past the restaurant, and take a left onto NY Road and go 3.3 mi. to course.

Facility Type: Public

Club Pro: Dennis Strigh
Discounts: None
Tee Times: No

Features: Driving Range, Practice Area, Pro Shop - Complete, Clubhouse, Lessons

Description: This is a flat and open course, but tougher than it sounds with hazards on more than half of the course.

Holes	Par	Yards Back Tees	Rating	Slope
9	35	3265	67.3	125

	9 Holes	18 Holes	Hours Mid Season
Weekday:	$10.00	$20.00	7:00 am - Dusk
Weekend:	$10.00	$20.00	7:00 am - Dusk
Cart Fees:	—	$10.00	

Mandatory Cart Rental: No
Club Rental: No

Hanover Country Club · NJ 46

133 Larrison Rd, Jacobstown NJ — **Tee Times:** (609)758-0300

Directions: NJ Trnpke to Exit 7A. Take 195 East 10 miles to Exit 16. Take 537 West. Course is 6.5 mi. on right side.

Facility Type: Public

Club Pro: None
Discounts: Seniors, Twilight
Tee Times: Yes, 2 weeks ahead recommended.

Features: Lessons, Showers/Lockers, Driving Range, Practice Area, Pro Shop - Complete, Clubhouse, Restaurant, Bar, Snack Bar, Banquet Facilities, Lodging Nearby

Description: This is a Robert Trent Jones course. The front 9 is rolling and the back 9 hilly and more challenging. 3 streams run through the course. The 18th is a 620 yd par 5 over a stream to an elevated, slanted green. What a way to finish! 10 holes are over 400 yds.

Coupon page 125

Holes	Par	Yards Back Tees	Rating	Slope
18	70	6720	69.9	—

	9 Holes	18 Holes	Hours Mid Season
Weekday:	—	$18.00	Dawn - Dusk
Weekend:	—	$22.00	Dawn - Dusk
Cart Fees:	—	$26.00	

Mandatory Cart Rental: See notes.
Club Rental: Yes

Notes: Carts are mandatory weekends and holidays from middle of April to the end of October until 1 pm. Facility includes a swimming pool. Open all year round.

Hendricks Field Golf Course

Franklin Ave, Belleville NJ — (201)751-0178

Directions: Garden St Pkwy going north past Bloom-field Toll stop. Take Hoover Ave (Exi t 150) and turn right at Jeroloman and right again on Franklin. Course on left. Pkwy south to Exit 149 (Belleville Ave) Right off ramp onto Belleville and 3rd light left on Franklin to course.

Facility Type: Public

Club Pro: Bob Schubert
Discounts: None
Tee Times: Yes, county ID holders may reserve Thursday in oerson for weekends No

Features: Showers/Lockers, Practice Area, Pro Shop - Complete, Clubhouse, Snack Bar

Description: A very level course, and a good walking course for seniors.

Holes	Par	Yards Back Tees	Rating	Slope
18	70	6088	68.9	108

	9 Holes	18 Holes	Hours Mid Season
Weekday:	—	$16.00	Dawn - Dusk
Weekend:	—	$ 20.00	Dawn - Dusk
Cart Fees:	—	$20.00	

Mandatory Cart Rental: No
Club Rental: Yes

Notes: Reduced rate for residents. Greens fees for out-of-state players $40. Cart rental fee above is for 2.

Hidden Acres Golf Course

Layton NJ — (201)948-9804

Directions: Rte 80 to Exit 36 (15 N). Take 15 to 206 North 15 mi. and left onto Rte 675. Take a left at Hainsville Food Store onto 645 then right onto 646 to top of hill.

Facility Type: Public

Club Pro: None
Discounts: None
Tee Times: No

Features: Practice Area, Pro Shop - Limited

Description: A rustic and well- maintained country course.

Holes	Par	Yards Back Tees	Rating	Slope
9	36	3000	—	—

	9 Holes	18 Holes	Hours Mid Season
Weekday:	$8.00	$8.00	7:00 am - Dusk
Weekend:	$8.00	$8.00	6:00 am - Dusk
Cart Fees:	$9.00	$18.00	

Mandatory Cart Rental: No
Club Rental: Yes

Hidden Hills Golf Course NJ 49

Rte 24, Hackettstown NJ — Tee Times: (908)852-5694

Directions: Rte 80 West to Exit 26 onto 46 W. Go 7 mi. to East Ave (the1st light in Hackettstown). Take a left and go 3/4 mi. to the end, and take a left on Mountain Ave. Go 1/2 mi. across the river and the course is on the left.

Facility Type: Public

Club Pro: Arnold D'Andrea
Discounts: Twilight, Seniors
Tee Times: Yes, 1 week ahead for any day

Features: Lessons, Showers/Lockers, Pro Shop - Limited, Clubhouse, Restaurant, Bar, Banquet Facilities, American Express

Description: This is a course where you must keep the ball in play. The front 9 is flat, the back 9 hillier. A favorite is the 11th hole, a 385 yard par 4. You have to carry your drive 275 yards to get beyond the dogleg to even think of parring this hole.

Holes	Par	Yards Back Tees	Rating	Slope
18	70	6307	69.7	—

	9 Holes	18 Holes	Hours Mid Season
Weekday:	—	$10.00	7:00 am - Dusk
Weekend:	—	$20.00	6:00 am - Dusk
Cart Fees:	—	$20.00	

Mandatory Cart Rental: No
Club Rental: Yes

High Mountain Golf Club NJ 50

845 Ewing Ave, Franklin Lakes NJ — Tee Times: (201)891-4653

Directions: Garden State Parkway to Exit 160. Get onto 208 North to Ewing Ave. Take a left to the course 1/2 mi. on the left.

Facility Type: Semi-private

Club Pro: Joe Lawler
Discounts: None
Tee Times: Yes, call Monday for following week

Features: Lessons, Showers/Lockers, Driving Range, Practice Area, Pro Shop - Complete, Clubhouse

Description: A good average playing course with a decent amount of water.

Holes	Par	Yards Back Tees	Rating	Slope
18	71	6350	68.6	116

	9 Holes	18 Holes	Hours Mid Season
Weekday:	—	$23.00	7:30 am - Dusk*
Weekend:	—	$30.00	2 pm - Dusk*
Cart Fees:	—	$28.00	

Mandatory Cart Rental: Yes
Club Rental: Yes

Notes: * Monday open to public on 1st come basis. Tues public after 12. Wed, Thurs, Fri public before 2, and weekends after 2.

High Point Country Club

Montague NJ — Tee Times: (201)293-3282

Directions: North on Rte 23 from Rte 80 over High Point Mountain. 3.5 mi. north of High Point State Park take left onto Close Rd (Rte 653). Course is 5 mi. on left.

Facility Type: Semi-private

Club Pro: John Di Meo
Discounts: Seniors, Twilight
Tee Times: Yes, 1 week ahead

Features: Lessons, Showers/Lockers, Driving Range, Practice Area, Pro Shop - Complete, Clubhouse, Restaurant, Snack Bar

Description: A well-kept and relatively even course built in a figure 8. It is pretty and challenging with trees and water on 14 holes. The complainers' hole is #10, a 518 yd par 5 over two ponds to a trapped green.

Holes	Par	Yards Back Tees	Rating	Slope
18	73	6665	69	129

	9 Holes	18 Holes	Hours Mid Season
Weekday:	$14.00	$27.00	8:00 am - Dusk
Weekend:	—	$40.00	6:00 am - Dusk
Cart Fees:	—	—	

Mandatory Cart Rental:
Club Rental: Yes

Notes: Cart fees included. Carts are mandatory.

Hillman's Golf Land

700 River Drive, Elmwood Park NJ — (201)796-1265

Directions: Exit 61 off Rte 80. South 1000 yds.

Facility Type: Pitch & Putt

Club Pro: Rodney Firth
Discounts: Seniors
Tee Times: No

Features: Lessons, Driving Range, Practice Area, Pro Shop - Complete, Clubhouse, Snack Bar

Description: Includes regular driving range and minature golf for the rest of the family.

Holes	Par	Yards Back Tees	Rating	Slope
18	54	920	—	—

	9 Holes	18 Holes	Hours Mid Season
Weekday:	—	$6.00	8:00 am - 11:00 pm
Weekend:	—	$8.00	8:00 am - midnight
Cart Fees:	—	—	

Club Rental: Yes

Notes: Senior discounts 8 am - 5 pm weekdays only.

Hillsborough Golf & CC

145 Wertsville Rd, Flemington NJ — **Tee Times:** (908)369-3322

Directions: Rte 287 to Exit 35S. Take 206 South 5 mi. past Somerville Circle and right onto Rte 514. Go 4.5 mi. to a stop. Go through the stop and make a left onto Wertsville Rd. The course is 3 mi. on the right.

Holes	Par	Yards Back Tees	Rating	Slope
18	70	6100	68.7	109

	9 Holes	18 Holes	Hours Mid Season
Weekday:	$15.00	$20.00	Dawn - Dusk
Weekend:	—	$25.00	Dawn - Dusk
Cart Fees:	—	$24.00	

Facility Type: Semi-private

Club Pro: Glen Shurts
Discounts: Seniors, Juniors, Twilight
Tee Times: Yes, 1 week in advance

Mandatory Cart Rental: Yes
Club Rental: Yes

Features: Lessons, Showers/Lockers, Driving Range, Practice Area, Pro Shop - Complete, Clubhouse, Restaurant, Bar, Snack Bar, Banquet Facilities

Description: Tom Fazio designed this course and it was Golf Digest's choice in both '90 and '91 for "Places to Play", for both its view and its challenge. The front 9 is open and the back 9 tight and hilly. Greens are small and undulating. This course puts a big value on your iron placements. The par 3 #8 is a favorite. It's a 190 yd shot to a narrow fairway with woods on both sides. The green is well-bunkered.

Holly Hills Golf Club

Alloway NJ — **Tee Times:** (609)935-2412

Directions: NJ Turnpike to Exit 2. Take 322 East toward Mullica Hill. Turn right onto Rte 45 which becomes Rte 77. At Pole Tavern Circle take 635 West 7 mi. to the course on right.

Holes	Par	Yards Back Tees	Rating	Slope
18	72	6400	70.8	118

	9 Holes	18 Holes	Hours Mid Season
Weekday:	—	$12.00	7:00 am - Dusk
Weekend:	—	$18.00	5:30 am - Dusk
Cart Fees:	—	$20.00	

Facility Type: Semi-private

Club Pro: Steve Keating
Discounts: Twilight
Tee Times: Yes, Wednesday for the weekend

Mandatory Cart Rental: See notes.
Club Rental: No

Features: Lessons, Showers/Lockers, Driving Range, Practice Area, Pro Shop - Complete, Clubhouse, Restaurant, Snack Bar, Banquet Facilities, American Express, VISA/MC, Bar, Lodging Nearby

Notes: Carts are mandatory on weekends until 1. A dress code is enforced. You must be a social club member to use the bar. The course is open all year round.

Description: This is an enjoyable course for any level of player. It has rolling hills, sparkling ponds and a mixture of tight and wider fairways. A favorite is the 10th, a par 5, 560 yard shot down a hill, over a water area and to an elevated green surrounded by large oaks. There is nothing but nature on this course after the 1st hole. The greens are in great shape, and management is proad of the service.

Hominy Hill Golf Course   NJ 55

92 Mercer Rd, Coltsneck NJ — Info: (908)462-9222   Tee Times: (908)758-8383

Directions: South on Garden State Parkway to Exit 123. Take Rte 9 South to Rte 18 South to Rte 537 East. The course is 1 mi. on the right. Or take NJ Turnpike to Exit 7A. Take Rte 195 East to Rte 537 East past Rte 18 to the course.

Facility Type: Public

Club Pro: None
Discounts: Twilight
Tee Times: Yes, County residents with ID 7 days prior after 8 pm Non residents purchase ID cards and can reserve 5 days prior, after 5 pm.

Features: Showers/Lockers, Practice Area, Pro Shop - Complete, Snack Bar

Description: This is a fairly flat and a well-kept course. Robert Trent Jones was the designer. Traps offer the challenge. It was a choice by Golf Digest for "Places to Play" in both '90 and '91.

Holes	Par	Yards Back Tees	Rating	Slope
18	72	6470	71.7	127

	9 Holes	18 Holes	Hours Mid Season
Weekday:	—	$27.00	7:00 am - Dusk
Weekend:	—	$29.00	6:00 am - Dusk
Cart Fees:	—	$24.00	

Mandatory Cart Rental: No
Club Rental: Yes

Notes: County residents with ID pay 1/2 for green fees.

Howell Park Golf Course   NJ 56

225 Southard Rd, Farmingdale NJ — Info: (908)938-4771   Tee Times: (908)758-8383

Directions: Garden State Parkway to Exit 98. Take Rte 195 to Exit 31B. At the light, take a left (Squamgum-Yellowbrook Rd). The course is 2 mi. on the left.

Facility Type: Public

Club Pro: David Laudien
Discounts: Twilight
Tee Times: Yes, Holders of county resident ID 7 days prior after 8 pm, holders of non-resident ID 5 days in advance after 5 pm.

Features: Practice Area, Pro Shop - Complete, Snack Bar, Lessons

Description: Lessons for the county courses are taught here. The course is in excellent condition for a county facility. Fairways are generally narrow with trees. There are a lot of traps and the greens are large. Golf Digest picked it for "Places to Play" in '90 and '91.

Holes	Par	Yards Back Tees	Rating	Slope
18	72	6885	72.9	128

	9 Holes	18 Holes	Hours Mid Season
Weekday:	—	$26.00	7:00 am - 6:00 pm
Weekend:	—	$28.00	6:00 am - 6:00 pm
Cart Fees:	—	$26..00	

Mandatory Cart Rental: No
Club Rental: Yes

Notes: County residents with ID pay 1/2 for green fees.

Indian Springs Golf Club   NJ 57

South Elmwood Rd, Marlton NJ —   Tee Times: (609)983-0222

Directions: NJ Turnpike to Exit 4. Take Rte 70 East to Elmwood Rd. Go right and 1/4 mi. to the course.

Facility Type: Public

Club Pro: Robin Sutton
Discounts: None
Tee Times: Yes, Tues for Saturday, Wed for Sunday

Features: Lessons, Showers/Lockers, Driving Range, Practice Area, Pro Shop - Complete, Restaurant, Bar, Banquet Facilities

Description: This is a relatively flat and straightforward course, but still offers a challenge for the average player.

Holes	Par	Yards Back Tees	Rating	Slope
18	70	6299	67.9	107

	9 Holes	18 Holes	Hours Mid Season
Weekday:	—	$14.00	6:30 am - Dusk
Weekend:	—	$17.00	6:00 am - Dusk
Cart Fees:	—	$17.00	

Mandatory Cart Rental: No
Club Rental: Yes

Jumping Brook Golf & CC   NJ 58

210 Jumping Brook Rd, Neptune NJ — Info: (908)922-8200   Tee Times: (908)922-6140

Directions: Garden State Parkway South to Exit 100B onto Rte 33 East. At the 2nd light (Jumping Brook Rd) take a left and the course is on the right. Going North on the Parkway Exit at 100A onto 66 East to the1st light, and take a right to the course.

Facility Type: Semi-private

Club Pro: Daniel Hollis
Discounts: Seniors, Juniors, Twilight
Tee Times: Yes, weekends only. Call same week.

Features: Lessons, Driving Range, Practice Area, Snack Bar, Pro Shop - Complete

Description: A challenging course, its a little hilly with small and well-bunkered greens.

Coupon page 126

Holes	Par	Yards Back Tees	Rating	Slope
18	72	6500	70.5	118

	9 Holes	18 Holes	Hours Mid Season
Weekday:	$10.00	$15.00	6:00 am - 7:00 pm
Weekend:	—	$20.00	6:00 am - 7:00 pm
Cart Fees:	—	$25.00	

Mandatory Cart Rental: See notes.
Club Rental:

Notes: Carts are mandatory on weekends. 9 hole play only after 3 on weekdays.

Knob Hill Country Club

360 Rte 33, Englishtown NJ — Tee Times: (908)446-4800

Directions: NJ Turnpike to Exit 8. Take Rte 33 West for 6 mi. and the course is on the left

Holes	Par	Yards Back Tees	Rating	Slope
9	34	2800	—	—

Facility Type: Public

	9 Holes	18 Holes	Hours Mid Season
Weekday:	$7.00	—	8:00 am - 6:00 pm
Weekend:	$9.00	—	7:00 am - 6:00 pm
Cart Fees:	$11.00	—	

Club Pro: John Piotrowski
Discounts: Seniors
Tee Times: Yes, 1 day ahead for weekend

Mandatory Cart Rental: No
Club Rental: No

Features: Lessons, Pro Shop - Complete

Description: An entirely new 18 hole course and development is under construction and at the time of publication, it had not been determined whether the old 9 hole course would be open in 1992. If it is open, it is not an easy course. It's hilly and wooded. Definately call to get the status.

Knoll East Golf Course

Knoll Rd, Parsippany NJ — (201)263-7115

Directions: Rte 80 to Exit 47 to Rte 46 to 2nd light. Take right onto Beverwick Rd and go 2 mi. to Mobil Station and take left. Course is 200 yds on right.

Holes	Par	Yards Back Tees	Rating	Slope
18	70	6000	67.8	108

	9 Holes	18 Holes	Hours Mid Season
Weekday:	—	$15.00	7:00 am - Dusk
Weekend:	—	$22.00	6:00 am - Dusk
Cart Fees:	$15.50	$24.00	

Facility Type: Public

Club Pro: Rich Williams
Discounts: None
Tee Times: No

Mandatory Cart Rental: No
Club Rental: No

Features: Lessons, Practice Area, Pro Shop - Complete, Clubhouse, Restaurant, Bar, Snack Bar, Banquet Facilities

Notes: 9 holes are playable only after 4 pm weekdays only.

Description: This is a short but challenging course in excellent shape. The fairways are tight.

Knoll West Golf Course

Parsippany NJ —(201)263-7110

Directions: Rte 80 going West to Exit 47 onto Rte
46. Take right at 2nd light onto Beverwick Rd. Go
2 mi. and make left at Mobil Station to course.
(past Knoll East GC)

Facility Type: Public

Club Pro: Steele King

Discounts: None

Tee Times: No, Tee times for members only. Non
members must book in person on the same day.

Features: Lessons, Practice Area, Pro Shop - Complete, Snack Bar, Showers/Lockers

Description: This is a long course with tough greens
and a lot of bunkers. The course is well kept. A favorite is the last hole, a 439 yard, par 4. It is long,
straight and bunkered to the green. The green is
long, narrow and trapped. You will hear from
those who par this one.

Holes	Par	Yards Back Tees	Rating	Slope
18	70	6716	72.4	127

	9 Holes	18 Holes	Hours Mid Season
Weekday:	—	$27.50	6:00 am - Dusk
Weekend:	—	$36.00	6:00 am - Dusk
Cart Fees:	$15.50	$24.50	

Mandatory Cart Rental: See notes.
Club Rental: No

Notes: Memberships available. 9 holes can be played
only after 3:30. Carts are mandatory any day before 3:30. Twilight after 3:30. Possibly a driving
range for '92 and reconstruction of a clubhouse for
middle to late '92.

Kresson Golf Course

Kresson/Gibbsboro Rd, Voorhees NJ — (609)424-1212

Directions: Take exit for Voorhees /Rte 561 South
off of 295. 9 lights from 295 take a left onto Kres-
son/Gibbsboro Rd. The course is 3/4 mi. on the
right.

Facility Type: Public

Club Pro: None
Discounts: Seniors, Twilight
Tee Times: No

Features: Showers/Lockers, Practice Area, Pro Shop
- Limited

Description: This is a short and challenging course
with the emphasis on irons. There is a lot of water.
It is scenic and steps back into the country after #7.

Holes	Par	Yards Back Tees	Rating	Slope
18	68	4800	—	—

	9 Holes	18 Holes	Hours Mid Season
Weekday:	—	$14.00	Dawn - Dusk
Weekend:	—	$18.00	Dawn - Dusk
Cart Fees:	—	$20.00	

Mandatory Cart Rental: No
Club Rental: Yes

Lake Lackawana Golf Course   NJ 63

155 Lake Drive, Stanhope NJ — (201)347-9701

Directions: Rte 80 West to Exit 25. Take 206 North 3 lights to Westminister Bank and make a right. The course is 1 mi. on the right.

Facility Type: Public

Club Pro: None
Discounts: Seniors
Tee Times: No

Features: Practice Area, Pro Shop - Limited, Snack Bar

Description: This is an executive-type course.

Holes	Par	Yards Back Tees	Rating	Slope
9	32	2240	—	—

	9 Holes	18 Holes	Hours Mid Season
Weekday:	$7.00	$10.00	7:00 am - Dusk
Weekend:	$9.00	$12.00	6:00 am - Dusk
Cart Fees:	—	—	

Club Rental: Yes

Lakewood Country Club   NJ 64

West County Line Rd, Lakewood NJ —   **Tee Times:** (908)363-9529

Directions: Garden State Parkway to the Lakewood Exit, 91. Take 526 West 7 mi. and course is on left.

Facility Type: Semi-private

Club Pro: Todd Toohey
Discounts: None
Tee Times: Yes, 1 week for weekends/holidays

Features: Lessons, Showers/Lockers, Driving Range, Practice Area, Pro Shop - Complete, Clubhouse, Restaurant, Bar, Snack Bar, Banquet Facilities, Lodging Nearby

Description: This is a championship course that was played by the Roosevelts. It is open, wooded and scenic. A favorite hole is the 15th, a 200 yd, par 3 over water. It is the #1 handicap hole.

Holes	Par	Yards Back Tees	Rating	Slope
18	71	6248	68.5	107

	9 Holes	18 Holes	Hours Mid Season
Weekday:	—	$12.00	Dawn - Dusk
Weekend:	—	$16.00	Dawn - Dusk
Cart Fees:	—	$20.00	

Mandatory Cart Rental: No
Club Rental: Yes

Notes: Memberships are available.

Latona Country Club

NJ 65

Oak & Cumberland Rds, Buena NJ — (609)692-8149

Directions: Rte 40 in Southern NJ going East. Take a right onto Rte 557, which is the first right turn after the intersection of Rtes 40 and 54. 557 turns into Cumberland (stay straight at fork) and go 1/4 mi. to the course on the left.

Facility Type: Public

Club Pro: None
Discounts: Twilight
Tee Times: No

Features: Practice Area, Pro Shop - Limited, Snack Bar

Description: This course is in excellent condition. It is relatively flat and open with no water. There is some sand around the greens. It is not as easy as it sounds.

Holes	Par	Yards Back Tees	Rating	Slope
9	35	3160	—	—

	9 Holes	18 Holes	Hours Mid Season
Weekday:	—	$8.00	7:00 am - Dusk
Weekend:	—	$12.00	6:00 am - Dusk
Cart Fees:	—	$12.00	

Mandatory Cart Rental: No
Club Rental: Yes

Notes: Cart fee is for double.

Lincoln Park Golf Center

NJ 66

369 Duncan Ave, Jersey City NJ — (201)332-5506

Directions: At the corner of Duncan Ave on Rtes 1 & 9 in Jersey City

Facility Type: Executive

Club Pro: None
Discounts: None
Tee Times: No

Features: Lessons, Pro Shop - Limited

Holes	Par	Yards Back Tees	Rating	Slope
9	27	720	—	—

	9 Holes	18 Holes	Hours Mid Season
Weekday:	$6.00	$8.00	9:00 am - 8:30 pm
Weekend:	$6.00	$8.00	9:00 am - 8:30 pm
Cart Fees:	—	—	

Club Rental: No

Marriott Seaview Golf Resort

Rte 9, Absecon NJ — Tee Times: (609)652-1800

Directions: Garden State Parkway to Exit 48. Take Rte 9 toward Absecon. The resort is 7 mi. on the right

Holes	Par	Yards Back Tees	Rating	Slope
18	71	6300	69.0	113
18	71	6800	73.0	132

Facility Type: Resort

	9 Holes	18 Holes	Hours Mid Season
Weekday:	$40.00	$68.00	7:00 am - Dusk
Weekend:	$40.00	$68.00	6:30 am - Dusk
Cart Fees:	—	—	

Club Pro: Rick Kline, Head Pro
Discounts: None
Tee Times: Yes, 3 days for weekday, 1 day for weekend. Guests have precedence.

Mandatory Cart Rental: Yes
Club Rental: Yes

Features: Lessons, Showers/Lockers, Driving Range, Practice Area, Pro Shop - Complete, Clubhouse, Restaurant, Bar, Snack Bar, Banquet Facilities, Lodging Nearby, American Express, VISA/MC

Notes: Cart fees are included with green fees.

Description: This was a Golf Digest pick for "Places to Play" in both '90 and '91. Built in 1915, this was one of the most exclusive resorts on the East Coast, and the site of the '42 PGA Championship. The shorter Bay course is a Donald Ross links design, with small undulating greens and steep-faced bunkers. The Pines is by Toomey, Flynn & Gordon, and cut through the pines for more of a park style. The golf shop was selected by Golf Shop Operations as one of the top 100 in country.

Mays Landing Country Club

Pleasantville NJ — Tee Times: (609)641-4411

Directions: Take the Atlantic City Expressway East to Exit 12. Go left on Rte 322 and 1/2 mi. to the course. Going West, take Exit 9 to Dillilah Rd, and turn left. Go 2 mi. to the Blackhorse Pike and turn left to the course.

Holes	Par	Yards Back Tees	Rating	Slope
18	72	6862	71.1	116

	9 Holes	18 Holes	Hours Mid Season
Weekday:	$15.00	$20.00	6:00 am - Dusk
Weekend:	$15.00	$25.00	6:00 am - Dusk
Cart Fees:	—	$22.00	

Facility Type: Public

Mandatory Cart Rental: No
Club Rental: Yes

Club Pro: Ron Ward
Discounts: Twilight
Tee Times: Yes, 1 week ahead for weekend

Features: Lessons, Showers/Lockers, Practice Area, Pro Shop - Limited, Clubhouse, Restaurant, Bar

Description: You'll use every club in your bag on this course. The fairways are tree-lined and narrow and there is water on 7 holes. A favorite hole is the 13th, a 430 yarder which you must carry over several interesting elevations.

Meadows Golf Club

79 Two Bridges Rd, Lincoln Pk NJ — Tee Times: (201)696-7212

Directions: I-80 West to Exit 52. Go off the ramp and take a left onto Two Bridges Rd. Go to the end and turn left (still Two Bridges Rd) and go1/2 mi. to course.

Facility Type: Semi-private

Club Pro: George O'Brian
Discounts: Twilight, Seniors
Tee Times: Yes, 1 week ahead for weekends

Features: Lessons, Showers/Lockers, Practice Area, Pro Shop - Complete, Clubhouse, Restaurant, Bar, Snack Bar, Banquet Facilities

Description: This is a challenging course. Water comes into play on all but 2 holes. A driving range is under construction, planned for use in '92.

Holes	Par	Yards Back Tees	Rating	Slope
18	68	6100	67.6	110

	9 Holes	18 Holes	Hours Mid Season
Weekday:	—	$15.00	Dawn - Dusk
Weekend:	—	$22.00	Dawn - Dusk
Cart Fees:	—	$22.00	

Mandatory Cart Rental: See notes.
Club Rental: Yes

Notes: Carts are mandatory on weekends.

Mercer Oaks Golf Course

Village Road West, West Windsor Township NJ — Info: (609)936-9603   Tee Times: (609)936-TIME

Directions: Take 295 to Exit 65A, Sloan Ave. Go East on Sloan to the 1st light and make a left onto Quakerbridge Rd. Go 2.3 mi. and make a right on Village Rd West. The course is 1.1 mi. on the right.

Facility Type: Public

Club Pro: None
Discounts: Seniors, Juniors, Twilight
Tee Times: Yes, Residents may call on Mon between 9 and 1 and Tuesday at the same time for Sun. Non residents can reserve on Thursday for weekends by phone.

Features: Driving Range, Practice Area, Pro Shop - Complete, Snack Bar

Holes	Par	Yards Back Tees	Rating	Slope
18	72	6318	69.6	113

	9 Holes	18 Holes	Hours Mid Season
Weekday:	—	$23.00	7:00 am - Dusk
Weekend:	—	$25.00	6:30 am - Dusk
Cart Fees:	—	$20.00	

Mandatory Cart Rental: No
Club Rental: No

Notes: Residents pay $13 weekdays and $15 weekends. Out of state pay $23 and $30. To qualify as a resident you must have ID from Princeton CC or Mountain View or proof of residency. Jr and Sr discounts are for county residents only.

Description: This is the newest public course in New Jersey at the time of publication. It opened in October and was rated without being played yet. The course is a Brian Ault design and like his TPC course, it has fairly high mounds and deep bunkers. The trees have been preserved, and although it is not a tight course, you do get that impression. The greens are large and undulating and afford a lot of pin placements. The signature will probably be #17, a 358 yard par 4 that plays next to a 300 acre man-made lake. We have not seen this course, but it is supposed to be very pretty.

Mountain View Golf Course
NJ 71
Bear Tavern Rd, Trenton NJ — (609)882-4093

Directions: I-95 to Exit 2. Take a left off the exit and course is on right.

Facility Type: Public

Club Pro: Steve Bowers
Discounts: Twilight, Seniors
Tee Times: No

Features: Lessons, Showers/Lockers, Practice Area, Pro Shop - Complete, Clubhouse, Bar, Snack Bar

Description: A well maintained course with water on several holes. The back 9 is a little hilly. There 3 par 5's on the back and 1 on the front. The fairways are wide open

Holes	Par	Yards Back Tees	Rating	Slope
18	72	6775	68.9	114

	9 Holes	18 Holes	Hours Mid Season
Weekday:	—	$18.00	7:00 am - Dusk
Weekend:	—	$22.00	6:00 am - Dusk
Cart Fees:	—	$18.00	

Mandatory Cart Rental: No
Club Rental: Yes

Notes: Sr discount only for residents of the county. Twilight after 5 midseason. Tee times may be instituted for '92. Call ahead 1st of the season to find out.

Oak Ridge Golf Club
NJ 72
136 Oak Ridge Rd, Clark — (908)574-0139

Directions: Garden State Parkway to Exit 135. Take Central Ave North to the 1st light (Raritan Rd) and take a left. This becomes Oak Ridge Rd. Go 3.5 mi. to the club.

Facility Type: Public

Club Pro: Dan Billy
Discounts: None
Tee Times: No

Features: Lessons, Showers/Lockers, Pro Shop - Complete, Clubhouse, Restaurant, Bar, Snack Bar

Description: This is a fairly straightforward course, flat, wide open, well trapped and irrigated.

Holes	Par	Yards Back Tees	Rating	Slope
18	70	6100	69.2	104

	9 Holes	18 Holes	Hours Mid Season
Weekday:	—	$16.00	Dawn - Dusk
Weekend:	—	$20.00	Dawn - Dusk
Cart Fees:	$12.00	$18.50	

Mandatory Cart Rental: No
Club Rental: Yes

Notes: Green fees are for those without county ID.. Out of state players pay $35 on weekdays and $50 on weekends for 18 holes.

Ocean Acres Country Club   NJ 73

925 Buckaneer Lane, Manahawkin NJ —   Tee Times: (609)597-9393

Directions: Grdn St Pkwy going south Exit 67. Take right at end of ramp. Take 1st left at Lighthouse Dr. Go 6 blocks to Buckaneer Lane and left to course. Going North on Pkwy take Exit 63 A to Rte 72 W. Go 1/4 mi. to Lighthouse and take a right. The course is approx 1 mi. on the right.

Facility Type: Semi-private

Club Pro: Bob Herman
Discounts: Twilight
Tee Times: Yes, up to 5 days ahead for weekends and holidays.

Features: Lessons, Practice Area, Pro Shop - Complete, Clubhouse, Restaurant, Bar, Snack Bar, Banquet Facilities

Description: A well maintained course with an open front 9 and wooded back 9. Water comes into play on two holes. A course favorite is the 10th, a par 3 island green. The 10th is featured on the scorecard.

Holes	Par	Yards Back Tees	Rating	Slope
18	72	6548	70.5	115

	9 Holes	18 Holes	Hours Mid Season
Weekday:	—	$20.00	Dawn - Dusk
Weekend:	—	$20.00	Dawn - Dusk
Cart Fees:	—	$20.00	

Mandatory Cart Rental: See notes.
Club Rental: Yes

Notes: Carts are mandatory between June 20 and Sept 13 from 7 am until noon every day. Memberships available.

Ocean City Golf Course   NJ 74

26th and Bay Ave, Ocean City NJ — (609)399-1315

Directions: Garden State Parkway to Exit 32 (Ocean City). Go across the bridge to Ocean City and take a right on Bay Ave to 26th. Or take Exit 25 toward Ocean City. At the 1st light, Bay Ave, take a left and go about 8 blocks to the course.

Facility Type: Executive

Club Pro: None
Discounts: Seniors
Tee Times: No

Features: Lessons, Pro Shop - Complete, Restaurant, Practice Area

Description: This is a 12 hole executive, part of the Ocean City airport complex. It's the only airport on the East Coast that you can fly into and walk to the beach from after a round of golf.

Holes	Par	Yards Back Tees	Rating	Slope
9	37	1750	—	—

	9 Holes	18 Holes	Hours Mid Season
Weekday:	$6.00	—	6:30 am - 7:30 pm
Weekend:	$6.00	—	6:30 am - 7:30 pm
Cart Fees:	—	—	

Mandatory Cart Rental:
Club Rental: Yes

Ocean County GC at Atlantis

Country Club Blvd, Tuckerton NJ — Tee Times: (609)296-2444

Directions: Garden St Parkway South to Exit 58. Go left off the exit onto 539 East. At the 1st light take a right (9 South). Go 1/4 mi. to Great Bay, and take a left. Go 1/4 mi. to Radio Rd, and right. Go 1 mi. Country Club Blvd, and turn left to the course. Going North on the Pkwy, take Exit 50 to 9 North. Go 3 mi. and turn right on Mathias Town Rd. Go 1 mi. to the light at Radio Rd, and turn left. 1/2 mi. to CC Blvd and left to the course.

Holes	Par	Yards Back Tees	Rating	Slope
18	72	6751	71.7	122

	9 Holes	18 Holes	Hours Mid Season
Weekday:	—	$16.00	7:00 am - Dusk
Weekend:	—	$19.00	6:00 am - Dusk
Cart Fees:	$12.00	$20.00	

Mandatory Cart Rental: No
Club Rental: Yes

Facility Type: Public

Club Pro: None
Discounts: Seniors, Twilight
Tee Times: Yes, 1 week ahead for any day.

Notes: Carts are mandatory from Mem Day through September on weekends and holidays from opening to 12 noon. Ocean County residents purchase ID card for $10 that allows reduced green fees.

Features: Lessons, Driving Range, Practice Area, Pro Shop - Complete, Clubhouse, Restaurant, Bar, Snack Bar, Banquet Facilities

Description: A George Fazio design, this course is long, flat and hard with narrow fairways and water on 4 holes. Formerly Atlantis Country Club, it was a choice of Golf Digest for "Places to Play" in both '90 and '91. This a beautiful and well-maintained facility.

Old Orchard Country Club

54 Monmouth Rd, Eatontown NJ — Tee Times: (908)542-7666

Directions: Garden State Parkway to Exit 105. This puts you on Rte 36 East. Just before the 6th light cut across 36 to Rte 71 North going toward Eatontown. The club 1/4 mi. on left.

Holes	Par	Yards Back Tees	Rating	Slope
18	72	6600	70.5	116

	9 Holes	18 Holes	Hours Mid Season
Weekday:	—	$20.00	Dawn - Dusk
Weekend:	—	$25.00	11:00 am - Dusk
Cart Fees:	—	$26.00	

Facility Type: Semi-private

Club Pro: George Craig
Discounts: Seniors, Twilight
Tee Times: Yes, up to 1 month in advance.

Mandatory Cart Rental: No
Club Rental: Yes

Features: Lessons, Showers/Lockers, Practice Area, Pro Shop - Complete, Clubhouse, Restaurant, Bar, Snack Bar, Banquet Facilities, Lodging Nearby

Notes: Members only play on weekends to 11 am. Cart fee is for double, $13 for single. Twilight begins at 4 pm mid-season

Description: This is a scenic course, built in 1929. The course is always in good condition. The terrain is flat, and there is water on 8 holes. The fairways offer a good mix of width. The 7th hole island green is a favorite. It's a par 5, 460 yds.

Orchard Hills Golf Course NJ 77

440 Paramus Rd, Paramus NJ — (201)447-3778

Directions: Garden State Parkway to Rte 4 West to Paramus Rd. Go North on Paramus and the course is approximately 3 mi. on right.

Facility Type: Public

Club Pro: None
Discounts: None
Tee Times: No, but a telephone reservation system may be established in'92.

Features:

Description: This course is undergoing major changes and is scheduled for opening in June of '92. Call for information.

Holes	Par	Yards Back Tees	Rating	Slope
9	35	3200	—	—

	9 Holes	18 Holes	Hours Mid Season
Weekday:	—	—	7:00 am - Dusk
Weekend:	—	—	6:30 am - Dusk
Cart Fees:	—	—	

Mandatory Cart Rental:
Club Rental:

Overpeck Golf Course NJ 78

Teaneck NJ — (201)837-3020

Directions: Garden St Pkwy to Rte 4 East. Take Teaneck Rd Exit and go south. Take a left at 2nd light, Cedar Lane directly to course.

Facility Type: Public

Club Pro: None
Discounts: None
Tee Times: No, but a telephone reservation system may be established in'92.

Features: Showers/Lockers, Practice Area, Pro Shop - Complete, Clubhouse, Restaurant

Description: This is a greatly improved course. It is very difficult from the back tees and fair from the front tees. Greens are average size and the fairways have been narrowed.

Holes	Par	Yards Back Tees	Rating	Slope
18	72	6890	69.6	108

	9 Holes	18 Holes	Hours Mid Season
Weekday:	—	$18.00	7:00 am - Dusk
Weekend:	—	$24.00	6:30 am - Dusk
Cart Fees:	—	$20.00	

Mandatory Cart Rental: No
Club Rental: No

Notes: Residents pay $11 weekdays and $14 on weekends for 18 holes. Out-of-state pay $40 anytime.

Paramus Golf & Country Club

314 Paramus Rd, Paramus NJ — (201)447-6067

Directions: Garden St Parkway North to Exit 161(Passaic St, Rochelle Park). Get off the exit and take a left onto Passaic St. When you cross Rte 4, it becomes Paramus Rd. Go 2 mi. to the club after Rte 4.

Facility Type: Public

Club Pro: Jake Zastko
Discounts: Seniors
Tee Times: No

Features: Lessons, Showers/Lockers, Practice Area, Pro Shop - Limited, Clubhouse, Restaurant, Bar, Snack Bar, Banquet Facilities

Description: This not too difficult a course. It is flat and wooded with some water hazards. The course is in the 2nd year of a 5 year improvement program reworking everything.

Holes	Par	Yards Back Tees	Rating	Slope
18	71	6100	67.6	109

	9 Holes	18 Holes	Hours Mid Season
Weekday:	—	$19.00	7:00 am - 6:30 pm
Weekend:	—	$25.00	6:00 am - 6:30 pm
Cart Fees:	—	$23.00	

Mandatory Cart Rental: No
Club Rental: Yes

Notes: Green fees are $23 weekdays and $25 weekends for out-of-state players. For a $25 registration fee, take $3 off green fees.

Pascack Brook Golf & CC

15 River Vale Rd, River Vale, NJ — Tee Times: (201)664-5886

Directions: Palisades Pkwy to Exit 2. Go South on 9W to the 1st traffic light. Take a right onto Bergan Rte 502 (Closter Dock Rd). Go 5 mi. on 502 to Bogert Mill Rd and take a right. Go to the end at the T stop and take a left onto Harriet Ave. The course is 1/2 mi. on the left.

Facility Type: Public

Club Pro: Yaz Consalvo
Discounts: Seniors
Tee Times: Yes, 1 week ahead for weekends/holidays

Features: Lessons, Practice Area, Clubhouse, Restaurant, Bar, Snack Bar, Pro Shop - Limited, Banquet Facilities

Description: This is a pleasant course and in good condition. It's mildly difficult, with its share of bunkers, water and trees. A good example is the 2nd hole, a 443 yd, par 4 dogleg left with traps to the right and front of green.

Holes	Par	Yards Back Tees	Rating	Slope
18	71	6287	70.9	120

	9 Holes	18 Holes	Hours Mid Season
Weekday:	—	$20.00	6:30 am - 7:00 pm
Weekend:	—	$42.00	6:00 am - 7:00 pm
Cart Fees:	—	$20.00	

Mandatory Cart Rental: See notes.
Club Rental: Yes

Notes: Weekend green fee includes cart.

Passaic County Golf Course

217 Totowa Rd, Wayne NJ — (201)696-5712

Directions: Garden St Parkway to Exit 154 onto Rte 3 West. 3 mi. to Rte 46 West. Another 3 mi. to River View Drive. Go north on River View Dr to just before the 4th light, Totowa Rd. Take a right and go 1/2 mi. to course.

Facility Type: Public

Club Pro: Al Perow, Club Pro
Discounts: Seniors
Tee Times: No

Features: Lessons, Showers/Lockers, Practice Area, Clubhouse, Restaurant, Snack Bar, Banquet Facilities, Pro Shop - Complete

Description: This 100 year-old course is in great condition considering how many rounds are accomodated. The red course is flat and wooded. The blue is hilly and wide open. Improvements to this facility are pretty constant.

Holes	Par	Yards Back Tees	Rating	Slope
18	69	6080	70.4	117
18	70	6457	69.8	115

	9 Holes	18 Holes	Hours Mid Season
Weekday:	—	$25.00	6:00 am - 7:00 pm
Weekend:	—	$25.00	5:00 am - 7:00 pm
Cart Fees:	—	$17.00	

Mandatory Cart Rental: No
Club Rental: Yes

Notes: Sr discount for county residents anytime and reciprocal on Thursdays. The driving range is a shag field. Rates for residents are $25 to join and $6 on weekdays and $7 on weekends.

Pennsauken Country Club

3800 Haddonfield Rd, Pennsauken NJ — **Tee Times:** (609)662-4961

Directions: NJ Turnpike to Exit 4. Take Rte 73 South to Rte 70 West 3 mi. to Racetrack Circle. Take the 1st right off the circle onto Haddonfield Rd. The course is 3 mi. on the right.

Facility Type: Semi-private

Club Pro: Quentin Griffith
Discounts: Twilight
Tee Times: Yes, 1 week ahead for any day

Features: Lessons, Showers/Lockers, Practice Area, Clubhouse, Restaurant, Bar, Snack Bar, Pro Shop - Complete, Banquet Facilities, Lodging Nearby

Description: This course is in very good condition. It was built in the '30s. It is well bunkered. The front is open and the back wooded. Greens are small.

Holes	Par	Yards Back Tees	Rating	Slope
18	70	6006	67.9	111

	9 Holes	18 Holes	Hours Mid Season
Weekday:	—	$17.00	Dawn - Dusk
Weekend:	—	$20.00	Dawn - Dusk
Cart Fees:	$15.00	$20.00	

Mandatory Cart Rental: No
Club Rental: Yes

Notes: Cart fee $15 single, $20 for double.

Pickatinny Golf Course

Bldg 121 A, Dover NJ — Info: (201)989-2460   Tee Times: (201)989-2466

Directions: I-80 to the Jefferson Exit. Take Rte 15 North for approximately 1 mi. to the entrance of Pickatinny Arsenal. Ask directions to the course.

Holes	Par	Yards Back Tees	Rating	Slope
18	72	6714	72.8	120

Facility Type: Semi-private

	9 Holes	18 Holes	Hours Mid Season
Weekday:	$9.00	$18.00	6:30 am - 6:00 pm
Weekend:	$12.00	$24.00	6:30 am - 6:00 pm
Cart Fees:	$12.00	$16.00	

Club Pro: Joe Kelly
Discounts: None
Tee Times: Yes, 1 day for weekdays, and 1 week for weekends

Mandatory Cart Rental: No
Club Rental: No

Features: Lessons, Showers/Lockers, Driving Range, Practice Area, Pro Shop - Complete, Clubhouse, Snack Bar, Restaurant, Bar, Banquet Facilities, VISA/MC

Notes: This course is open only to active and retired military personel, active reservists or retired reservists with 20 years of service.

Description: The front 9 is flat, the back 9 rolls a little more. The fairways are a good mix of width and difficulty. The greens are essentially flat. Water comes into play on 4 holes. The course is also well-bunkered throughout and considered tough.

Pinch Brook Golf Course

234 Ridgedale Ave, Florham Park NJ — Info: (201)377-2039   Tee Times: (201)644-4022

Directions: Rte 287 to Rte 10. East on Rte 10 for 2 mi. to Ridgedale and take a right. 3 mi. to course on the left.

Holes	Par	Yards Back Tees	Rating	Slope
18	65	5000	63.7	98

Facility Type: Public

	9 Holes	18 Holes	Hours Mid Season
Weekday:	—	$15.00	7:00 am - 7:00 pm
Weekend:	—	$22.00	7:00 am - 7:00 pm
Cart Fees:	$14.00	$23.00	

Club Pro: Cindy Cooper
Discounts: None
Tee Times: Yes, registered players up to one week in advance.

Mandatory Cart Rental: No
Club Rental: Yes

Features: Lessons, Showers/Lockers, Pro Shop - Complete, Clubhouse, Snack Bar, Bar, Practice Area

Notes: Green fees for Morris County residents are 1/2. See county System details at the beginning of this section. Sr discounts for registered county residents only.

Description: This is an easy course to walk but a difficult one to play. It is relatively flat, wooded and water comes into play.

Pinebrook Golf Course

1 Covered Bridge Rd, Englishtown NJ — Info: (908)536-7272   Tee Times: (908)758-8383

Directions: Garden State Parkway to Exit 123. Take Rte 9 South to the course, approx 12 mi.,

Facility Type: Public

Club Pro: None
Discounts: Twilight
Tee Times: Yes, County residents with ID 7 days prior or after 8 pm, non-residents with ID 5 days prior after 5 pm.

Features: Practice Area, Pro Shop - Complete, Clubhouse, Snack Bar

Description: This course is up and down a little and in excellent shape. It's a good course for your irons.

Holes	Par	Yards Back Tees	Rating	Slope
18	61	4168	58.1	90

	9 Holes	18 Holes	Hours Mid Season
Weekday:	—	$23.00	7:00 am - Dusk
Weekend:	—	$25.00	6:00 am - Dusk
Cart Fees:	—	$22.00	

Mandatory Cart Rental: No
Club Rental: No

Notes: County residents with ID pay 1/2 for green fees.

Pinecrest Golf Course

561 Spur, Hammonton NJ —   Tee Times: (609)561-6110

Directions: Atlantic City Expressway going West or East, take Exit 28. Go South on Rte 54. Make a right at the 1st light (561 spur) and go 2.3 mi. to the course.

Facility Type: Public

Club Pro: Robert Martell
Discounts: Twilight
Tee Times: Yes, Friday before for weekends/holidays

Features: Lessons, Showers/Lockers, Driving Range, Practice Area, Pro Shop - Complete, Clubhouse, Restaurant, Bar, Banquet Facilities

Description: This is a scenic and relatively challenging course. It's narrow and wooded with water coming into play on two holes. #6 is a favorite. It's a 581 yd par 5 - difficult to reach the two-tiered and bunkered green in 2 shots over water.

Holes	Par	Yards Back Tees	Rating	Slope
18	72	6200	69.7	113

	9 Holes	18 Holes	Hours Mid Season
Weekday:	—	$11.00	Dawn - Dusk
Weekend:	—	$15.00	Dawn - Dusk
Cart Fees:	—	$22.00	

Mandatory Cart Rental: No
Club Rental: No

Pitman Golf Club

Pitman NJ 08071 — Tee Times: (609)589-8081

Directions: Rte 55 to Rte 322 West. Go right at the 1st light (no name on road). Take that 2 mi. to a blinking light and take a left. Go 600 yds to course on the right.

Facility Type: Public

Club Pro: John Tyrell
Discounts: None
Tee Times: Yes, 1 week ahead for weekends/holidays

Features: Lessons, Driving Range, Practice Area, Pro Shop - Limited, Snack Bar

Description: This is a wide open and flat course with water on 6 holes. If you par #11, you've done well. It's a 435 yd par 4, dogleg left over a ravine to a trapped green on a hill.

Holes	Par	Yards Back Tees	Rating	Slope
18	71	6190	68.3	111

	9 Holes	18 Holes	Hours Mid Season
Weekday:	—	$12.00	Dawn - Dusk
Weekend:	—	$16.00	Dawn - Dusk
Cart Fees:	—	$22.00	

Mandatory Cart Rental: No
Club Rental: No

Notes: Cart rental fee during week is $20, per 2 players.

Plainfield CC West 9

Woodland and Maple Aves, Edison NJ — (908)769-3672

Directions: Garden State Parkway to Exit 135. Take Central Ave West to the 1st light, Raritan Rd, and turn left. Go 4 mi. to the end and take a right on Inman to the end. Go left 150 yds to the course.

Facility Type: Public

Club Pro: Ed Famula
Discounts: Seniors, Juniors, Twilight
Tee Times: No

Features: Lessons, Practice Area, Clubhouse, Restaurant, Bar, Snack Bar, Pro Shop - Limited, Lodging Nearby

Description: Built in the 1930's, this course is rolling , fairly open, and has a little water. The greens are in excellent shape. #6 is a par 4, 340 yard iron shot to the top of a hill and a chip down to a postage stamp green.

Holes	Par	Yards Back Tees	Rating	Slope
9	33	2493	62.8	103

	9 Holes	18 Holes	Hours Mid Season
Weekday:	$15.00	$15.00	7:00 am - Dusk
Weekend:	$21.00	$21.00	7:00 am - Dusk
Cart Fees:	$17.00	$17.00	

Mandatory Cart Rental: No
Club Rental: Yes

Notes: The green fees are for all day play. Memberships available for reduced green fee advantages.

Pomona Golf Club

400 W Moss Mill Rd, Pomona NJ — (609)965-3232

Directions: Garden State Parkway going South to Exit 44. Take a right onto Moss Mill Rd and go approx 3 mi. to the course.

Holes	Par	Yards Back Tees	Rating	Slope
9	34	2426	—	—

Facility Type: Public

	9 Holes	18 Holes	Hours Mid Season
Weekday:	$10.00	$10.00	8:00 am - 7:00 pm
Weekend:	$12.00	$12.00	8:00 am - 7:00 pm
Cart Fees:	—	—	

Club Pro: Elwood Myers
Discounts: Twilight
Tee Times: No

Club Rental: Yes

Features: Lessons, Driving Range, Snack Bar

Description: This is a level and wooded course with doglegs through the woods. Accuracy is a must. It's a great course for your irons.

Princeton Country Club

1 Wheeler Way, Princeton NJ — (609)452-9382

Directions: Take US 1 for 4 miles South of Princeton Circle. Make a right onto Emmons Drive and the 1st left onto Wheeler Way to the course. Going North on US 1, get off on Meadow Rd and make a left back onto Rte 1, then turn right on Emmons Drive.

Holes	Par	Yards Back Tees	Rating	Slope
18	70	6200	68.6	—

	9 Holes	18 Holes	Hours Mid Season
Weekday:	—	$18.00	7:00 am - Dusk
Weekend:	—	$22.00	6:00 am - Dusk
Cart Fees:	—	$18.00	

Facility Type: Public

Mandatory Cart Rental: No
Club Rental: Yes

Club Pro: Steve Bowers
Discounts: Seniors, Twilight
Tee Times: No

Features: Lessons, Showers/Lockers, Practice Area, Clubhouse, Restaurant, Bar, Snack Bar, Banquet Facilities, Pro Shop - Complete

Notes: County residents pay half the above rates with ID. Out-of-state pay $30 on weekends. Tee times may be instituted for '92. Call to inquire. Sr discount limited to Mercer County residents. Twilight at 5 midseason.

Description: This is a busy, well-maintained course. You cannot spray your shots here, because it's tight and wooded. Greens are elevated. Water comes into play on the 13th. The course is flat and well-bunkered.

Quail Brook Golf Course

New Brunswick Rd, Somerset NJ — Info: (908)560-9199 Tee Times: (908)560-1500

Directions: 287 to Exit 6. Going South on 287 get off ramp and go to 2nd light (Cedar Grove Lane). Take a right and go 1.5 mi. to New Brunswick Rd and take a left. 7/10 mi. to course.

Facility Type: Public

Club Pro: None
Discounts: None
Tee Times: Yes, County residents are placed in system to call 7 days prior. Non-residents in the system call 1 day prior for $6 charge.

Features: Driving Range, Practice Area, Pro Shop - Complete, Clubhouse, Snack Bar

Description: The front 9 is flat, the back 9 more aggressive. A picturesque course. The course has a lot of woods, forcing straight hits.

Holes	Par	Yards Back Tees	Rating	Slope
18	71	6474	70.8	119

	9 Holes	18 Holes	Hours Mid Season
Weekday:	—	$14.00	7:00 am - Dusk
Weekend:	—	$17.00	6:00 am - Dusk
Cart Fees:	$11.80	$18.00	

Mandatory Cart Rental: No
Club Rental: Yes

Notes: Out of county players can be put in the system for $50. The driving range is complete.

Quail Ridge Golf World

3410 Hurley Pond Rd, Wall Tnshp NJ — (908)681-0918

Directions: On Highway 34 in Wall Township.

Facility Type: Pitch & Putt

Club Pro: None
Discounts: None
Tee Times: No

Features: Driving Range, Lessons, Pro Shop - Complete, Snack Bar

Description: Clubs are supplied here. The facility has a driving range and miniature golf.

Holes	Par	Yards Back Tees	Rating	Slope
18	56	960	—	—

	9 Holes	18 Holes	Hours Mid Season
Weekday:	$3.00	$6.00	8:00 am - 9:30 pm
Weekend:	$3.00	$6.00	8:00 am - 9:30 pm
Cart Fees:	—	—	

Club Rental:

Ramblewood Country Club

200 Country Club Pkwy, Mt Laurel NJ — Tee Times: (609)235-2119

Directions: Rte 295 to the Mt Laurel Exit (36A) to Rte 73 South. 60 ft past the 3rd light take a left onto Church Rd and go 1/2 mi. to signs for the club.

Facility Type: Public

Coupon page 126

Club Pro: None
Discounts: Twilight, Seniors
Tee Times: Yes, 1 week ahead for any day.

Features: Lessons, Showers/Lockers, Clubhouse, Restaurant, Bar, Banquet Facilities, Pro Shop - Complete, Snack Bar, Lodging Nearby, VISA/MC

Description: This is a fairly flat course in great shape. The blue course is shorter and carved out of the trees. The red is longer and the hardest, especially #8. This is a par 4, 418 yd dogleg over a creek. The green is on a small hill with hazards left and right. The red/white course rating and slope are 71.1/120, white/blue are 69.5/116, and the blue/red are 70.3/118.

Holes	Par	Yards Back Tees	Rating	Slope
9	R 36	3485	71.1	120
9	W 36	3392	69.5	116
9	B 36	3232	70.3	118

	9 Holes	18 Holes	Hours Mid Season
Weekday:	—	$23.50	7:00 am - 7:00 pm
Weekend:	—	$28.50	7:00 am - 7:00 pm
Cart Fees:	—	$25.00	

Mandatory Cart Rental: No
Club Rental: Yes

Notes: Greens fees listed are for unlimited play. The cart fee on weekdays is $23.50.

Rancocas Golf Club

Club House Drive, Willingboro NJ — Tee Times: (609)877-5344

Directions: Rte 295 to Exit 45 B onto Beverly-Roncocas Rd. Take the 2nd left after the 5th light (JFK Way) onto Country Club Drive. Take 2nd left again onto Club House Drive to course.

Facility Type: Public

Coupon page 126

Club Pro: Greg Fields
Discounts: Seniors, Juniors, Twilight
Tee Times: Yes, 1 week ahead for any day. Members can make 8 days in advance.

Features: Lessons, Driving Range, Practice Area, Clubhouse, Snack Bar, VISA/MC, Pro Shop - Complete

Description: A Robert Trent Jones course, it is flat and well bunkered (99 traps). The front 9 is tree-lined and the back 9 open. The challenge here is the 2nd shot on #4, a 585 yd par 5, with a narrow bunkered fairway to an elevated well-bunkered green.

Holes	Par	Yards Back Tees	Rating	Slope
18	71	6800	73.0	130

	9 Holes	18 Holes	Hours Mid Season
Weekday:	$16.00	$21.00	6:30 am - Dusk
Weekend:	$25.00	$38.00	Dawn - Dusk
Cart Fees:	—	$10.00	

Mandatory Cart Rental: See notes.
Club Rental: Yes

Notes: Cart included and mandatory for 18 holes on weekends before noon. Afternoon $20 for 9 and $30 for 18. Memberships available for reduced green fees.

River Vale Country Club

660 River Vale Rd, River Vale NJ — Tee Times: (201)391-2300

Directions: Garden St Parkway to Exit 172. Go East on Grand to Middletown Rd at the stop. Make a right and the course is on the left 1 mi. Or take the Palisades Pkwy to Exit 6W. Make a left at the 4th light (Blue Hill Rd) and go to the end. Make a left onto RiverVale Rd and go 1/4 mi. to course.

Facility Type: Public

Club Pro: Jeff Glass
Discounts: Twilight
Tee Times: Yes, 2 weeks ahead for any day.

Features: Lessons, Showers/Lockers, Driving Range, Practice Area, Pro Shop - Complete, Clubhouse, Restaurant, Bar, Snack Bar, American Express, VISA/MC, Banquet Facilities, Lodging Nearby

Description: This course was designed by Orin Smith and built in 1930. It is a shot-makers golf club. It's fairly wooded and water comes into play. The signature here is the 5th hole, a par 3, 233 yd shot uphill - tough and pretty.

Holes	Par	Yards Back Tees	Rating	Slope
18	72	6470	70.1	116

	9 Holes	18 Holes	Hours Mid Season
Weekday:	—	$58.00	6:00 am - 6:00 pm
Weekend:	—	$78.00	6:00 am - 6:00 pm
Cart Fees:	—	—	

Mandatory Cart Rental: Yes
Club Rental: Yes

Notes: Carts are included in green fees and mandatory. Dress code applies. Normally open all year round, the club will close for the winter for renovations. Irrigation and cement cart paths are planned. Call for numerous specials.

Rock View Golf Club

Montague NJ — (201)293-9891

Directions: Rte 84 West to Exit 1. Take Rte 6 toward Port Jervis. Make a left at the 2nd light, Rte 521. Go 4 mi. to the club.

Facility Type: Public

Club Pro: None
Discounts: None
Tee Times: No

Features: Pro Shop - Complete, Clubhouse, Bar, Snack Bar, Lodging Nearby

Description: This is a short and tricky course with 7 doglegs. It's a good walking course.

Holes	Par	Yards Back Tees	Rating	Slope
9	35	2500	—	—

	9 Holes	18 Holes	Hours Mid Season
Weekday:	$7.00	$10.00	8:00 am - 6:00 pm
Weekend:	$8.00	$11.00	6:00 am - 6:00 pm
Cart Fees:	$10.00	$20.00	

Mandatory Cart Rental: No
Club Rental: Yes

Rockleigh Golf Course

15 Paris Ave, Rockleigh NJ — **Info:** (201)768-6353

Directions: Palisades Pkwy to Exit 5S. Take Rte 303 South, and it becomes Livingston Ave. Take a left at the 4th light, Paris Ave, and proceed to the course.

Holes	Par	Yards Back Tees	Rating	Slope
9	36	3282	35.0	117
9	36	2961	34.5	117
9	36	3127	34.0	117

Facility Type: Public

	9 Holes	18 Holes	Hours Mid Season
Weekday:	—	$18.00	6:30 am - Dusk
Weekend:	—	$24.00	6:30 am - Dusk
Cart Fees:	$12.00	$20.00	

Club Pro: George Phillips
Discounts: Seniors
Tee Times: No, but a telephone reservation system may be established in '92.

Mandatory Cart Rental: No
Club Rental: Yes

Features: Lessons, Showers/Lockers, Practice Area, Pro Shop - Complete, Snack Bar, Restaurant

Notes: Residents pay $11 weekdays and $14 weekends. Out-of-state pay $40 all times.

Description: White is the shortest course and red the longest. The slope on any combination is 117. The course is generally wide open with 50 yd fairways and very few trees. The rough is short and there is water on two holes.

Rolling Greens Golf Club

214 Newton-Sparta Rd, Newton NJ — (201)383-3082

Directions: Rte 80 to Exit 25. Take 206 North into Andover Township. Just past the Exxon Station on the right, turn onto Limecrest Rd. Go approximately 4 mi. to the 1st light. Take a left onto Rte 616. The course is 1/2 mi. on the left.

Holes	Par	Yards Back Tees	Rating	Slope
18	66	5300	—	—

Facility Type: Public

	9 Holes	18 Holes	Hours Mid Season
Weekday:	—	$13.00	Dawn - Dusk
Weekend:	—	$17.00	Dawn - Dusk
Cart Fees:	—	$17.00	

Coupon page 127

Club Pro: None
Discounts: Twilight
Tee Times: No

Mandatory Cart Rental: No
Club Rental: Yes

Features: Pro Shop - Limited, Snack Bar

Description: This is an interesting course - difficult for being so short. It is relatively flat and open with lots of bunkers and a fair amount of water. A favorite is #9, a par 3, 180 yd tough shot over water to a well-bunkered green.

Ron Jawarski's Eagle's Nest

Sewell NJ — Tee Times: (609)468-3542

Directions: Rte 55 South from Phila to Exit 53B. 1.5 mi. on left on Rte 553.

Facility Type: Semi-private

Club Pro: Joe Russo
Discounts: Seniors
Tee Times: Yes, any day for weekdays. For weekends/holidays, Monday prior.

Features: Lessons, Showers/Lockers, Practice Area, Pro Shop - Complete, Clubhouse, Restaurant, Bar, Snack Bar, Banquet Facilities, VISA/MC, Lodging Nearby

Description: This course is in excellent shape and one of the toughest in the area. The original front 9 is relatively flat. The course becomes hillier on the back 9. The signature hole is #15, a 482 yd par 5. It takes a lengthy tee shot by a hazard and trap on the right to lay up correctly. The landing area before the green is over a creek and the green is guarded on 3 sides with water and sand.

Holes	Par	Yards Back Tees	Rating	Slope
18	71	6376	70	115

	9 Holes	18 Holes	Hours Mid Season
Weekday:	—	$15.00	7:00 am - Dusk
Weekend:	—	$20.00	6:00 am - Dusk
Cart Fees:	—	$20.00	

Mandatory Cart Rental: Yes
Club Rental: Yes

Notes: Carts are mandatory on weekends and holidays before noon.

Rutgers Golf Course

777 Hoes Lane, Piscataway NJ — Tee Times: (908)932-2631

Directions: Rte 287 to Exit 5 (River Rd South) towards Highland Park. Make a left at the 3rd light, Hoes Lane. The course is 1/4 mi.

Facility Type: Public

Club Pro: Art DeBlasio
Discounts: Twilight, Seniors
Tee Times: Yes, 1 week in advance for weekends in person. Previous Friday for weekdays.

Features: Lessons, Practice Area, Pro Shop - Complete, Snack Bar

Description: A short but tricky course, it is open and wooded with water throughout the back 9. There are 5 par 3's.

Holes	Par	Yards Back Tees	Rating	Slope
18	71	6267	69.9	110

	9 Holes	18 Holes	Hours Mid Season
Weekday:	—	$12.00	7:00 am - 7:30 pm
Weekend:	—	$18.00	6:00 am - 7:30 pm
Cart Fees:	—	$25.00	

Mandatory Cart Rental: No
Club Rental: No

Scotch Hills Country Club   NJ 101

Jerusalem Rd, Scotch Plains NJ — (908)232-9748

Directions: Rte 22 going West, exit at Mountain Ave. Go 3 blocks and make a left onto Jerusalem Ave and go to the end, approx 1 m, to the club. Heading East on 22, exit at Park Ave (Scotch Plains). Make a left at the 1st light, Mountain Ave, and a right onto Jerusalem to the course.

Holes	Par	Yards Back Tees	Rating	Slope
9	33	2200	31.4	104

	9 Holes	18 Holes	Hours Mid Season
Weekday:	$8.00	$8.00	7:00 am - Dusk
Weekend:	$12.00	$12.00	6:30 am - Dusk
Cart Fees:	$8.00	—	

Facility Type: Public

Club Pro: John Turnbull
Discounts: Twilight
Tee Times: No

Mandatory Cart Rental: No
Club Rental: Yes

Notes: Resident memberships are available.

Features: Lessons, Driving Range, Practice Area, Pro Shop - Complete, Snack Bar

Description: This course looks easy, but it's not. It's hilly, with some varied lies, and it sports some of the best greens in the area. Left is out-of-bounds on most of the holes.

Shark River Golf Course   NJ 102

Old Corlies Ave, Neptune NJ — Info: (908)636-7272   Tee Times: (908)758-8383

Directions: Garden State Parkway to Exit 100 from either direction. Go East on Rte 33. Watch for brown Monmouth County signs to the course just before the Rte 18 overpass.

Holes	Par	Yards Back Tees	Rating	Slope
18	71	6180	68.9	112

	9 Holes	18 Holes	Hours Mid Season
Weekday:	—	$24.00	7:00 am - Dusk
Weekend:	—	$26.00	6:00 am - Dusk
Cart Fees:	—	$24.00	

Facility Type: Public

Club Pro: None
Discounts: Twilight
Tee Times: Yes, County residents with ID 7 days prior or after 8 pm, non-residents with ID 5 days prior after 5 pm.

Mandatory Cart Rental: No
Club Rental: No

Notes: County residents with ID pay 1/2 for green fees.

Features: Practice Area, Pro Shop - Complete, Clubhouse, Restaurant

Description: This was fashioned from the famous Asbury Park Golf Course. It is an old style course with small, well-bunkered greens. It is relatively flat with little water. The fairways are watered.

Spa Executive 9

McAffee NJ — Tee Times: (201)827-3710

Directions: Rte 80 West to Exit 53 (Rte 23 N) to Hamburg. Take a right onto Rte 94 North. Go 4 miles to the light and bear right. Go approximately 2 miles to The Great Gorge Resort, The Spa and Great Gorge Village.

Facility Type: Executive

Coupon page 127

Club Pro: None
Discounts: Seniors
Tee Times: Yes, 1 week ahead for any day

Features: Practice Area, Pro Shop - Limited, Snack Bar, American Express, VISA/MC, Restaurant, Bar, Banquet Facilities, Lodging Nearby

Description: An executive-type course designed by Robert Trent Jones, it is scenic, tight and challenging.

Holes	Par	Yards Back Tees	Rating	Slope
9	31	2369	—	—

	9 Holes	18 Holes	Hours Mid Season
Weekday:	$18.00	$28.00	8:00 am - 7:30 pm
Weekend:	$21.00	$34.00	7:00 am - 7:30 pm
Cart Fees:	—	—	

Mandatory Cart Rental: See notes.
Club Rental: Yes

Notes: The cart fee is included in the above prices. Carts are mandatory on weekends only. The restaurant and bar are off site in the hotel.

Spooky Brook Golf Course

North Branch NJ — Info: (908)873-2242   Tee Times: (908)560-1500

Directions: 287 to Exit 7 (Weston-Canal Rd). Go to the light and turn toward South Boundbrook. Go 2 mi. to 621 (Elizabeth Ave) and take a right and course is 3 mi. on right.

Facility Type: Public

Club Pro: None
Discounts: Seniors, Juniors
Tee Times: Yes, County residents are placed in system and can call 7 days prior. Non-residents in the system can call 1 day prior for $6 charge.

Features: Driving Range, Practice Area, Pro Shop - Complete, Clubhouse, Snack Bar

Description: A flat and wide open straightforward course.

Holes	Par	Yards Back Tees	Rating	Slope
18	71	6630	69.2	111

	9 Holes	18 Holes	Hours Mid Season
Weekday:	—	$14.00	7:00 am - Dusk
Weekend:	—	$17.00	6:00 am - Dusk
Cart Fees:	$11.80	$18.00	

Mandatory Cart Rental: No
Club Rental: Yes

Notes: Non residents of Somerset County can be put into the reservation system for $50.

Spring Meadow Golf Course NJ 105

4181 Atlantic Ave, Farmingdale NJ — (908)449-0806

Directions: Garden State Parkway to Exit 98. Follow the signs for Allaire State Park. The course is 1 mi. East of Allaire State Park on 524.

Holes	Par	Yards Back Tees	Rating	Slope
18	71	5800	65.3	113

Facility Type: Public

	9 Holes	18 Holes	Hours Mid Season
Weekday:	—	$13.00	Dawn - Dusk
Weekend:	—	$16.00	Dawn - Dusk
Cart Fees:	—	$20.00	

Club Pro: None
Discounts: Seniors, Twilight
Tee Times: No

Mandatory Cart Rental: No
Club Rental: Yes

Features: Driving Range, Practice Area, Pro Shop - Limited, Clubhouse, Restaurant, Bar, Snack Bar, Banquet Facilities

Description: This is the only course owned by the state. It is about 70 yrs old and picturesque.

Springfield Golf Center NJ 106

855 Jacksonville/ Mt Holly Rd, Mt Holly NJ — (609)267-8440

Directions: NJ Turnpike to Exit 5. Take a right onto Rte 541. At the 2nd light take a jug handle left onto Wood Lane Rd/Rte 630. At the 1st light make a left onto Rte 628 (Jacksonville/Mt Holly Rd). The course is 2 mi. on right.

Holes	Par	Yards Back Tees	Rating	Slope
18	54	697	—	—
18	68	5872	66.6	—

	9 Holes	18 Holes	Hours Mid Season
Weekday:	—	$10.00	Dawn - Dusk
Weekend:	—	$12.00	Dawn - Dusk
Cart Fees:	—	$19.00	

Facility Type: Public

Club Pro: Jack Williams
Discounts: Seniors, Twilight
Tee Times: No

Mandatory Cart Rental: No
Club Rental: Yes

Features: Lessons, Driving Range, Practice Area, Pro Shop - Limited, Clubhouse, Bar, Snack Bar, Lodging Nearby

Description: The front 9 is quite tight and watery, the back 9 wide open. It's flat and a good walking course.

Notes: Members have preference on weekend mornings until 8:00 am. This is a complete golf facility for everyone in the family, including a pitch & putt course, a complete 24 tee driving range and miniature golf. The driving range is open untill 11 pm in the summer.

Stony Brook Golf Club NJ 107

Stonybrook Rd, Hopewell NJ — Tee Times: (609)466-2215

Directions: Rte 295 to Exit 4. Take Rte 31 North toward Pennington. Go approximately 2.5 mi. and take a right onto Rte 654. Follow 654 as it bends and go past Hopewell CC to Stony Brook.

Facility Type: Public

Club Pro: Dale Shankland
Discounts: Seniors, Juniors, Twilight
Tee Times: Yes, 2 days in advance for weekends

Features: Lessons, Practice Area, Clubhouse, Snack Bar, Banquet Facilities, VISA/MC, Pro Shop - Complete

Description: Robert Kraeger designed this links-type course. It is not quite an executive course. It appeals to the shot maker.

Holes	Par	Yards Back Tees	Rating	Slope
18	62	3603	57.3	91

	9 Holes	18 Holes	Hours Mid Season
Weekday:	$9.00	$13.00	7:00 am - Dusk
Weekend:	$9.00	$16.00	6:30 am - Dusk
Cart Fees:	$11.00	$22.00	

Mandatory Cart Rental: No
Club Rental: Yes

Notes: A limited number of memberships are available. Open all year round.

Sunset Valley Golf Club NJ 108

Pompton Plains NJ — Info: (201)835-1515   Tee Times: (201)644-4022

Directions: Rte 80 to Rte 23 North. Go 1 mi. and jug handle at Newark Pompton Turnpike. Go to the first light and make a left. Go approx 2.5 mi. to Sunset and make a right to the course.

Facility Type: Public

Club Pro: Dave Nelson
Discounts: None
Tee Times: Yes, those in the computer sustem may call 1 week in advance.

Features: Lessons, Showers/Lockers, Practice Area, Pro Shop - Complete, Clubhouse, Bar, Snack Bar

Description: This is a difficult course with large undulating greens, tree-lined fairways and several water hazards.

Holes	Par	Yards Back Tees	Rating	Slope
18	70	6439	71.7	129

	9 Holes	18 Holes	Hours Mid Season
Weekday:	—	$15.00	7:00 am - Dusk
Weekend:	—	$22.00	7:00 am - Dusk
Cart Fees:	—	$23.00	

Mandatory Cart Rental: No
Club Rental: Yes

Notes: See county system details at the beginning of this section.

Tamarack Golf Course   NJ 109
97 Hardenburg, E Brunswik NJ — (908)821-8881

Directions: NJ Turnpike to Exit 9. Take Rte 18
North to Rte 1 South to the 2nd Milltown Exit.
You are on Main Street in Milltown. Go to Riva
Ave and take a right. Take a left at the 2nd blink-
ing light onto Hardenburg Rd to the course.

Facility Type: Public

Club Pro: Ed Heuser
Discounts: Juniors
Tee Times: No

Features: Lessons, Showers/Lockers, Driving Range,
Practice Area, Pro Shop - Complete, Restaurant,
Bar, Snack Bar

Description: The longer red/white is a full championship course. The gold/blue course is not as
long, but it is still challenging. There is something
for every golfer here. The course was desihned by
Hal Purdy.

Holes	Par	Yards Back Tees	Rating	Slope
18	71	6244	69.4	107
18	72	7025	73.0	118

	9 Holes	18 Holes	Hours Mid Season
Weekday:	—	$16.00	7:00 am - 6:00 pm
Weekend:	—	$20.00	6:00 am - 6:00 pm
Cart Fees:	$12.50	$20.00	

Mandatory Cart Rental: No
Club Rental: No

Notes: Out of state players pay $50, unless accompa-
nied by a Middlesex County resident, where fees
are $24 on weekdays and $30 on weekends. Non-
resident prices apply to New Jersey residents not
residing in Middlesex county.

Tara Greens Golf Center   NJ 110
1111 Somerset St, Somerset NJ — (908)247-8284

Directions: NJ Trnpke to Exit 9. Follow signs to New
Brunswick. Take Rte 27 South toward Princeton.
The course is on Rte 27, 2 miles South of New
Brunswick on the right.

Facility Type: Public

Club Pro: Mike Bonetate, Brendan Boyle
Discounts: Seniors
Tee Times: No

Features: Lessons, Driving Range, Practice Area, Pro
Shop - Complete, Clubhouse, Snack Bar

Description: This is a complete golf facility with a
well-manicured flat 9 hole course with water and
sand, a "pitch & putt" course, a driving range and
miniature golf course - something for the whole
family.

Holes	Par	Yards Back Tees	Rating	Slope
9	27	592	—	—
9	38	3139	35.5	108

	9 Holes	18 Holes	Hours Mid Season
Weekday:	—	$10.00	7:00 am - 11:00 pm
Weekend:	—	$12.00	6:00 am - 11:00 pm
Cart Fees:	—	$18.00	

Mandatory Cart Rental: No
Club Rental: Yes

Valleybrook Golf Course

NJ 111

Little Gloucester Rd, Blackwood NJ — Tee Times: (609)227-3171

Directions: Rte 42 South out of Phila to the Black-wood/Clementon Exit. Take a right off the ramp and go 6/10 mi. to light (Little Gloucester Rd). Take a left and the course is on the left approx 1.2 mi.

Facility Type: Public

Club Pro: Kevin Kotter
Discounts: Twilight
Tee Times: Yes, 1 week for weekend

Features: Lessons, Driving Range, Practice Area, Pro Shop - Complete, Clubhouse, Snack Bar, Banquet Facilities

Description: Renovations were completed in '91. This is a mix of flat and hilly terrain with fairly tight fairways. A creek crosses the course several times.

Holes	Par	Yards Back Tees	Rating	Slope
18	72	6100	70.0	124

	9 Holes	18 Holes	Hours Mid Season
Weekday:	—	$12.00	7:00 am - Dusk
Weekend:	—	$16.00	6:00 am - Dusk
Cart Fees:	—	$19.00	

Mandatory Cart Rental: No
Club Rental: No

Notes: Call for weekday specials.

Warrenbrook Golf Course

NJ 112

500 Warrenville Rd, Warren Township NJ — Info: (908)754-8402 Tee Times: (908)560-1500

Directions: Rte 22 in Greenbrook to Warrenville Rd North. The course is approx 2 mi. on Warrenville Rd.

Facility Type: Public

Club Pro: None
Discounts: Seniors, Juniors
Tee Times: Yes, County residents are put in system for reservations and can call 7 days prior. Non-residents in the system can call 1 day prior for $6 charge.

Features: Practice Area, Clubhouse, Snack Bar, Pro Shop - Complete

Description: This is a heavily treed and hilly course with an element of difficulty. An example is the 5th, a 559 yd par 5 sharp dogleg left with water on the right. There are no short cuts to a large sloping green.

Holes	Par	Yards Back Tees	Rating	Slope
18	71	6462	71.7	129

	9 Holes	18 Holes	Hours Mid Season
Weekday:	—	$14.00	7:00 am - Dusk
Weekend:	—	$17.00	6:00 am - Dusk
Cart Fees:	$11.80	$18.00	

Mandatory Cart Rental: No
Club Rental: Yes

Notes: Changes expected for '92 season are a new irrigation system, and new cart paths. Non-residents of Somerset County can be put into the reservation system for $50. Sr. an Jr. discount for County residents only.

Washington Tnshp GC

Friesmille Rd, Turnersville NJ — (609)227-1435

Directions: NJ Turnpike ot Exit 3. Take the Black Horse Pike into Turnersville. Take a right on Friesmille Rd and the course is 1/2 mi. on the right behind Birch's Apts.

Holes	Par	Yards Back Tees	Rating	Slope
9	27	1251	—	—

	9 Holes	18 Holes	Hours Mid Season
Weekday:	—	$7.50	7:00 am - 8:00 pm
Weekend:	—	$8.50	7:00 am - 8:00 pm
Cart Fees:	—	—	

Facility Type: Executive

Club Pro: None
Discounts: Seniors
Tee Times: No

Club Rental: Yes

Features: Practice Area, Pro Shop - Limited

Description: This is a flat and wide-open course, with no water. If you loose a ball here, you're blind, according to the pro-shop. The greens are in superb shape.

Wedgwood Country Club

Turnersville NJ — **Tee Times:** (609)227-5522

Directions: New Jersey Turnpike to Exit 3. Take the Black Horse Pike, Rte 168, East approximately 5 miles to Wilson Rd. Take a right and the road ends at the club.

Holes	Par	Yards Back Tees	Rating	Slope
18	72	6933	72.7	122

	9 Holes	18 Holes	Hours Mid Season
Weekday:	—	$12.00	6:30 am - Dusk
Weekend:	—	$15.00	6:00 am - Dusk
Cart Fees:	—	$18.00	

Facility Type: Semi-private

Club Pro: None
Discounts: Twilight
Tee Times: Yes, 1 week ahead for weekends

Mandatory Cart Rental: No
Club Rental: Yes

Features: Showers/Lockers, Practice Area, Pro Shop - Complete, Clubhouse, Restaurant, Bar, Banquet Facilities

Notes: Twilight starts at 4 pm mid-season.

Description: A flat and deceptive course, not in the least forgiving. The greens are small and the course is well-trapped. A good example is the 13th, a par 4, 439 yd shot over either of 2 ponds. One may get you on the way to a well trapped green.

Weequahic Park Golf Course   NJ 115
Weequahic Park, Newark NJ — (201)923-1838

Directions: Grd St Pkwy Exit 143 B onto Lyons Ave East toward Newark. Take it to the end and make a right onto Elizabeth Ave. Make a left at the 3rd light to the course.

Facility Type: Public

Club Pro: Jim Feaster
Discounts: Seniors
Tee Times: Yes,. county ID holders may reserve on Thursday in person for weekends.

Features: Lessons, Showers/Lockers, Pro Shop - Complete, Clubhouse, Snack Bar

Description: Rolling hills and small greens. There are no level lies and no straight putts.

Holes	Par	Yards Back Tees	Rating	Slope
18	70	5609	66	106

	9 Holes	18 Holes	Hours Mid Season
Weekday:	—	$16.00	7:00 am - 7:00 pm
Weekend:	—	$20.00	6:00 am - 7:00 pm
Cart Fees:	$10.00	$20.00	

Mandatory Cart Rental: No
Club Rental: No

Westwood Golf Course   NJ 116
850 Kings Highway, Woodbury NJ — Tee Times: (609)845-2000

Directions: Rte 295 to Exit 20. Go East toward Woodbury to Kings Highway and take a left. The course is on the right.

Facility Type: Public

Club Pro: None
Discounts: Twilight
Tee Times: Yes, Monday prior for the weekends/holidays

Features: Showers/Lockers, Driving Range, Practice Area, Pro Shop - Complete, Restaurant, Bar, Snack Bar, Banquet Facilities

Description: This is a pleasantly easy course, although it is well-bunkered, and water comes into play on 4 holes. The course is slightly hilly.

Holes	Par	Yards Back Tees	Rating	Slope
18	71	5931	67.9	108

	9 Holes	18 Holes	Hours Mid Season
Weekday:	—	$12.00	Dawn - Dusk
Weekend:	—	$15.00	Dawn - Dusk
Cart Fees:	—	$20.00	

Mandatory Cart Rental: No
Club Rental: No

Wild Oaks Country Club   NJ 117

75 Wild Oaks Drive, Salem NJ — (609)935-0705

Directions: New Jersey Turnpike to Exit 1 onto Rte 49 East. Go through Pennsville, Salem and into Quinton. Turn right on Sickler Street, the2nd street after the light in Quinton. Go 1 mile to the course.

Facility Type: Public

Club Pro: None
Discounts: Twilight
Tee Times: No

Features: Showers/Lockers, Practice Area, Clubhouse, Restaurant, Bar, Snack Bar, Banquet Facilities, Pro Shop - Limited

Description: These are flat, open and walkable courses (red, yellow and white) in a nice country setting. Water comes into play. #3 on the yellow is a favorite. It's a par 4, 365 yd dogleg, across a ravine to a 3-tiered green with traps on both sides.

Holes	Par	Yards Back Tees	Rating	Slope
9	36	3385	71.4	113
9	36	3285	71.4	117
9	36	3165	—	—

	9 Holes	18 Holes	Hours Mid Season
Weekday:	$7.00	$9.00	Dawn - Dusk
Weekend:	$9.00	$13.00	Dawn - Dusk
Cart Fees:	—	$13.00	

Mandatory Cart Rental: No
Club Rental: Yes

Notes: A weekday special includes lunch. Cart rental fee is per person.

Willowbrook Country Club   NJ 118

Bridgeboro Rd, Morrestown NJ —   **Tee Times:** (609)461-0131

Directions: Rte 295 to Exit 40B. Take a right onto Marter Ave. Go 1 mi. to the 2nd light and take a left onto Westfield Ave. Go 1 mi. to the light and make a right onto Bridgeboro Rd, to the course.

Facility Type: Public

Club Pro: Brian Feld
Discounts: Seniors, Twilight
Tee Times: Yes, 1 week ahead for weekends/holidays

Features: Lessons, Showers/Lockers, Driving Range, Practice Area, Clubhouse, Restaurant, Bar, Banquet Facilities, Pro Shop - Complete, Lodging Nearby

Description: This is an open course with a moderate amount of water. The 18th hole is particularly interesting. It's a 418 yd par 4. A pond lays to the right of the 2nd shot and a stream in front of the green.

Holes	Par	Yards Back Tees	Rating	Slope
18	72	6392	71.9	125

	9 Holes	18 Holes	Hours Mid Season
Weekday:	—	$16.50	Dawn - Dusk
Weekend:	—	$25.00	Dawn - Dusk
Cart Fees:	—	$18.00	

Mandatory Cart Rental: No
Club Rental: Yes

Notes: Cart rental fee $17 during the week.

Woodlake Golf & CC

25 New Hampshire Ave, Lakewood NJ — Info: (908)367-4500   Tee Times: (908)367-4500

Directions: Garden State Parkway South to Exit 91. Bear right off the ramp onto Lanes Mill Rd. Go 3 lights and take a right onto Rte 88. The next light is New Hampshire Ave. Take a right and look for the course on the right.

Facility Type: Semi-private

Club Pro: Bob Issler
Discounts: Twilight
Tee Times: Yes, up to 2 days in advance.

Features: Lessons, Driving Range, Practice Area, Pro Shop - Complete, Clubhouse, Restaurant, Bar, Snack Bar, Banquet Facilities, Showers/Lockers, VISA/MC, Lodging Nearby

Description: This course is a lot of water and woods. Bring a lot of balls unless your game is accurate. One of the reasons is the 566 yd, par 5, 5th hole. It's straight off the tee, but the 3rd shot has water on the right and the green has water in front and on the right.

Holes	Par	Yards Back Tees	Rating	Slope
18	72	6766	72.5	126

	9 Holes	18 Holes	Hours Mid Season
Weekday:	—	$20.00	7:00 am - Dusk
Weekend:	—	$27.00	6:00 am - Dusk
Cart Fees:	—	$10.00	

Mandatory Cart Rental: See notes.
Club Rental: Yes

Notes: Weekend green fee includes cart, but the cart is mandatory only until 2 pm on weekends.. Green fee then drops to $20 without cart. Cart fee on weekends is $12. This course is open all year round.

NJ 3   **Warren**

APPLE MOUNTAIN GOLF & CC

Belvedere NJ

1 800 PLA GOLF

A public course with a country club atmosphere.
Tee times by phone. Full PGA staff led by Head
Pro Bob Dacey

You are invited to play a COMPLI-
MENTARY 9 or 18 hole round of golf
when accompanied with one fully
paid round of equal value one time
during the 1992 season.

Valid all day Mon thru Fri (except
holidays) and on weekends and holidays after 3

**Must call ahead for assured tee
times.**

POWER CART RENTAL REQUIRED

❏ Validation

PLEASE READ VALIDATION RESTRICTIONS CAREFULLY.

NJ 8   **Monmouth**

BEL-AIRE GOLF COURSE

Highway 34, Allenwood NJ

(908) 449-6024

A beautiful 18 hole Par 60 course and a
challenging Par 3 course with holes to 183 yds.
Excellent pro shop facility.

You are invited to play a COMPLI-
MENTARY 9 or 18 hole round of golf
when accompanied with one fully
paid round of equal value one time
during the 1992 season.

Valid anytime until May 1 and after
Nov 1

Call ahead for assured tee times

❏ Validation

OFFER IS NOT VALID IF DETACHED FROM BOOK.

NJ 11   **Morris**

BOWLING GREEN GOLF CLUB

Schoolhouse Rd, Milton NJ

(201)697-8688

Come enjoy 18 challenging holes of golf at
beautiful Bowling Green, rated as one of New
Jersey's top 3 public courses

You are invited to play a COMPLI-
MENTARY 9 or 18 hole round of golf
when accompanied with one fully
paid round of equal value one time
during the 1992 season.

Valid anytime Mon thru Thurs.

Call 48 hours in advance of starting
time.

**POWER CART RENTAL IS RE-
QUIRED.**

❏ Validation

NJ 12 **Atlantic**

BRIGANTINE GOLF LINKS

Roosevelt Blvd & The Bay, Brigantine, NJ
(609)266-1388

Come experience the flavor of a British Open Course in Atlantic City. 18 challenging ocean-side golf holes await your conquest.

You are invited to play a COMLPIMENTARY 9 or 18 hole round of golf when accompanied with one fully paid round of equal value one time during the 1992 season.

Valid Mon thru Fri (except holidays) from 11 am to 6 pm.

Must call ahead for tee times.

POWER CART RENTAL IS REQUIRED.

❑ Validation

OFFER IS NOT VALID IF DETACHED FROM BOOK.

NJ 20 **Merser**

CRANBURY GOLF CLUB

49 Southfield Rd, Cranbury NJ
(609)799-0341

A beautiful 18 hole course in the country setting of West Windsor. Specializing in golf outings. Restaurant and Pub. Driving range. Memberships are available.

You are invited to play a COMPLIMENTARY 9 or 18 hole round of golf when accompanied with one fully

paid round of equal value 2 times durting the 1992 season

Valid Mon thru Fri (except holidays) from 7 am to 7 pm. Must call ahead for tee times.

POWER CART RENTAL IS REQUIRED

❑ 1st Time Validation

❑ 2nd Time Validation

COUPONS ARE NOT VALID FOR LEAGUE PLAY, SPECIAL EVENTS, OR OUTINGS.

NJ 28 **Warren**

FAIRWAY VALLEY GOLF CLUB

Minehill Rd, Washington, NJ
(908)689-1530

You are invited to play a COMPLIMENTARY 9 or 18 hole round of golf when accompanied with one fully paid round of equal value one time during the 1992 season.

Valid Mon thru Fri (except holidays) only from 9:00 am to 4:00 pm in June, July and Aug and any day after Labor Day.

Must call ahead for tee times

POWER CART RENTAL IS REQUIRED

❑ Validation

NJ 37   Monmouth

GAMBLER RIDGE GOLF CLUB
Burlington Path Rd, Cream Ridge NJ
(609)758-3588

Outings are our specialty. Private club service and atmosphere at public facility prices. Special prices and arrangements for any size golf outing.

You are invited to play a COMPLIMENTARY 9 or 18 hole round of golf when accompanied with one fully paid round of equal value two times during the 1992 season.

Valid Mon thru Fri (except holidays) only after 12:00 noon.

Must call ahead for tee times.

POWER CART RENTAL IS REQUIRED.

☐ 1st Time Validation

☐ 2nd Time Validation

PLEASE READ VALIDATION RESTRICTIONS CAREFULLY.

NJ 40   Sussex

GREAT GORGE'S COUNTRY CLUB
McAffee, NJ
(201)827-5757

27 holes of challenging golf designed by George Fazio. Excellent conditions, scenic setting. Fully-stocked pro shop. PGA instruction available. Outings welcome. Catering available.

You are invited to play an 18 hole round of golf for the local resident rate two times during the 1992 season. Also receive a free bucket of range balls.

Valid Mon thru Fri (except holidays) only from 7 am to 6 pm.

Must call ahead for tee times.

POWER CART RENTAL IS REQUIRED.

☐ 1st Time Validation

☐ 2nd Time Validation

OFFER IS NOT VALID IF DETACHED FROM BOOK.

NJ 46   Burlington

HANOVER COUNTRY CLUB
133 Larrison Rd, Jacobstown NJ
(609)758-0300

We have special discounted winter, afternoon and senior rates.

You are invited to play a COMPLIMENTARY 9 or 18 hole round of golf when accompanied with one fully paid round of equal value 2 times during the 1992 season.

Valid anytime of the day Mon thru Fri (except holidays).

Must call ahead for tee times.

POWER CART RENTAL REQUIRED.

☐ 1st Time Validation

☐ 2nd Time Validation

NJ 58　　　　　　　　　　　　　　　　　**Monmouth**

JUMPING BROOK GOLF & CC

210 Jumping Brook Rd, Neptune NJ
(908)922-6140

Play one of the Jersey Shore's oldest courses,
built in 1925, with its original character intact.
Excellent clubhouse facilities. Outings welcome.
Convenient to Jersey Beaches.

You are invited to play a COMPLI-
MENTARY 9 or 18 hole round of golf
when accompanied with one fully
paid round of equal value one time
during the 1992 season.

Valid Mon thru Fri (except holidays)
from 7 am to 4 pm.

Must call ahead for tee times.

POWER CART RENTAL IS RE-
QUIRED

❏ Validation

OFFER IS NOT VALID IF DETACHED FROM BOOK.

NJ 93　　　　　　　　　　　　　　　　　**Burlington**

RAMBLEWOOD COUNTRY CLUB

200 Country Club Parkway, Ramblewood, NJ
(609)235-2119

This public golf course offers flat terrain and fairly
wide driving areas. The fairways should be easy
to navigate as there are few bunkers to impede
your progress. The greens are very large and flat
but bunkers will make your approach shot count.

You are invited to play a COMPLI-
MENTARY 9 or 18 hole round of golf
when accompanied with one fully
paid round of equal value two times
during the 1992 season.

Valid Mon thru Fri (except holidays)
from 11:00 am to 4:00 pm and
weekends and holidays after 4:00
pm Must call ahead for tee times.

POWER CART RENTAL IS RE-
QUIRED.

❏ 1st Time Validation

❏ 2nd Time Validation

COUPONS ARE NOT VALID FOR LEAGUE PLAY, SPECIAL EVENTS, OR OUTINGS.

NJ 94　　　　　　　　　　　　　　　　　**Burlington**

RANCOCAS GOLF CLUB

Club House Drive, Willingboro, NJ
(609)877-5344

Challenge yourself to 6800 yards of vintage
Robert Trent Jones Sr championship golf.
Experience fairways cut out of mature
hardwoods, 3 greens protected by water and over
95 sand bunkers to test your shot-making ability.

You are invited to play a COMPLI-
MENTARY 9 or 18 hole round of golf
when accompanied with one fully-
paid round of equal value 2 times
during the 1992 season.

Valid Mon thru Fri from 11 am to 4
pm and weekends and holidays after 4 pm. Must call ahead for assured tee times.

POWER CART RENTAL IS RE-
QUIRED

❏ 1st Time Validation

❏ 2nd Time Validation

NJ 98   Sussex

ROLLING GREENS GOLF CLUB
214 Newton-Sparta Rd, Newton, NJ
(201)383-3082

Our course is under new management. 18 Holes.
Par 66. No tee times necessary. Open to the
public.

You are invited to play a COMPLI-
MENTARY 9 or 18 hole round of golf
when accompanied with one fully
paid round of equal vlaue one time
during the 1992 season.

Valid Mon thru Fri (except holidays)
only from 7 am to 7 pm.

Call ahead for tee times

**POWER CART RENTAL IS RE-
QUIRED**

☐ Validation

PLEASE READ VALIDATION RESTRICTIONS CAREFULLY.

NJ 103   Sussex

SPA EXECUTIVE 9
McAffee, NJ
(201)827-3710

A picturesque and challenging course located in
the mountains of Great Gorge, 60 minutes from
Manhattan. Designed by Robert Trent Jones.

You are invited to play a COMPLI-
MENTARY 9 or 18 hole round of golf
when accompanied by a fully paid
round of equal value 2 times during
the 1992 season.

Valid Mon thru Fri (except holidays)
from 7 am to 5 pm.

Must call ahead for tee times.

**POWER CART RENTAL IS RE-
QUIRED.**

☐ 1st Time Validation

☐ 2nd Time Validation

OFFER IS NOT VALID IF DETACHED FROM BOOK.

NJ DR1   Bergen

LT'S MEADOWLANDS GOLF CNTR.
56 Paterson Plank Rd, East Rutherford NJ
(201)507-5656

Driving range. 50 heated tees. 18 hole miniature
golf. Practice putting green. Sand & bunker
practice. Marine slips. Pro shop. Indoor teaching
facility and PGA staffed Golf Acadamy

You are entitled to a free bucket of
balls for every one purchased of
equal value anytime during the
1992 season.

Valid anytime.

☐ 1st Time Validation

☐ 2nd Time Validation

New York

Southern New York

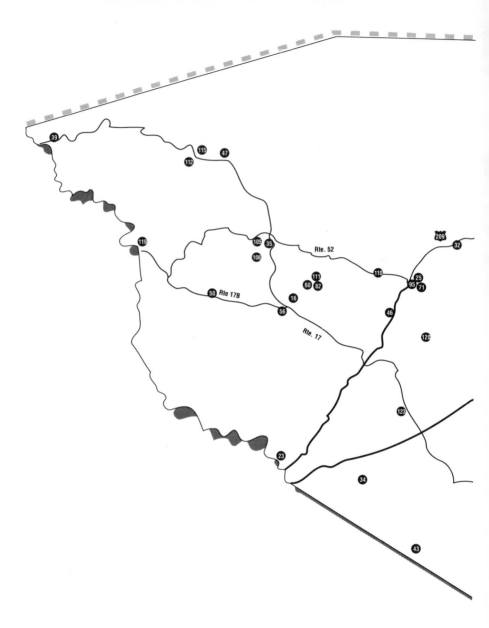

Southern New York

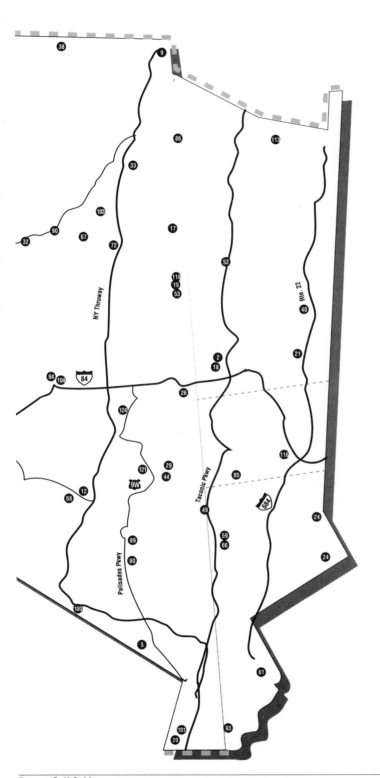

Long Island
and Five Boroughs

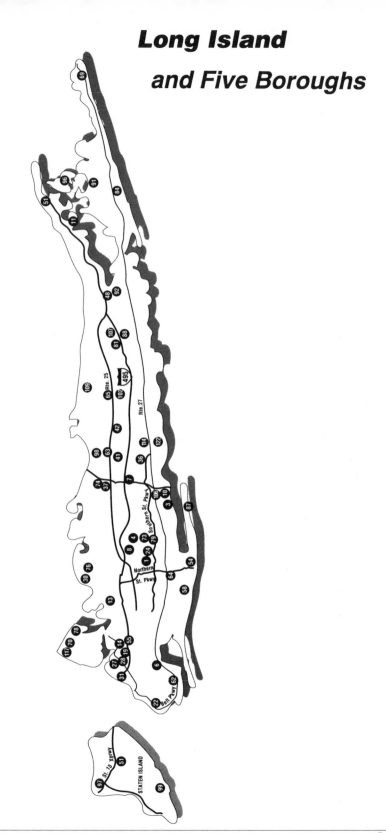

New York County Systems

NASSAU COUNTY: Eisenhower, Bay Park, Cantiague, Cristopher Morley, and North Woodmere.
Residents may obtain a "Leisure Pass" at any of the courses by showing a drivers licence and paying $7. The pass is good for 3 years and entitles the holder to reduced green fees and the ability to reserve tee times at Eisenhower. "Leisure Passes" for seniors are good for life.

SUFFOLK COUNTY: West Sayville, Bergen Point, Indian Island, Timber Point
You may not play without a "Green Key Card" or without someone who has one on Suffolk County courses. The card may be obtained at any of the course pro shops by showing a drivers licence or picture ID. Non-residents can walk on and will be paired with a card holder. The card entitles holders to reserve tee times on the phone system. See courses for details.

WESTCHESTER COUNTY: Dunwoodie, Maple Moor, Sprain Lake, Saxon Woods, Mohansic
In order to qualify for resident rates in Westchester, a "Park Pass" must be obtained with a drivers licence or ID showing residence. The pass is $15 and is good for up to 3 years, depending on when in the year it is purchased.

Bay Park Golf Course

Bay Park, NY — (516)593-8840

Directions: Southern St Pkwy to Exit 17 South. Go 3 mi. on Ocean Ave and look for signs for Bay County Park.

Facility Type: Public

Club Pro: None
Discounts: Seniors
Tee Times: No

Features: Practice Area, Clubhouse, Snack Bar

Description: A short and hilly course, not as easy as it looks. It's by the water - very pretty.

Holes	Par	Yards Back Tees	Rating	Slope
9	30	1956	—	—

	9 Holes	18 Holes	Hours Mid Season
Weekday:	$16.00	—	Dawn - Dusk *
Weekend:	$18.00	—	Dawn - Dusk
Cart Fees:	—	—	
Club Rental: No			

Notes: Above prices are non-resident. Residents $7 and $8. Srs $3.50 during the week. *Course 15 is-closed Wednesday.

Beekman Country Club

11 Country Club Rd, Hopewell Junction NY — **Tee Times:** (914)226-7700

Directions: Taconic Pkwy (Exit 16N off of I-84). Go North on the Taconic 4 mi. and exit on Beekman Rd. Go left off the ramp and 1 mile to the course.

Facility Type: Public

Club Pro: Jimmy Bergholtz
Discounts: Twilight, Juniors, Seniors
Tee Times: Yes, 2 weeks ahead for weekends

Features: Lessons, Showers/Lockers, Practice Area, Pro Shop - Complete, Clubhouse, Restaurant, Bar, Snack Bar, Banquet Facilities, Lodging Nearby

Description: This is the most widely played course in the area. The lower 18, the "Hyland" and "Valley" 9s, are fairly open. The "Taconic" 9 is tighter, wooded and more challenging. Major improvements are in the works.

Holes	Par	Yards Back Tees	Rating	Slope
9	H 35	3050	69.3	123
9	V 35	2920	70.1	124
9	T 36	2980	70.1	123

	9 Holes	18 Holes	Hours Mid Season
Weekday:	$10.00	$25.00	7:00 am - Dusk
Weekend:	$14.00	$34.50	Dawn - Dusk
Cart Fees:	$12.50	$12.50	

Mandatory Cart Rental: See notes.
Club Rental: Yes

Notes: Weekday 18 includes cart and lunch. Weekend 18 includes cart. Otherwise cart fee is per person. Twilight weekends only after 3 pm.

Bergen Point Golf Course NY 3

Bergen Ave, West Babylon NY — Info: (516)661-8282 Tee Times: 516 244 PARK

Directions: Southern State Parkway to Rte 109 E. Go to Great Eastneck Rd, which becomes Bergen Ave, to the course.

Facility Type: Public

Club Pro: Chuck Workman
Discounts: Seniors, Juniors
Tee Times: Yes, Up to 1 week and as late as 24 hours only on a touch tone phone and only with a Green Key Card.

Features: Lessons, Showers/Lockers, Driving Range, Practice Area, Pro Shop - Complete, Clubhouse, Restaurant, Bar, Snack Bar, Banquet Facilities, Lodging Nearby, American Express, VISA/MC

Description: This is a links style course designed by Bill Mitchell. It was a choice of Golf Digest for "Places to Play" in '90 and '91. The signature hole is #6, a 232 yd par 3. Water lies to the right of the fairway and the green slopes down with sand left and right.

Holes	Par	Yards Back Tees	Rating	Slope
18	71	6600	71.6	122

	9 Holes	18 Holes	Hours Mid Season
Weekday:	—	$13.00	7:00 am - Dusk
Weekend:	—	$15.00	6:00 am - Dusk
Cart Fees:	—	$22.00	

Mandatory Cart Rental: No
Club Rental: Yes

Notes: Non-residents and those without Green Key Cards may walk on and will be paired with a Card holder.

Bethpage State Park NY 4

Bethpage State Park, Farmingdale NY — Info: (516)249-0700

Directions: Long Island Expressway to Exit 44 S (Seaford-Oyster Bay Expressway) to Exit 8 and follow the signs. Or take the Southern State Pkwy to the Seaford-Oyster Bay Expressway North to Exit 8.

Facility Type: Public

Club Pro: Chuck Workman
Discounts: Seniors, Twilight
Tee Times: No, see notes.

Features: Lessons, Showers/Lockers, Driving Range, Practice Area, Pro Shop - Complete, Clubhouse, Restaurant, Bar, Snack Bar, Banquet Facilities, Lodging Nearby

Description: This is a golf mecca, picked by Golf Digest in both '90 and '91 for "Places to Play". All five course are of championship calaber. The black course is the longest and one of Golf Digest's "75 Best Public Courses", and one of Golf Mags top 100. Yellow and green are for starters. Blue has a tough front and an easy back. Red is noted for long par 4 doglegs. Red, black and some of blue are AW Tillinghast designs.

Holes	Par	Yards Back Tees	Rating	Slope
18	R 70	6756	72.7	126
18	B 72	6687	72.2	123
18	G 71	6265	70.1	117
18	Y 71	6316	69.9	116
18	Black 71	7065	74.0	139

	9 Holes	18 Holes	Hours Mid Season
Weekday:	$7.00	$12.00	6:00 am - Dusk
Weekend:	$8.00	$14.00	Dawn - Dusk
Cart Fees:	$13.00	$21.00	

Mandatory Cart Rental: No
Club Rental: Yes

Notes: Tickets are available on weekends at 4 am and on weekdays at 5 am. There is less of a wait after 2 pm. You must walk the green and black courses. The green fee on black is $2 extra. 9 holes on weekdays are playable only after 10, and only after 12 on weekends.

Blue Hill Golf Course

NY 5

285 Blue Hil Rd, Pearl River NY — **Tee Times:** (914)735-2094

Directions: Palisades Parkway to Exit 6W. Get onto Orangeburg Rd going West. At the 3rd light make a right and the course is approximately 1/2 mile on the left.

Facility Type: Public

Club Pro: James Stewart
Discounts: Twilight
Tee Times: Yes, 24 hours in advance for any day. Residents are allowed preference for weekend times.

Features: Lessons, Showers/Lockers, Practice Area, Pro Shop - Complete, Clubhouse, Restaurant, Bar, Snack Bar, Banquet Facilities, Lodging Nearby

Holes	Par	Yards Back Tees	Rating	Slope
18	72	6402	69.7	117

	9 Holes	18 Holes	Hours Mid Season
Weekday:	$12.00	$20.00	7:30 am - Dusk
Weekend:	$14.00	$26.00	6:30 am - Dusk
Cart Fees:	$11.00	$22.00	

Mandatory Cart Rental: No
Club Rental: No

Notes: 9 hole play only after 4 pm. If you're not resident, your best shot is to play weekday afternoons.

Description: Stephen Kay was the architect of this pretty and well-maintained course. It is wide open and hilly! Water comes into play. It used to be that this was not an overly difficult course, but '92 will be the 5th year of an improvement program adding bunkers and moving cart paths. Many of the trees planted years ago are coming of age and making things tighter. The 18th is going to par 5 and from a fairly wide open shot to one that will require absolute accuracy. #15 is the toughest par 4 around and the par 3's offer a challenge to the wide range of capabilities.

Breezy Point Executive GC

NY 6

Brooklyn NY — (718)253-6816

Directions: Belt Parkway to Exit 11S. Go over the Marine Pkwy Bridge (also known as Gil Hodges) into Riis Park and see signs for the course.

Facility Type: Executive

Club Pro: None
Discounts: Seniors
Tee Times: No

Features: Snack Bar

Description: A driving range and pro shop are nearby.

Holes	Par	Yards Back Tees	Rating	Slope
18	55	1696	—	—

	9 Holes	18 Holes	Hours Mid Season
Weekday:	—	$6.50	6:30 am - 5:30 pm
Weekend:	—	$9.00	6:00 am - 5:30 pm
Cart Fees:	—	—	

Brentwood Country Club　　　NY 7

100 Pennsylvania Ave, Brentwood NY — Info: (516)436-6060　Tee Times: (516)224-5648

Directions: 495 to Exit 54. Go across Wicks Rd to Washington and take a right. Look for course sign 1m on left and take a left after sign.

Holes	Par	Yards Back Tees	Rating	Slope
18	72	6173	67.3	111

Facility Type: Public

	9 Holes	18 Holes	Hours Mid Season
Weekday:	—	$20.00	6:30 am - 6:00 pm *
Weekend:	—	$26.00	6:30 am - 6:00 pm
Cart Fees:	—	$21.00	

Club Pro: Richie Loughlin
Discounts: None
Tee Times: Yes, non residents can reserve weekend time after 11 for $4. Call Fri 9 - 4.

Mandatory Cart Rental: No
Club Rental: Yes

Features: Showers/Lockers, Practice Area, Pro Shop - Complete, Clubhouse, Restaurant, Bar, Snack Bar, Banquet Facilities, Lessons

Notes: * The course is closed on Monday. 1st time non-residents must also buy a $7 card good for all subsequent season play.

Description: This is a fairly flat and fairly easy course with no water. The fairways are bordered by pine trees.

Cantiague Park Golf Course　　　NY 8

W John St, Hicksville NY — (516)571-7061

Directions: 495 to Exit 43 onto Rte 106/107 South 1 mi. to West John Street. Take right to course 1/2 mi.

Holes	Par	Yards Back Tees	Rating	Slope
9	30	2900	—	—

Facility Type: Executive

	9 Holes	18 Holes	Hours Mid Season
Weekday:	$16.00	—	Dawn - Dusk *
Weekend:	$18.00	—	Dawn - Dusk
Cart Fees:	—	—	
Club Rental:	Yes		

Club Pro: Bill McCumiskey
Discounts: Seniors
Tee Times: No

Notes: *The course is closed Tuesdays. Resident rates are $7 weekdays and $8 weekends. Senior rate is $3.50 and applies to weekdays only. Lessons are taught at the driving range adjacent to the course. Waiting times can be learned by calling 571-7062.

Features: Lessons, Practice Area, Driving Range, Pro Shop - Complete

Description: This is a great course for seniors.

Catskill Golf Club

NY 9

27 Brooks Lane, Catskill NY — Tee Times: (518)943-0302

Directions: NY Thruway to Exit 21. Take Jefferson Hts Rd toward Catskill. Turn left approx 1 mi. onto Brooks Lane to the course.

Facility Type: Semi-private

Coupon page 197

Club Pro: None
Discounts: Twilight
Tee Times: Yes, 3 days ahead for weekends/holidays

Features: Lessons, Showers/Lockers, Practice Area, Pro Shop - Complete, Clubhouse, Restaurant, Bar, Banquet Facilities, Lodging Nearby

Description: This is a challenging course for first-timers not use to the terrain. It is hilly with a few blind shots to the green. The greens are average in size and a few are elevated. A lake comes into play on #3 and #12. The course is well-maintained with watered fairways.

Holes	Par	Yards Back Tees	Rating	Slope
9dt	71	6156	69.2	115

	9 Holes	18 Holes	Hours Mid Season
Weekday:	$12.00	$20.00	8:00 am - 6:00 pm
Weekend:	$ 12.00	$20.00	8:00 am - 6:00 pm
Cart Fees:	$7.00	$12.00	

Mandatory Cart Rental: Yes
Club Rental: Yes

Notes: 9 holes on weekends after 2 pm only.

Cedar Beach Golf Course

NY 10

17 Ross Rd, Babylon NY — (516)669-9382

Directions: Ocean Pkwy 8 mi. East of Jones Beach.

Facility Type: Pitch & Putt

Club Pro: None
Discounts: None
Tee Times: No

Features: Pro Shop - Limited, Snack Bar

Description: This is a wide open course with an ocean view. It's ideal for the beginner and the experienced golfer's short game.

Holes	Par	Yards Back Tees	Rating	Slope
18	54	1500	—	—

	9 Holes	18 Holes	Hours Mid Season
Weekday:	—	$4.00	8:00 am - 6:00 pm
Weekend:	—	$4.00	8:00 am - 6:00 pm
Cart Fees:	—	—	
Club Rental:	Yes		

Cedars Golf Club
NY 11

Cases Lane, Cutchogue NY — (516)734-6363

Directions: Take the last Exit on 495 onto Rte 58 East, which runs into Rte 25. Go approx 12 mi. after exiting 495 to Cutchogue. At "Village Green" take a right onto Cases Lane and follow signs to the course.

Facility Type: Executive

Club Pro: None
Discounts: Seniors
Tee Times: No

Features: Lessons, Clubhouse

Description: This is a pretty par 3 course that was professionally designed with lots of woods and water on 3 holes. The longest hole is 175 yds, the shortest 100 yds, the avarage 117.

Holes	Par	Yards Back Tees	Rating	Slope
9	27	1100	—	—

	9 Holes	18 Holes	Hours Mid Season
Weekday:	$4.50	$6.75	7:00 am - 8:00 pm
Weekend:	$5.00	$7.50	7:00 am - 8:00 pm
Cart Fees:	$.75	$.75	

Mandatory Cart Rental: No
Club Rental: Yes

Notes: Non-golfers and children under 7 are not allowed on this course.

Central Valley Golf Club
NY 12

210 Smith Clove Rd, Central Valley NY — **Tee Times:** (914)928-6924

Directions: NY Thruway to Exit 16. Take a right onto 32 North. Go 1 mile and take a right onto Smith Clove. 1 mile to club.

Facility Type: Semi-private

Coupon page 197

Club Pro: Wendy Fayo
Discounts: Seniors, Twilight
Tee Times: Yes, 1 week in advance for any day

Features: Lessons, Showers/Lockers, Practice Area, Pro Shop - Complete, Clubhouse, Restaurant, Bar, Banquet Facilities, American Express, VISA/MC

Description: This is a scenic course that cuts through the Northern Ramapo Mountains. The fairways are tight and the greens are small making it an enjoyable challenge for the average golfer.

Holes	Par	Yards Back Tees	Rating	Slope
18	71	5639	67.5	122

	9 Holes	18 Holes	Hours Mid Season
Weekday:	—	$20.00	7:00 am - dark
Weekend:	$17.00	$30.00	6:00 am - dark
Cart Fees:	$13.00	$22.00	

Mandatory Cart Rental: No
Club Rental: Yes

Notes: Annual green fees are available. The course sports a newly renovated $3 million clubhouse. It has a long season, weather permitting.

Christopher Morley Park GC NY 13

Searingtown Rd, North Hills NY — (516)621-9107

Directions: Exit 36 off 495. North on Searingtown Rd to course on right.

Holes	Par	Yards Back Tees	Rating	Slope
9	29	1520	—	—

Facility Type: Public

	9 Holes	18 Holes	Hours Mid Season
Weekday:	$16.00	—	6:00 am - Dusk *
Weekend:	$18.00	—	6:00 am - Dusk
Cart Fees:	$1.50	—	
Club Rental:	No		

Club Pro: None

Discounts: Seniors

Tee Times: No

Features: Snack Bar

Description: A good beginners course. There are no power carts.

Notes: * The course is closed on Monday. Green fees listed are for non residents. Resident rates are $7 during the week and $8 weekends/holidays. Senior rates are $3.50 and apply on weekdays only.

Clearview Golf Course NY 14

202-12 Willets Point Blvd, Queens NY — **Info:** (718)229-2570 **Tee Times:** 718 225 GOLF

Directions: Clearview Expressway North from 495 to Willets Point Blvd. Take a left at the end of the ramp. The course is on the left approx 100 yds. From the Bronx take the Whitestone Bridge to Cross Island Pkwy. Exit at Clearview Expressway and the course is right there.

Holes	Par	Yards Back Tees	Rating	Slope
18	70	6268	69.1	115

	9 Holes	18 Holes	Hours Mid Season
Weekday:	—	$13.50	Dawn - Dusk
Weekend:	—	$15.50	Dawn - Dusk
Cart Fees:	—	$21.00	

Facility Type: Public

Coupon page 197

Club Pro: Tony Chateauvert

Discounts: Twilight

Tee Times: Yes, 7 days for weekday, 10 days for weekends/holidays for a $2 reservation fee

Mandatory Cart Rental: No

Club Rental: Yes

Features: Lessons, Practice Area, Pro Shop - Complete, Clubhouse, Snack Bar, VISA/MC, Showers/Lockers

Notes: Tournament packages are available for all types and sizes of tournaments. A feature of this course is its proximaty to La Gauardia Airport.

Description: With great views of Long Island Sound, this fairly flat course slopes up from the first hole and then gradually back down. The fairways are tree-lined and wide. It is a forgiving course for the average golfer, yet offers a challenge for the low handicapper. The signature is #8 with a view of the bridge and City Island.

College Hill Golf Club

North Clinton St, Poughkeepsie NY — (914)486-9112

Directions: On Rte 9 North of the Mid Hudson Bridge take 44/55 East for 2-3 mi. to the light at Clinton St. Take a left, go through 5 lights and the course is on the right.

Facility Type: Public

Club Pro: Bruce Flesland
Discounts: Juniors
Tee Times: No

Features: Lessons, Snack Bar, Showers/Lockers, Practice Area, Pro Shop - Complete

Description: This is a great nine hole rolling course. It is harder than it appears - good for the average player. The course is in excellent condition.

Holes	Par	Yards Back Tees	Rating	Slope
9	34	2530	32.2	—

	9 Holes	18 Holes	Hours Mid Season
Weekday:	$5.00	—	7:00 am - Dusk
Weekend:	$6.00	—	7:00 am - Dusk
Cart Fees:	$10.00	—	

Mandatory Cart Rental: No
Club Rental: Yes

Notes: Club repair is available at the pro shop.

Concord Hotel Golf Course

Kiamesha Lake NY — **Tee Times:** (914)794-4000

Directions: Take Rte 17 to Exit 105B and follow signs to the hotel.

Facility Type: Resort

Club Pro: Mike Castelluzzi
Discounts: None
Tee Times: Yes, 72 hour cancellation policy, months in advance for Monster and International. The 9 hole course for guests only.

Features: Lessons, Showers/Lockers, Driving Range, Practice Area, Pro Shop - Complete, Clubhouse, Restaurant, Bar, Snack Bar, Banquet Facilities, Lodging Nearby, American Express, VISA/MC

Description: The "Monster" has been the sight of many tournaments. It is a Joe Finger design and one of the worlds most challenging courses. It was a Golf Digest pick in '90 and '91 for "Places to Play" for the public and one of their picks for best all around in the country. This is a low handicapper's course. The "International" is a shotmakers course with accuracy at a premium.

Holes	Par	Yards Back Tees	Rating	Slope
9	31	2200	—	—
18	M 72	7450	76.4	142
18	I 71	6600	71.0	—

	9 Holes	18 Holes	Hours Mid Season
Weekday:	—	$ 70.00*	7:00 am - 6:00 pm
Weekend:	—	$ 85.00*	7:00 am - 6:00 pm
Cart Fees:		—	

Mandatory Cart Rental: Yes
Club Rental: Yes

Notes: *Greens fees listed above are for the Monster. Greens fees for the "International" are $45 on weekdays and $50 on weekends. Cart included in all prices.

Dinsmore Golf Course

Staatsburg NY — (914)889-4071

Directions: On the West side of Rte 9, 4 miles North of Hyde Park. From the Taconic exit at Willow Rd. Go West to Rte 9, take a left and go 1/4 mi. The course is in Mills-Norrie State Park.

Facility Type: Public

Club Pro: Ralph Montoya
Discounts: Seniors, Juniors
Tee Times: No

Features: Lessons, Showers/Lockers, Pro Shop - Complete, Clubhouse, Restaurant, Bar, Banquet Facilities, Practice Area

Description: Thi is one of the oldest courses in the country. It is wide open and hilly with no water. It has a beautiful view of the Hudson. The South 9 is a championship course, a par 36. The greens are trapped, and the course is well-maintained.

Holes	Par	Yards Back Tees	Rating	Slope
18	70	4070	68.0	—

	9 Holes	18 Holes	Hours Mid Season
Weekday:	$6.00	$10.00	8:00 am - Dusk
Weekend:	$7.00	$12.00	6:00 am - Dusk
Cart Fees:	$11.00	$18.00	

Mandatory Cart Rental: No
Club Rental: Yes

Notes: Open the 1st Friday of April and closes the 1st Tuesday of November. At publication date, plans were in the works for a reservation system. Call ahead for information on 889-4071, or 4751.

Dogwood Knolls Golf Course

Hopewell Junction NY — (914)226-7317

Directions: Taconic Pkwy to Rte 52 (North of Rte 84). Go East on 52 and take a right at the 1st light onto 376. The course is approximately 4 miles.

Facility Type: Public

Club Pro: Heinz Mews
Discounts: Seniors
Tee Times: No

Features: Showers/Lockers, Practice Area, Pro Shop - Limited, Clubhouse, Bar, Snack Bar

Description: This is a semi-hilly course with small greens - somewhat of a shotmakers course. The 165 yd par 3 #8 is a good example. Its a short downhill hit with a lot of problems out-of-bounds if you miss.

Holes	Par	Yards Back Tees	Rating	Slope
9	36	3300	71.0	—

	9 Holes	18 Holes	Hours Mid Season
Weekday:	$6.00	$10.00	7:00 am - Dusk
Weekend:	$8.00	$12.00	6:00 am - Dusk
Cart Fees:	$9.00	$16.00	

Mandatory Cart Rental: No
Club Rental: Yes

Douglaston Golf Course

6320 Marathon Pkwy, Douglaston NY — Info: (718)428-1617   Tee Times: (718)224-6566

Directions: 495 to Exit 31 going East or to Exit 32 going West. Take the Marathon Pkwy to the course.

Facility Type: Public

Club Pro: Kenny McLodye and Helen Finn
Discounts: Seniors
Tee Times: Yes, 1 week for weekdays, Thursday 10 days prior for weekends/holidays

Features: Lessons, Practice Area, Pro Shop - Complete, Restaurant, Bar, Snack Bar, VISA/MC

Description: This is short course with 7 par 3s. But #18 stands out. It is 540 yd par 5 that tees off out of a narrow chute to a lot of undulations. You'll be left with a blind shot if you don't clear them.

Holes	Par	Yards Back Tees	Rating	Slope
18	67	5482	65.4	116

	9 Holes	18 Holes	Hours Mid Season
Weekday:	—	$13.50	Dawn - Dusk
Weekend:	—	$15.50	Dawn - Dusk
Cart Fees:	$11.75	$21.00	

Mandatory Cart Rental: No
Club Rental: Yes

Dunwoodie Golf Course

Wasylenko Lane, Yonkers NY — (914)969-9217

Directions: Major Deegan to Yonkers Ave West 1 mi. to course. Exit 4 from the Cross County or the Sawmill to the course.

Facility Type: Public

Club Pro: Andy Macko
Discounts: Twilight
Tee Times: Yes, reserve 1 week ahead in person.

Features: Lessons, Showers/Lockers, Driving Range, Practice Area, Pro Shop - Complete, Clubhouse, Snack Bar, Banquet Facilities, Restaurant, Bar

Description: Course is tight for the 1st 5 holes and then loosens up. Hilly for first 9 and flatter for back 9. The pro says it's the best conditioned course in the county.

Holes	Par	Yards Back Tees	Rating	Slope
18	70	5780	68.3	117

	9 Holes	18 Holes	Hours Mid Season
Weekday:	—	$35.00	7:00 am - Dusk
Weekend:	—	$40.00	6:00 am - Dusk
Cart Fees:	$12.00	$18.00	

Mandatory Cart Rental: No
Club Rental: Yes

Notes: Reduced green fees for county residents.

Dutcher Golf Course

135 East Main, Pawling NY — (914)855-9845

Directions: Rte 22 North. Take a left at the sign for Pawling, and the course is on the left.

Facility Type: Public

Club Pro: Sal Golisano

Coupon page 198

Discounts: Twilight
Tee Times: No

Features: Lessons, Driving Range, Practice Area, Pro Shop - Complete, Snack Bar

Description: This course lays claim to being the oldest course in the country, designed by John Dutcher and built in 1890. It is scenic and challenging. It has a good variety of holes. The greens and tees are especailly well maintained.

Holes	Par	Yards Back Tees	Rating	Slope
9dt	68	4880	60.2	113

	9 Holes	18 Holes	Hours Mid Season
Weekday:	—	$11.00	7:00 am - Dusk
Weekend:	—	$13.00	7:00 am - Dusk
Cart Fees:	$10.00	$15.00	

Mandatory Cart Rental: No
Club Rental: Yes

Dyker Beach Golf Course

86th St & 7th Ave, Brooklyn NY — Info: (718)836-9722 Tee Times: 718 225 GOLF

Directions: From Long Island take the Belt Pkwy to the Bay Ave/8th St Exit. At the 1st light, Cropsy Ave, take a left. Go 1 light to 86th Ave and take a left to 7th Ave to course. From NYC take the BQE towards Staten Is. Exit at 86th St, make a left and the course is 3 blocks. Or take the RR subway to 86th and 4th Ave and walk 3 blocks.

Facility Type: Public

Coupon page 198

Club Pro: None
Discounts: Twilight
Tee Times: Yes, 2 weeks for weekend/holiday. 1 week for weekday. There is a $2 reservation charge.

Features: Lessons, Showers/Lockers, Practice Area, Clubhouse, Snack Bar, VISA/MC, Lodging Near-by, Pro Shop - Limited

Description: It is hard to believe you're in New York on most of this course. Picked by Golf Digest in '90 and'91 for "Places to Play", the course is challenging enough, but can also be forgiving. It was designed by John Van Kleek in 1928.

Holes	Par	Yards Back Tees	Rating	Slope
18	71	6548	68.8	115

	9 Holes	18 Holes	Hours Mid Season
Weekday:	—	$13.50	Dawn - Dusk
Weekend:	—	$15.50	Dawn - Dusk
Cart Fees:	—	$21.00	

Mandatory Cart Rental: No
Club Rental: Yes

Notes: Inquire about tournament packages.

Eddy Farm Resort & GC

Sparrowbush NY — (914)856-2225

Directions: Rte 84 to Exit 1 West through Port Jervis. The course is 2 mi. West of Port Jervis on Rte 97.,

Facility Type: Resort

Club Pro: Robert Barna
Discounts: None
Tee Times: No, Public walk on after 4 pm.

Features: Lessons, Pro Shop - Complete, Snack Bar, Lodging Nearby

Description: A very scenic course, along the cliffs of the Delaware River.

Holes	Par	Yards Back Tees	Rating	Slope
9	27	860	—	—
9	35	2600	—	—

	9 Holes	18 Holes	Hours Mid Season
Weekday:	$7.00	$11.00	4:00 pm - Dusk *
Weekend:	$7.00	$11.00	4:00 pm - Dusk *
Cart Fees:	—	—	
Club Rental: Yes			

Notes: Public play after 4 pm in the afternoon.

Eisenhower Park Golf Course

East Meadow NY — Info: (516)542-4528   Tee Times: (516)542-GOLF

Directions: 495 to Exit 38 onto Northern State Pkwy to the Meadowbrook Pkwy. Exit at Stuart Ave to the park and course.

Facility Type: Public

Club Pro: None
Discounts: None
Tee Times: Yes, Liesure Pass holders can call ahead Mon for Friday, Tues for Sat, and Wed for Sun from 9 am to 1 pm, and can call Thursday for remaining slots for a $4 charge.

Features: Lessons, Showers/Lockers, Driving Range, Pro Shop - Complete, Clubhouse, Restaurant, Snack Bar, Practice Area, Bar, Banquet Facilities

Description: Excellent shape for public courses. There is a lot of golf palyed here. Lessons are taught at the driving range, adjacent to the course.

Holes	Par	Yards Back Tees	Rating	Slope
18	72	6836	—	—
18	72	6263	—	—
18	72	6035	—	—

	9 Holes	18 Holes	Hours Mid Season
Weekday:	$16.00	$26.00	Dawn - Dusk
Weekend:	—	$30.00	Dawn - Dusk
Cart Fees:	—	$20.00	

Mandatory Cart Rental: No
Club Rental: No

Notes: Greens fees listed are for non-residents. Resident green fees are $12 weekdays and $14 weekends and holidays for 18 and $8 for 9 holes. Srs during the week play for $6 for 18, and $4 for 9. There is no 9 hole play on weekends.

Fallsview Hotel & CC

Ellenville NY — Tee Times: (914)647-4960

Directions: Rte 17 to Exit 113. Take Rte 209 North 12 miles to hotel.

Holes	Par	Yards Back Tees	Rating	Slope
9	35	3432	72.5	126

Facility Type: Resort

Club Pro: Werner Teichmann
Discounts: None
Tee Times: Yes, 3 days ahead for weekends

	9 Holes	18 Holes	Hours Mid Season
Weekday:	$10.00	$16.00	8:00 am - 6:00 pm
Weekend:	$12.00	$18.00	7:00 am - 6:00 pm
Cart Fees:	$11.00	$21.00	

Mandatory Cart Rental: No
Club Rental: Yes

Features: Lessons, Showers/Lockers, Driving Range, Practice Area, Pro Shop - Limited, Restaurant, Bar, Lodging Nearby, Snack Bar, Banquet Facilities

Notes: Open April to Thanksgiving, weather permitting.

Description: This is a Robert Trent Jones course in the very scenic Catskill Mountains. The course offers a challenge for any golfer. A good example is the 8th, a 470 yd par 4. It is uphill to an exact placement for a shot at the green and then a difficult green, even with no traps.

Fishkill Golf Course

Fishkill NY 12524 — (914)896-5220

Directions: The facility is on the West side of Rte 9, 3/4 of a mile South of I-84.

Holes	Par	Yards Back Tees	Rating	Slope
9	29	1521	—	—

Facility Type: Executive

Club Pro: None
Discounts: Seniors
Tee Times: No

	9 Holes	18 Holes	Hours Mid Season
Weekday:	$7.00	$12.00	Dawn - Dusk
Weekend:	$7.00	$12.00	Dawn - Dusk
Cart Fees:	—	—	

Mandatory Cart Rental:
Club Rental: Yes

Features: Lessons, Practice Area, Pro Shop - Limited, Snack Bar

Description: The facility includes a driving range that is open until 10 pm. It has 25 mat tees and 30 grass tees. There is also miniature golf and batting cages.

Flushing Meadow Golf Course   NY 27

Flushing Meadow Park, Corona NY — (718)271-8182

Directions: Grand Central Pkwy to Shea
Stadium/National Tennis Center Exit. The course
is 200 yds from Tennis Center.

Holes	Par	Yards Back Tees	Rating	Slope
18	54	1035	—	—

Facility Type: Pitch & Putt

	9 Holes	18 Holes	Hours Mid Season
Weekday:	—	$5.00	8:00 am - 7:00 pm
Weekend:	—	$5.50	8:00 am - 7:00 pm
Cart Fees:	—	—	
Cart Rental:			
Club Rental: Yes			

Club Pro: None
Discounts: Seniors
Tee Times: No

Features: Snack Bar

Forest Park Golf Course   NY 28

Woodhaven NY —   **Tee Times:** (718)296-0999

Directions: Grand Central Parkway to the Interbor-
ough Parkway going West. Take the Forest Park
Dr Exit. Course is directly off the exit.

Holes	Par	Yards Back Tees	Rating	Slope
18	67	5820	65.6	108

Facility Type: Public

	9 Holes	18 Holes	Hours Mid Season
Weekday:	$8.00	$13.50	6:00 am - Dusk
Weekend:	$8.00	$15.50	6:00 am - Dusk
Cart Fees:	—	$21.65	

Club Pro: Tom Strafaci
Discounts: Seniors, Twilight
Tee Times: Yes, 1 week in advance at a charge of $2.

Mandatory Cart Rental: No
Club Rental: Yes

Features: Lessons, Practice Area, Pro Shop - Limited,
Snack Bar

Description: Hills make this course good exercise for
the walker. Greens are slightly elevated. Water
comes in on 3 holes. Course offers a good challenge for the average golfer.

Garrison Golf Club

Rte 9, Garrison NY —   Tee Times: (914)424-3605

Directions: Rte 84 to Rte 9 South into Garrison. The course is on Rte 9 in Garrison.

Holes	Par	Yards Back Tees	Rating	Slope
18	72	6412	71.6	132

Facility Type: Semi-private

Club Pro: Tony DeStefano

Discounts: None

Tee Times: Yes, Non-members can call 1 week ahead for weekend play after 12.

	9 Holes	18 Holes	Hours Mid Season
Weekday:	$ 15.00	$20.00	7:30 am - 6:00 pm
Weekend:	$15.00	$30.00	7:00 am - 6:00 pm
Cart Fees:	—	$28.00	

Mandatory Cart Rental: No
Club Rental: Yes

Features: Lessons, Driving Range, Practice Area, Pro Shop - Complete, Clubhouse, Restaurant, Bar, Banquet Facilities, Lodging Nearby

Notes: 9 hole play only after 4 pm. This course is open all year, weather permitting.

Description: Dick Wilson designed this scenic course overlooking the Hudson. The front 9 is hilly and tight. The signature hole is #14, a 215 yd par 3. This hole is all carry to a peninsula green.

Glen Cove Golf Course

Lattingtown Rd, Glen Cove NY — (516)671-0033

Directions: 495 to Exit 39 N (Glen Cove Rd) to the end. At the fire house take a right turn onto Brewster St which becomes Forest Ave. At the 4th light make a left onto Dosoris Lane. Go to 1st stop and turn right onto Lattingtown Rd to course 2/10 mi. on the left.

Holes	Par	Yards Back Tees	Rating	Slope
18	64	5000	64.4	109

Facility Type: Semi-private

Club Pro: Mal Galletta

Discounts: None

Tee Times: No, 1st come, but you must have a permit to play at this course. See notes.

	9 Holes	18 Holes	Hours Mid Season
Weekday:	$6.00	$8.00	7:00 am - Dusk
Weekend:	$7.00	$10.00	6:00 am - Dusk
Cart Fees:	$12.00	$17.00	

Mandatory Cart Rental: No
Club Rental: Yes

Notes: Permits are not restricted to Glen Cove residents. Inquire about memberships, both inclusive and not inclusive of green fees. There are lockers but no showers.

Features: Lessons, Showers/Lockers, Driving Range, Practice Area, Pro Shop - Complete, Restaurant, Bar, Snack Bar

Description: This is a tight course. Nevertheless, it's forgiving. It's a beautifully maintained course with a view of Connecticut. The greens are fast and well kept. There's a lot of water coming into play.

Governor's Island Golf Course NY 31

Gov's Island NY — (212)668-7329

Directions: Staten Island Ferry to Gov's Isand.

Facility Type: Semi-private

Club Pro: None
Discounts: None
Tee Times: No, Restricted to military personel, active and retired and US Gov't Dept of Transportation personel.

Features: Practice Area, Pro Shop - Complete, Snack Bar

Description: This course plays around Fort Jay with a view of Manhattan. 5 holes intersect.

Holes	Par	Yards Back Tees	Rating	Slope
9	36	1893	—	—

	9 Holes	18 Holes	Hours Mid Season
Weekday:	—	—	9:00 am - 8:00 pm *
Weekend:	—	—	7:30 am - 8:00 pm
Cart Fees:	—	—	
Club Rental:			

Notes: * The course is closed on Tuesdays. Greens fees start at $10 for lower ranking personel and go down to $5.

Granit Hotel & Golf Course NY 32

Kerhonkson NY — (914)626-3141

Directions: NY Thruway to Exit 18, New Paltz. Follow 299 West through New Paltz to Rte 44-55. At that junction, make a right turn. Go over the mountain and look for signs to the the hotel.

Facility Type: Public

Club Pro: John Magaletta
Discounts: None
Tee Times: No

Coupon page 198

Features: Lessons, Driving Range, Practice Area, Pro Shop - Complete, Restaurant, Bar, Banquet Facilities, Lodging Nearby

Description: A rolling and scenic course, it is moderately difficult. The #6, 610 yard par 5 is an interesting hole.

Holes	Par	Yards Back Tees	Rating	Slope
18	70	6355	69.5	117

	9 Holes	18 Holes	Hours Mid Season
Weekday:	$10.00	$18.00	7:00 am - 6:00 pm
Weekend:	$10.00	$18.00	6:00 am - 6:00 pm
Cart Fees:	$12.00	$22.00	

Mandatory Cart Rental: No
Club Rental: Yes

Green Acres Golf Course

Kingston NY — (914)331-2283

Directions: NY Thruway to Exit 19. At the traffic circle take the 2nd Kingston Exit, Col Chandler Dr. approx 2.5 into town. Make a left at the light, Albany Ave, and go approx 3 mi. Take the 1st left after McDonalds, Horwich St, to the course.

Facility Type: Public

Club Pro: None
Discounts: None
Tee Times: No

Holes	Par	Yards Back Tees	Rating	Slope
9	36	2900	—	—

	9 Holes	18 Holes	Hours Mid Season
Weekday:	$4.00	$6.00	Dawn - Dusk
Weekend:	$5.00	$8.00	Dawn - Dusk
Cart Fees:	$7.00	$14.00	

Mandatory Cart Rental: No
Club Rental: Yes

Description: A straightforward short and flat course, great for beginners and walkers.

Green Ridge Golf Club

Gregory Rd, Johnson NY — (914)355-1317

Directions: This course is 6 miles North of the New Jersey state line in SW Orange County. Take Rte 84 to Exit 3. Take Rte 6 West to 284 South for 3 miles. Turn right at the sign for town of Johnson. Take the next 2 left turns to the course.

Facility Type: Public

Club Pro: None
Discounts: Twilight
Tee Times: No

Coupon page 199

Features: Pro Shop - Complete, Clubhouse, Bar, Snack Bar

Description: This is a challenging little course that sits right in a valley. The greens are small and a river and 3 ponds come into play.

Holes	Par	Yards Back Tees	Rating	Slope
9	36	2800	34	—

	9 Holes	18 Holes	Hours Mid Season
Weekday:	$11.00	$11.00	Dawn - Dusk
Weekend:	$15.00	$15.00	Dawn - Dusk
Cart Fees:	$11.00	$20.00	

Mandatory Cart Rental: No
Club Rental: Yes

Grossinger Golf Course

Ferndale NY — Tee Times: (914)292-1450

Directions: Rte 17 going North to Exit 100. Take a left off the exit and follow the signs. Going South take the same exit. Make a left off the exit and a left at the 2nd light. Follow the signs.

Holes	Par	Yards Back Tees	Rating	Slope
9	36	3268	—	—
18	71	6791	72.7	134

Facility Type: Semi-private

	9 Holes	18 Holes	Hours Mid Season
Weekday:	—	$33.00	7:00 am - 5:30 pm
Weekend:	—	$33.00	7:00 am - 5:30 pm
Cart Fees:	—	$24.00	

Club Pro: Kevin Shaw
Discounts: None
Tee Times: Yes, 1 week in advance for any day.

Mandatory Cart Rental: Yes
Club Rental: Yes

Features: Lessons, Showers/Lockers, Driving Range, Practice Area, Pro Shop - Complete, Clubhouse, Restaurant, Bar, Snack Bar, VISA/MC, Lodging Nearby

Notes: Memberships available

Description: The 18 hole course is "Big G" and was designed by Joe Finger. It is the NY State Open and Amateur site. The Front 9 is "Lake", and the back 9 "Valley". A favorite hole is #4, a par 5, 512 shot with water down the left of a well-bunkered fairwy to an island green. The 3rd 9 is "Vista". All are in great shape, and they can be played in any combination. Golf Digest picked the course for "Places to Play" in '90 and '91. It's the best kept secret in the Catskills. Open April 15 to Nov 1.

Gull Haven Golf Course

Gull Haven Drive, Central Islip NY 11772 — (516)436-6059

Directions: 495 to Exit 56. Go South on Rte 111. A left fork becomes Carlton Ave. 3 miles after the fork, take left onto Gull Haven Dr to course.

Holes	Par	Yards Back Tees	Rating	Slope
9dt	70	5640	—	—

Facility Type: Public

	9 Holes	18 Holes	Hours Mid Season
Weekday:	—	$14.00	6:00 am - 6:00 pm
Weekend:	—	$19.00	6:00 am - 6:00 pm
Cart Fees:	—	$16.00	

Club Pro: Richie Loughlin
Discounts: None
Tee Times: No

Mandatory Cart Rental: No
Club Rental: No

Features: Lessons, Practice Area, Pro Shop - Limited, Clubhouse, Restaurant, Bar, Snack Bar

Description: This is a fairly straightforward and easy course with no water.

Hamlet Golf & Country Club NY 37

Hauppauge Rd, Commack NY — Tee Times: (516)499-0345

Directions: 495 to Exit 52. Take Commack Rd North 2 mi. to Hauppauge Rd. Take a left and go 1/2 mi. to course.

Holes	Par	Yards Back Tees	Rating	Slope
9	27	1255	—	—
18	70	6300	69.0	115

Facility Type: Semi-private

Club Pro: Mike Borsuk, Head pro
Discounts: Twilight, Seniors
Tee Times: Yes, Tuesday morning for weekends. Members (permit holders) have preference on weekends.

	9 Holes	18 Holes	Hours Mid Season
Weekday:	$7.00	$20.00	7:00 am - 6:00 pm
Weekend:	$9.00	$25.00	6:00 am - 6:00 pm
Cart Fees:	$13.00	$25.00	

Mandatory Cart Rental: See notes.
Club Rental: No

Features: Lessons, Practice Area, Pro Shop - Complete, Clubhouse, Restaurant, Bar, Snack Bar, Banquet Facilities

Description: The course is very flat and wide open. There is no water but a lot of sand. Yet it's a very forgiving course.

Notes: 9 hole play on the regulation course only after twilight. The 9 hole green fees above refer to executive course. Carts are mandatory on weekends/holidays up to 2 pm. Sr rate during the week only. Inquire about permits.

Hanah Country Resort NY 38

Hanah Country Resort, Maragaretville NY — Info: (914)586-4841   Tee Times: (800)752-6494

Directions: NY Thruway to the Kingston Exit. Take Rte 28 West approx 45 mi. to Margaretville. Take a right on Rte 30 to the hotel and course.

Holes	Par	Yards Back Tees	Rating	Slope
18	72	7000	—	—

Facility Type: Resort

Club Pro:
Discounts:
Tee Times:

	9 Holes	18 Holes	Hours Mid Season
Weekday:	—	—	
Weekend:	—	—	
Cart Fees:	—	—	

Mandatory Cart Rental:
Club Rental:

Features:

Description: A new 7000 yd bent grass course is opening July of '92. Call for details.

Hancock Golf Course

Golf Course Drive, Hancock NY — (607)637-2480

Directions: Rte 17 to Exit 87. Going West take a right off the ramp and the first right at Golf Course Dr to the course. Going East on 17, take a right off the exit ramp, another right back under Rte 17 and a right at Golf Course Dr to the course.

Facility Type: Public

Club Pro: None
Discounts: None
Tee Times: No

Features: Lessons, Practice Area, Pro Shop - Limited, Clubhouse, Snack Bar

Description: This is a Robert Trent Jones course - hills, traps and water holes. The Binghamton Press rated the 3rd and 5th in the top 18 holes in the Catskills. #3 is a 525 yard par 5 shot to a dogleg and then to a narrow fairway over water. The green is flat , but well-bunkered.

Holes	Par	Yards Back Tees	Rating	Slope
9dt	72	6418	70.1	113

	9 Holes	18 Holes	Hours Mid Season
Weekday:	$8.00	$9.00	Dawn - Dusk
Weekend:	$11.00	$12.00	Dawn - Dusk
Cart Fees:	$9.00	$13.00	

Mandatory Cart Rental: No
Club Rental: Yes

Harlem Valley Golf Club

Wingdale NY — (914)832-9957

Directions: 684 North continuing on Rte 22 to Wingdale. Take a left at the light in Wingdale to the course. (No name on road).

Facility Type: Semi-private

Club Pro: None
Discounts: Seniors
Tee Times: No

Features: Lessons, Showers/Lockers, Practice Area, Snack Bar

Description: This course is hilly and wide open, but challenging and a hard one to par. Water comes into play on #8 and #9. The signature hole is #17, a 587 yd par 5 dogleg left with out-of-bounds to the right. The shot to the green is over maples if your set up is not perfect.

Holes	Par	Yards Back Tees	Rating	Slope
9dt	34	5996	68.9	118

	9 Holes	18 Holes	Hours Mid Season
Weekday:	$8.50	$15.00	7:00 am - 7:00 pm *
Weekend:	$11.00	$18.00	1:00 pm - 7:00 pm *
Cart Fees:	$11.00	$20.00	

Mandatory Cart Rental: No
Club Rental: No

Notes: * Closed to public Tues before 1pm and Wed after 3 for league play and weekends before 1 pm.

Hauppauge Country Club

Hauppauge NY — (516)724-7500

Directions: 495 to Exit 56. North on Rte 111 to Veterens Hwy. Make left and bear to right, 1/4 mi. to course.

Facility Type: Public

Club Pro: Dan Malawista
Discounts: Seniors, Twilight
Tee Times: No

Features: Lessons, Driving Range, Practice Area, Pro Shop - Complete, Clubhouse, Restaurant, Bar, Snack Bar, Banquet Facilities

Description: This is a fairly flat course with a lot of water on the back 9. The 17th is surrounded by water and sand.

Holes	Par	Yards Back Tees	Rating	Slope
18	72	6525	71.5	126

	9 Holes	18 Holes	Hours Mid Season
Weekday:	$16.00	$44.00	6:00 am - Dusk
Weekend:	—	—	closed to Public
Cart Fees:	$7.00	—	

Mandatory Cart Rental: Yes
Club Rental: No

Notes: 9 hole play during week only after 4 pm. Cart fee included in 18 hole green fee. Driving range enlarged for '92.

Heatherwood Golf Club

303 Arrowhead Lane, Centereach NY — **Tee Times:** (516)473-9000

Directions: 495 to Exit 62. Go North on Rte 97 to Rte 347. East on 347 approx 2 miles to course.

Facility Type: Semi-private

Club Pro: Bob Freund
Discounts: Twilight
Tee Times: Yes, Pay $12 to get into the system to call ahead day before as a one time seasonal fee.

Features: Lessons, Showers/Lockers, Practice Area, Pro Shop - Complete, Clubhouse, Restaurant, Bar, Banquet Facilities, Snack Bar

Description: This course has rolling tree-lined fairways and plays longer than it reads.

Holes	Par	Yards Back Tees	Rating	Slope
18	60	4109	62.1	104

	9 Holes	18 Holes	Hours Mid Season
Weekday:	—	$15.00	6:00 am - 7:00 pm
Weekend:	—	$17.00	11:00 am - 7:00 pm *
Cart Fees:	—	$20.00	

Mandatory Cart Rental: No
Club Rental: Yes

Notes: * Closed to non-members weekend mornings before 11 am. Pay annual fee to have access to starting times on weekend mornings. Twilight after 5. A yearly senior rate is available for weekday play only. A driving net is expected for '92.

Hickory Hill Golf Course

Call Stony Ford 9C at (914)457-3000

Directions: Rte 17 to Goshen Exit. Take 17A through Warwick. Course on 17A.

Holes	Par	Yards Back Tees	Rating	Slope
18	—	—	—	—

Facility Type: Public

Club Pro: None
Discounts: Twilight
Tee Times: Yes, call for information..

	9 Holes	18 Holes	Hours Mid Season
Weekday:	—	—	5:30 am - Dusk
Weekend:	—	—	5:30 am - Dusk
Cart Fees:	—	—	

Mandatory Cart Rental: No
Club Rental:

Features: Driving Range, Practice Area, Pro Shop - Limited, Clubhouse, Restaurant, Bar, Banquet Facilities, Lodging Nearby

Description: A new Hal Purdy favorite design 18 hole course is scheduled to open in July of '92 as a new Orange County facility. The rates, schedules and tee times will generally be the same as Stony Ford Golf Course in Montgomery. The facility will include a driving range and lodge.

Highland Country Club

Rte 9D, Garrison NY — (914)424-3727

Directions: Intersection of Rtes 9D and 403 in Garrison.

Holes	Par	Yards Back Tees	Rating	Slope
9	33	4538	62.5	115

Facility Type: Semi-private

Club Pro: Joe Cristello
Discounts: Seniors
Tee Times: No

	9 Holes	18 Holes	Hours Mid Season
Weekday:	—	$15.00	Dawn - Dusk
Weekend:	—	$20.00	see notes
Cart Fees:	—	$20.00	

Mandatory Cart Rental: No
Club Rental: No

Features: Lessons, Practice Area, Pro Shop - Limited

Description: This is a difficult course. It is wooded, features some water and demands a good deal of accuracy. The 119 yd #6 plays over a pond.

Notes: Several holes have double tees. The course is closed to the public on weekends from Memorial Day to Labor Day. Otherwise the public can play after 1 pm on weekends. There is limited access to the restaurant for non-members.

Hollow Hills CC

49 Ryder Ave, Dix Hills NY — (516)242-0010

Directions: 495 to Exit 51. Go South 1 mile and take the 2nd right onto Ryder Ave. The course is 1 mi. on the left.

Facility Type: Public

Club Pro: Joe Bifulco
Discounts: Seniors
Tee Times: No

Features: Lessons, Driving Range, Practice Area, Pro Shop - Limited, Clubhouse, Restaurant, Bar, Banquet Facilities

Description: This is a hilly and challenging little course.

Holes	Par	Yards Back Tees	Rating	Slope
9	35	2170	30.5	—

	9 Holes	18 Holes	Hours Mid Season
Weekday:	$8.00	$16.00	7:00 am - Dusk
Weekend:	$9.00	$18.00	6:00 am - Dusk
Cart Fees:	$16.00	$22.00	

Mandatory Cart Rental: No
Club Rental: Yes

Homowack Hotel Golf Course

Spring Glen NY — (914)647-6800 ext 1147

Directions: Rte 17 to Exit 113. Take Rte 209 North 7.5 mi. to hotel on left.

Facility Type: Resort

Club Pro: Ed Gray
Discounts: None
Tee Times: No

Features: Lessons, Driving Range, Practice Area, Pro Shop - Limited, Lodging Nearby, Snack Bar

Description: If you get out of the woods on this course, you're lucky. 5 scenic and challenging holes in woods and 4 more forgiving holes in the valley. Excellent greens. Grass and matt tees on driving range.

Holes	Par	Yards Back Tees	Rating	Slope
9	36	3045	—	—

	9 Holes	18 Holes	Hours Mid Season
Weekday:	$7.00	$9.00	8:00 am - Dusk
Weekend:	$8.00	$9.00	7:00 am - Dusk *
Cart Fees:	$10.00	$16.00	

Mandatory Cart Rental: No
Club Rental: Yes

Notes: * The course is closed on Saturdays. Complete resort facilities.

Huff House Golf Course

Roscoe NY — (607)498-9953

Directions: Rte 17 to Exit 94. Follow the signs.

Facility Type: Executive

Coupon page 199

Club Pro: None
Discounts: None
Tee Times: No

Description: An executive course on the top of a mountain.

Holes	Par	Yards Back Tees	Rating	Slope
9	27	1094	—	—

	9 Holes	18 Holes	Hours Mid Season
Weekday:	$8.00	$8.00	8:00 am - Dusk
Weekend:	$8.00	$8.00	8:00 am - Dusk
Cart Fees:	—	—	
Club Rental: No			

Indian Island Golf Course

NY 48

Riverside Dr, Riverhead NY — **Info:** (516)727-7776   **Tee Times:** 516 244 PARK

Directions: 495 to Exit 71. Go South on Rte 24 approx 7 mi. to Rte 105. Take a left, go over the bridge and the course is on the right.

Facility Type: Public

Club Pro: Bob Fox
Discounts: Seniors, Twilight
Tee Times: Yes, Up to 1 week and as late as 24 hours only on a touch tone phone and only with a Green Key Card.

Features: Lessons, Showers/Lockers, Driving Range, Practice Area, Pro Shop - Complete, Clubhouse, Restaurant, Bar, Snack Bar

Description: A tight front 9 and watery back 9. The greens are high and tough. The driving range is lit and open till 10 pm.

Holes	Par	Yards Back Tees	Rating	Slope
18	72	6353	71.0	124

	9 Holes	18 Holes	Hours Mid Season
Weekday:	—	$27.00	7:00 am - 6:00 pm
Weekend:	—	$31.00	6:00 am - 6:00 pm
Cart Fees:	—	$22.00	

Mandatory Cart Rental: No
Club Rental: Yes

Notes: Suffolk Co residents pay $13 on weekdays and $15 on weeends. Non-residents or those without Green Key Cards may walk on and will be paired with a Card holder.

Indian Valley Golf Course

Shrub Oak NY — (914)245-9816

Directions: Taconic Pkwy to Rte 6 East, 300 yds to the course.

Holes	Par	Yards Back Tees	Rating	Slope
9	27	1300	—	—

Facility Type: Executive

	9 Holes	18 Holes	Hours Mid Season
Weekday:	$6.00	$8.00	8:00 am - Dusk
Weekend:	$7.00	$9.00	8:00 am - Dusk
Cart Fees:	—	—	
Club Rental: No			

Club Pro: None
Discounts: None
Tee Times: No

Features: Bar, Snack Bar

Description: Tight for an executive course. A lot of water. Good practice for your irons.

Island Glen Country Club

NY 50

Bethel NY — (914)583-9898

Directions: Rte 17 to Exit 104. This will put you on 17 B (You can only go one way). The course is on Rte 17B, 16 mi. on the right side. It's past the Racetrack in Bethel.

Holes	Par	Yards Back Tees	Rating	Slope
9	36	3000	—	—

	9 Holes	18 Holes	Hours Mid Season
Weekday:	$10.00	$10.00	8:00 am - 7:00 pm
Weekend:	$12.00	$12.00	7:30 am - 7:00 pm
Cart Fees:	$12.00	$20.00	

Facility Type: Public

Coupon page 199

Club Pro: None
Discounts: Twilight
Tee Times: No

Mandatory Cart Rental: No
Club Rental: Yes

Features: Showers/Lockers, Practice Area, Pro Shop - Complete, Snack Bar, Clubhouse, Bar

Notes: Major improvements are planned for the '92 season.

Description: This challenging little course is situated in a valley. Wildlife is abundant, especially deer. The course is moderately hilly. You must play over a barn on #4.

Island's End Golf & CC

Greenport NY — Tee Times: (516)477-9457

Directions: 495 to the last exit. Take Rte 25 1 mi. past Greenport to the course.

Holes	Par	Yards Back Tees	Rating	Slope
18	72	6639	71.4	125

Facility Type: Semi-private

	9 Holes	18 Holes	Hours Mid Season
Weekday:	—	$23.00	7:00 am - Dusk
Weekend:	—	$27.00	6:00 am - Dusk
Cart Fees:	—	$11.00	

Club Pro: Chris Vedder

Discounts: None

Tee Times: Yes, 12 noon of the day prior for non-members. A $5/person tee time charge.

Mandatory Cart Rental: No

Club Rental: Yes

Features: Lessons, Showers/Lockers, Driving Range, Pro Shop - Complete, Clubhouse, Restaurant, Bar, Banquet Facilities, Lodging Nearby

Notes: Dress code applies. If in doubt, please call. Cart fee is per person.

Description: This is a beautifully situated course on Long Island Sound. The course is relatively flat. The back 9 stretches to the Sound with the par 3 #16 running along a cliff. Out of bounds is the Sound.

James Baird State Park GC

Pleasant Valley NY — Info: (914)452-1489

Directions: The course is just off the Taconic Pkwy, 1 mi. North of the Rte 55 Exit. Heading South, look for sign in Pleasant Valley.

Holes	Par	Yards Back Tees	Rating	Slope
18	71	6616	71.2	124

	9 Holes	18 Holes	Hours Mid Season
Weekday:	$ 6.00	$10.00	7:00 am - 7:00 pm
Weekend:	$ 7.00	$12.00	6:00 am - 7:00 pm
Cart Fees:	$10.00	$18.00	

Facility Type: Public

Club Pro: Brad Davis

Discounts: Seniors, Juniors

Tee Times: No

Mandatory Cart Rental: No

Club Rental: Yes

Features: Lessons, Showers/Lockers, Driving Range, Practice Area, Pro Shop - Complete, Clubhouse, Restaurant, Bar, Banquet Facilities

Notes: 9 hole play only after 4 pm. At the time of publication, plans were in the works for a reservation system. Call for information.

Description: This is a very pretty Robert Trent Jones course. It is fairly flat with a few water holes and some interesting challenges.

James J. McCann Mem. GC NY 53

155 Wilbur Blvd, Poughkeepsie NY — (914)471-3917

Directions: On Rte 9 North or South to Spackenkill Rd in Poughkeepsie near IBM plant. Take Spackenkill East to Wilbur Blvd and left to the course.

Facility Type: Public

Club Pro: Ronald Jensen
Discounts: None
Tee Times: Yes, in person Fri for weekends. Tickets at 454 1968

Features: Lessons, Showers/Lockers, Driving Range, Practice Area, Pro Shop - Complete, Restaurant, Bar, Snack Bar

Description: This is a rolling course in excellent condition. Fairways are cut to definition. Traps are well kept and greens are large.

Holes	Par	Yards Back Tees	Rating	Slope
18	72	6524	70.7	120

	9 Holes	18 Holes	Hours Mid Season
Weekday:	$6.00	$ 17.00	7:00 am - Dusk *
Weekend:	$7.00	$20.00	7:00 am - Dusk
Cart Fees:	$11.00	$18.00	

Mandatory Cart Rental: No
Club Rental: Yes

Notes: * Monday play begins at 12 pm. City and town residents pay $9 weekdays and $11 weekends. County residents pay $11 weekdays and $13 weekends for 18 holes.

Jones Beach Golf Course NY 54

Wantagh NY — (516)785-1600

Directions: Meadowbrook Pkwy South. It becomes Ocean Dr and runs into fields 4 or 5 at the park.

Facility Type: Pitch & Putt

Club Pro: None
Discounts: Seniors
Tee Times: No

Holes	Par	Yards Back Tees	Rating	Slope
18	56	—	—	—

	9 Holes	18 Holes	Hours Mid Season
Weekday:	—	$3.00	8:00 am - 6:00 pm
Weekend:	—	$3.00	8:00 am - 6:00 pm
Cart Fees:	—	—	
Club Rental:	Yes		

Notes: Sr discounts for holders of NY Drivers License.

Kissena Park Golf Course NY 55

164-15 Booth Memorial Ave, Flushing NY — **Tee Times:** (718)939-4594

Directions: 495 to Exit 24, Kissena Blvd. Go north one block to Booth Memorial Ave, and make a right. Go to 164th St, cross over and the course is on the left.

Facility Type: Public

Club Pro: Dale Shankland
Discounts: Twilight
Tee Times: Yes, $2 charge to reserve up to 1 week in advance

Features: Lessons, Showers/Lockers, Practice Area, Pro Shop - Complete, Snack Bar

Description: The course is hilly and has a great view of Manhattan from the 11th hole. The fairways are tight in places. This course is harder than it reads.

Holes	Par	Yards Back Tees	Rating	Slope
18	64	4727	61.8	101

	9 Holes	18 Holes	Hours Mid Season
Weekday:	—	$13.50	Dawn - Dusk
Weekend:	—	$15.50	Dawn - Dusk
Cart Fees:	—	$20.00	

Mandatory Cart Rental: No
Club Rental: Yes

Notes: Cart fee listed is for two. Twilights are at 3 and 5:30 pm, mid-season.

Kutsher's Country Club NY 56

Monticello NY — **Tee Times:** (914)794-6000 ext 2320

Directions: Rte 17 to Exit 105 B and follow the signs.

Facility Type: Resort

Club Pro: None
Discounts: None
Tee Times: Yes, 2 weeks in advance recommended.

Features: Lessons, Showers/Lockers, Practice Area, Pro Shop - Complete, Clubhouse, Restaurant, Bar, Snack Bar, Banquet Facilities, Lodging Nearby, Driving Range

Description: A William Mitchell design, the course is carved out of the forest. It is scenic and narrow with a heavy premium on accuracy. The course was a selection by Golf Digest for "Places to Play" in '90 and '91. The signature is a 440 yd, par 4 #2. It's a straight out tee-off, out-of-bounds right and trees left to a well-bunkered green, reachable with a long iron.

Holes	Par	Yards Back Tees	Rating	Slope
18	72	7157	73.5	123

	9 Holes	18 Holes	Hours Mid Season
Weekday:	—	$24.00	7:30 am - 6:00 pm *
Weekend:	—	$24.00	7:00 am - 6:00 pm
Cart Fees:	—	$24.00	

Mandatory Cart Rental: Yes
Club Rental: Yes

Notes: * Weekday is Mon through Thurs. Driving range will be available summer of '92.

LaTourette Park Golf Course

NY 57

1001 Richmond Hill Rd, Staten Island NY — Info: (718)351-1889 Tee Times: 718 225 GOLF

Directions: From Long Island and Brooklyn, take the Varranzano Bridge to 278 West. Exit at Bradley Ave onto the service road to the 2nd light, Wooley Ave. Go left 5 lights to course. From NJ take the Goethals Bridge to 278 East. Exit at Victory Blvd, go to the light, and turn left. Bear right just after next light onto the service road. At the 1st light, Wooley Ave, make a right and go 4 lights to Richmond Hill Rd. Turn left and course is at the crest of the hill.

Facility Type: Public

Club Pro: Eddie Sorge
Discounts: Twilight
Tee Times: Yes, 10 days for any day

Features: Lessons, Driving Range, Practice Area, Clubhouse, Snack Bar, Pro Shop - Complete, Bar, VISA/MC

Description: This course was a WPA project, designed by John Van Kleek. It is long and hilly. #14 is nice. It's a straight 354 yd par 4 shot from an elevated tee to a bunkered green. It's a challenging course. The greens have been greatly improved.

Holes	Par	Yards Back Tees	Rating	Slope
18	72	6500	69.7	117

	9 Holes	18 Holes	Hours Mid Season
Weekday:	—	$13.50	Dawn - Dusk
Weekend:	—	$15.50	Dawn - Dusk
Cart Fees:	—	$21.00	

Mandatory Cart Rental: No
Club Rental: No

Notes: Inquire about tournament packages.

Coupon page 200

Lido Golf Course

NY 58

Lido Beach NY — Info: (516)431-8778 Tee Times: (516)889-8181

Directions: Southern State Pkwy to Meadowbrook Pkwy South. Take the Meadowbrook to the Loop Pkwy and to the end. Make a right onto Lido Blvd and the course is 2 mi. on right.

Facility Type: Public

Club Pro: Leo Tabick
Discounts: Twilight
Tee Times: Yes, in person for weekdays up to 2 weeks prior. A lottery for weekends 10 days prior, can be done by mail.

Features: Driving Range, Practice Area, Pro Shop - Complete, Clubhouse, Restaurant, Snack Bar, Banquet Facilities

Description: This is a Robert Trent Jones Scottish links-style design. Wind and water are the operative words. # 16 is a signature hole. It's a 465 yd par 5 with water as a big concern. This is a challenging course.

Holes	Par	Yards Back Tees	Rating	Slope
18	71	6387	71.1	128

	9 Holes	18 Holes	Hours Mid Season
Weekday:	—	$25.00	6:30 am - 6:00 pm
Weekend:	—	$25.00	6:30 am - 6:00 pm
Cart Fees:	—	$20.00	

Mandatory Cart Rental: No
Club Rental: Yes

Notes: Facility features a new indoor golf school.

Loch Ledge Golf Course

Yorktown Hts NY — Info: (914)962-2922

Directions: Taconic Pkwy to Underhill Ave Exit. Take Underhill Ave East 1.5 mi. to light at Rte 118. Make right and course is 2 mi. on the right.

Facility Type: Public

Club Pro: Orlando Fiore
Discounts: Twilight
Tee Times: No

Features: Lessons, Practice Area, Pro Shop - Limited

Description: A scenic course that is challenging due to tight, tree-lined and sloping fairways. Water comes in on 2 holes and the greens are average to small. #11 is a 501 yd par 5 straight, tight shot to a dog-leg left and to the smallest green on the course. The temptation is to simplify. There are 4 more long par 5's.

Holes	Par	Yards Back Tees	Rating	Slope
18	71	6100	66.8	114

	9 Holes	18 Holes	Hours Mid Season
Weekday:	—	$12.00	8:00 am - Dusk
Weekend:	—	$16.00	Dawn - Dusk
Cart Fees:	—	$22.00	

Mandatory Cart Rental: No
Club Rental: Yes

Notes: Twilight after 4 pm midseaon.

Lochmor Golf Course

Hurleyville, NY — Tee Times: (914)434-9079

Directions: Rte 17 to Exit 105B to Rte 42 North. Take 1st left onto Anawana Lake Rd. Go 10 mi. to course (1 mi. past Hurleyville)

Facility Type: Public

Club Pro: Glen Sonnenschein
Discounts: Twilight
Tee Times: Yes, 3 days ahead for weekends

Features: Lessons, Showers/Lockers, Driving Range, Practice Area, Pro Shop - Complete, Clubhouse, Bar, Snack Bar

Description: This is a scenic and hilly course with wide fairways and little water, although the course overlooks a lake. The drives are easy but the approach shots deceptively hard and the greens are small. A Golf Digest pick for "Places to Play" in '90 and '91.

Holes	Par	Yards Back Tees	Rating	Slope
18	72	6248	69.9	119

	9 Holes	18 Holes	Hours Mid Season
Weekday	$12.00	$20.00	7:00 am - 6:30 pm
Weekend	$12.00	$20.00	6:30 am - 6:30 pm
Cart Fees:	—	$22.00	

Mandatory Cart Rental: See notes.
Club Rental: No

Notes: Carts are mandatory on weekend mornings

Maple Moor Golf Course   NY 61

1128 North St, White Plains NY — **Info:** (914)946-1830   **Tee Times:** (914)949-6752

Directions: Hutchinson River Pkwy to Exit 25 W directly to course.

Facility Type: Public

Club Pro: Rick Poanessa
Discounts: Seniors, Twilight
Tee Times: Yes, 1 week in person. A park pass is $15 for 3 years for county residents.

Features: Lessons, Showers/Lockers, Practice Area, Pro Shop - Complete, Clubhouse, Restaurant, Snack Bar, Bar

Description: The course is generally flat and wide open. The front 9 is tighter and a little longer. The greens are in good shape and fast for most golfers.

Holes	Par	Yards Back Tees	Rating	Slope
18	71	6300	69.1	112

	9 Holes	18 Holes	Hours Mid Season
Weekday:	—	$35.00	7:00 am - 6:00 pm
Weekend:	—	$40.00	5:30 am - 6:00 pm
Cart Fees:	—	$19.50	

Mandatory Cart Rental: No
Club Rental: Yes

Notes: County residents pay $11 on weekdays and $14 on weekends.

Marine Park Golf Course   NY 62

2880 Flatbush Ave, Brooklyn NY — **Info:** (718)338-7113   **Tee Times:** (718)338-7149

Directions: Belt Pkwy to Exit 11N. Take a left at the 2nd light into course.

Facility Type: Public

Club Pro: John Vuono
Discounts: Twilight
Tee Times: Yes, 7 days ahead is suggested.

Features: Lessons, Practice Area, Pro Shop - Complete, Clubhouse, Restaurant, Bar, VISA/MC

Description: This is a links-type course, flat and open with no water. #3, a 465 yd par 4 dogleg right to a small green is a favorite. This is one of those courses where it's hard to believe you're in New York at times.

Holes	Par	Yards Back Tees	Rating	Slope
18	72	6866	70.5	118

	9 Holes	18 Holes	Hours Mid Season
Weekday:	—	$13.50	Dawn - Dusk
Weekend:	—	$15.50	Dawn - Dusk
Cart Fees:	—	$21.00	

Mandatory Cart Rental: No

Marriott Windwatch

1717 Vanderbilt, Hauppauge NY — Tee Times: (516)232-9850

Directions: 495 to Exit 57. Take Rte 90 North (Motor Pkwy). The Marriott is 3/4 mi. on the left.

Facility Type: Resort

Club Pro: Steven Schaller, Head Pro
Discounts: None
Tee Times: Yes, 3 days ahead for any day

Features: Showers/Lockers, Driving Range, Practice Area, Pro Shop - Complete, Clubhouse, Restaurant, Bar, Snack Bar, Banquet Facilities, Lodging Nearby, American Express, VISA/MC, Lessons

Description: Joe Lee was the architect of this well balanced course. The course is 15 acres of lakes with 62 white sand traps. Golf Digest picked this in "91 after it opened as one of its "Places to Play". It is the home of the John Jacobs Golf School. The 16th is the signature hole. It's a 338 yard par 4. The tee shot is a 210 - 220 carry through water on both sides.

Holes	Par	Yards Back Tees	Rating	Slope
18	71	6408	71.1	133

	9 Holes	18 Holes	Hours Mid Season
Weekday:	$ 32.00	$59.00	7:30 am - 7:00 pm
Weekend:	$ 34.00	$65.00	7:00 am - 7:00 pm
Cart Fees:	—	—	

Mandatory Cart Rental: Yes
Club Rental: Yes

Notes: 9 hole play before 8:30 in the morning and after 4 only. Cart is included in green fees. The above prices are subject to change.

Merrick Road Park GC

2550 Club House Road, Merrick NY — (516)868-4650

Directions: 495 to the Northern State Parkway. Take the Meadowbrook Parkway South to Exit M9East (Merrick Road East). After getting off the parkway, take a right at the 1st light to the rear of the parking lot

Facility Type: Public

Club Pro: Mike Wade
Discounts: None
Tee Times: No

Features: Lessons, Driving Range, Practice Area, Pro Shop - Complete, Clubhouse, Snack Bar

Description: This is a flat course with trapped greens and some water. It is more challenging than it's advertised to be.

Holes	Par	Yards Back Tees	Rating	Slope
9	36	3200	—	—

	9 Holes	18 Holes	Hours Mid Season
Weekday:	$7.00	—	6:00 am - 6:00 pm
Weekend:	$7.00	—	6:00 am - 6:00 pm
Cart Fees:	—	—	
Club Rental: No			

Notes: Pull carts only on this course. There is a small surcharge for non-residents. There are teaching clinics throughout the year, including the winter.

Middle Island Country Club

Middle Island NY — (516)924-5100

Directions: 495 to Exit 66. Take County Rd 101 (Yaphank Rd) north. Road forks in Yaphank. Bear to the right at the fork. This is Main Street. Go 1/4 mile to another fork and bear left (Middle Island -Yapank Rd). The course is on the right about 1.5 mi.

Holes	Par	Yards Back Tees	Rating	Slope
9	36	3461	71.9	126
9	36	3473	71.9	126
9	36	3554	71.9	126

Facility Type: Semi-private

	9 Holes	18 Holes	Hours Mid Season
Weekday:	$10.00	$20.00	6:30 am - Dusk
Weekend:	$12.50	$25.00	1:00 pm - Dusk *
Cart Fees:	$12.50	$25.00	

Club Pro: Mike Wands
Discounts: None
Tee Times: No, 1st come basis.

Mandatory Cart Rental: See notes.
Club Rental: Yes

Features: Lessons, Showers/Lockers, Practice Area, Pro Shop - Complete, Clubhouse, Restaurant, Bar, Snack Bar, Banquet Facilities

Notes: * Weekends until 1pm reserved for seasonal list of players. Carts are mandatory on weekends until 2 pm from April 13 to Oct 13.

Description: A beautifully landscaped course, it was designed by a professional landscaper whose estate it was converted from. The "Spruce" 9 is the longest and flattest. "Dogleg" and "Oak" are tight and tougher. Play in any combination.

Mohansic Golf Course

Yorktown Hts NY — Info: (914)962-4049 Tee Times: (914)962-4065

Directions: Taconic Parkway Southbound to Baldwin Rd Exit in Yorktown Hts. Going North, cross over the highway from the same exit.

Holes	Par	Yards Back Tees	Rating	Slope
18	70	6550	69.8	118

Facility Type: Public

	9 Holes	18 Holes	Hours Mid Season
Weekday:	—	$35.00	7:00 am - 7:00 pm
Weekend:	—	$40.00	5:30 am - 7:00 pm
Cart Fees:	—	$19.05	

Club Pro: John Paonessa
Discounts: Seniors, Juniors, Twilight
Tee Times: Yes, 1 week in person

Mandatory Cart Rental: No
Club Rental: Yes

Features: Lessons, Showers/Lockers, Driving Range, Practice Area, Pro Shop - Complete, Clubhouse, Restaurant, Bar, Snack Bar

Notes: County residents pay $11 weekdays and $14 weekends for 18 holes.

Description: The site of the Pro Am, this course is a good mix of holes and fairways. The course is hilly and the greens are manicured. The signature hole is the 443 yd par 4 #4, a dogleg left with a left-to-right sloping fairway. The approach shot is to a well-guarded, elevated and narrow green with a long iron.

Mohonk Golf Course

1000 Mountain Rest Rd, New Paltz NY — (914)256-2154

Directions: NY Thruway to New Paltz, Exit 18. Take Rte 299 through New Paltz and follow signs to the course.

Facility Type: Public

Club Pro: None
Discounts: None
Tee Times: No

Features: Practice Area, Pro Shop - Complete, Snack Bar, Lodging Nearby, Banquet Facilities, Restaurant, VISA/MC

Description: A hilly course with marker flags on 2, 6 and 9. Carved out of the woods, the course is fairly challenging. Greens are in good shape. The signature hole is the 1st, a par 3, 185 yd. Your shots are around a massive ash to an elevated two trapped green, behind which sits one of the oldest club houses in the country. Don't be surprised with a bogey.

Holes	Par	Yards Back Tees	Rating	Slope
9	35	2569	—	—

	9 Holes	18 Holes	Hours Mid Season
Weekday:	$7.50	$11.00	7:30 am - Dusk
Weekend:	$8.50	$13.00	7:00 am - Dusk
Cart Fees:	$10.50	$18.00	

Mandatory Cart Rental: No
Club Rental: Yes

Notes: A weekday special before noon.

Monroe Country Club

Still Rd, Monroe NY 10950 — (914)783-9045

Directions: NY Thruway to Harriman Exit. After the toll, take the 1st exit, Rte 131. Make a left off of the exit onto Rte 17-32. At the 2nd light, the junction of 32 and 17M, make a horseshoe right onto 17M North. Make a left at the 1st light, Still Rd, and the course is on the right.

Facility Type: Semi-private

Club Pro: Bob Trueslow
Discounts: Twilight, Seniors
Tee Times: No

Features: Lessons, Showers/Lockers, Practice Area, Pro Shop - Complete, Clubhouse, Restaurant, Bar, Banquet Facilities, Lodging Nearby

Description: This is a somewhat challenging course in good condition. The greens are in excellent shape and they undulate. There are no straight putts on any of them. The terrain is hilly, and the fairways are fairly wide. # 8 is the signature. It's a par 4, 298 yard relatively easy shot to the green, but this green will keep you from parring.

Holes	Par	Yards Back Tees	Rating	Slope
9dt	70	5458	65.7	109

	9 Holes	18 Holes	Hours Mid Season
Weekday:	—	$16.00	8:00 am - Dusk
Weekend:	—	$22.00	2:00 pm - Dusk *
Cart Fees:	—	$24.00	

Mandatory Cart Rental: No
Club Rental: Yes

Notes: * Weekends before 2 pm reserved for members. Senior special on Thursday.

Montauk Downs State Park

South Fairview Ave, Montauk NY — (516)668-5000

Directions: 495 to Exit 70. Take 101 south to 27 West to the end of Long Island and the Village of Montauk. Make a left on West Lake Dr and go 1/4 mi. to Fairview and make another left to the course.

Holes	Par	Yards Back Tees	Rating	Slope
18	72	6762	73.3	133

	9 Holes	18 Holes	Hours Mid Season
Weekday:	—	$14.00	6:00 am - 7:00 pm
Weekend:	—	$16.00	6:00 am - 7:00 pm
Cart Fees:	—	$22.00	

Facility Type: Public

Club Pro: Kevin Smith
Discounts: Twilight
Tee Times: No

Mandatory Cart Rental: No
Club Rental: No

Features: Showers/Lockers, Driving Range, Practice Area, Pro Shop - Complete, Clubhouse, Restaurant, Bar, Snack Bar, Banquet Facilities

Description: Rated one of the top public courses in the country, it was a Golf Digest pick for "Places to Play" in both '90 and '91. This Robert Trent Jones design is a true links-type and a pretty challenging course. #12 is a good example. It's a 215 yd par 3 blind tee shot to a dogleg over a gorge.

Mosholu Golf Course
NY 70

Jerome and Bainbridge Ave, Bronx NY — Tee Times: (212)655-9164

Directions: North on Major Deegan to Exit 13, East 233rd. Right at 1st light onto Jerome Ave and right at 1st light to course. Going South on Deegan exit at East 233rd St and turn right at the 2nd light. Manhattan golfers can get to the course on the #4 train. Get off at last stop,. the Woodlawn Station.

Holes	Par	Yards Back Tees	Rating	Slope
9dt	71	6236	70.6	124

	9 Holes	18 Holes	Hours Mid Season
Weekday:	$9.00	$13.50	6:15 am - 9:00 pm
Weekend:	$11.50	$15.50	6:15 am - 9:00 pm
Cart Fees:	$11.00	$21.00	

Facility Type: Public

Club Pro: Brian Fitzpatrick
Discounts: Seniors, Juniors, Twilight
Tee Times: Yes, 5 days prior for weekends/holidays

Mandatory Cart Rental: No
Club Rental: Yes

Features: Lessons, Showers/Lockers, Driving Range, Practice Area, Snack Bar, VISA/MC, Pro Shop - Limited, Clubhouse

Description: A narrow course that requires accuracy. The driving range stays open until 9.

Nevele Golf Course

Ellenville NY — Tee Times: (914)647-6000 ext 643

Directions: Rte 17 to Exit 113 to 209 North. Follow signs to course.

Facility Type: Resort

Coupon page 200

Club Pro: Jack Breno
Discounts: None
Tee Times: Yes, 2 weeks prior for any day.

Features: Lessons, Showers/Lockers, Driving Range, Practice Area, Pro Shop - Complete, Restaurant, Bar, Snack Bar, Banquet Facilities, Lodging Nearby, American Express, VISA/MC

Description: This course was redesigned by Tom Fazio. It was a pick by Golf Digest in '90 and '91 for "Places to Play". It is a challenging course with a particularly interesting 18th hole right along a lake. The 16th is another challenge. From the blue tee, you must carry 215 over water.

Holes	Par	Yards Back Tees	Rating	Slope
18	70	6500	71.9	128

	9 Holes	18 Holes	Hours Mid Season
Weekday:	—	$25.00	7:00 am - 7:00 pm
Weekend:	—	$30.00	6:30 am - 7:00 pm
Cart Fees:	$13.00	$26.00	

Mandatory Cart Rental: No
Club Rental: Yes

New Paltz Golf Course

215 Huguenot St, New Paltz NY — (914)255-8282

Directions: NY Thruway to the New Paltz Exit. Go West on Rte 299 into New Paltz. Just before crossing the bridge take a right on Huguenot St. Go 1.3 miles and the course is on the left.

Facility Type: Public

Club Pro: Larry Furey
Discounts: Seniors
Tee Times: No

Features: Lessons, Driving Range, Practice Area, Pro Shop - Complete, Restaurant, Bar, Clubhouse, Banquet Facilities, Lodging Nearby

Description: This course is tougher than it sounds. It is flat with swamps and long holes. The match-breaker is the 8th hole, a 200 yd par 3. Your carry off the tee is 170 yds over water to the right side, since the left is treed. The green is contoured - and to distract you, the view is magnificent.

Holes	Par	Yards Back Tees	Rating	Slope
9	36	3450	73.0	126

	9 Holes	18 Holes	Hours Mid Season
Weekday:	$8.00	$11.00	6:30 am - Dusk
Weekend:	$12.00	$17.00	6:00 am - Dusk
Cart Fees:	$12.00	$18.00	

Mandatory Cart Rental: No
Club Rental: Yes

N. Woodmere Park GC

N. Woodmere NY — (516)791-7705

Directions: Southern St Pkwy to Exit 19. South on Peninsula Blvd, take right on Branch in Woodmere. Course is 1 mi. on left.

Facility Type: Executive

Club Pro: None
Discounts: Seniors
Tee Times: No

Features: Driving Range, Practice Area

Description: Flat and short and an easy walk.

Holes	Par	Yards Back Tees	Rating	Slope
9	31	2285	—	—

	9 Holes	18 Holes	Hours Mid Season
Weekday:	$ 16.00	—	Dawn - Dusk *
Weekend:	$18.00	—	Dawn - Dusk
Cart Fees:	—	—	
Club Rental:			

Notes: * The course is closed Thursdays. Residents pay $7 and $8. The driving range is separate and pro shop is at driving range. The pro shop/dr # is 516 791 8100.

Northport Vet. Mem. Hosp GC

Northport NY — (516)261-4400

Directions: 495 to Exit 54. Take Sunken Meadow-Sagtikos Pkwy North to the end. Make a left onto Rte 25 going West about 2.5 mi. At Ronaldo Rd, take a left to course.

Facility Type: Public

Club Pro: None
Discounts: Twilight
Tee Times: No

Features: Pro Shop - Limited

Description: A scenic little course. It is hilly with small greens.

Holes	Par	Yards Back Tees	Rating	Slope
9	34	4694	—	—

	9 Holes	18 Holes	Hours Mid Season
Weekday:	—	$7.50	7:00 am - Dusk
Weekend:	—	$8.50	7:00 am - Dusk
Cart Fees:	—	—	

Mandatory Cart Rental: No
Club Rental: No

Otterkill Golf & Country Club NY 75

Otter Rd, Campbell Hall NY — (914)427-2301

Directions: Rte 17 to Goshen and Rte 207 North. Go approximately 8 m, and take a left onto Otter Rd and go 1/2 mi. to the course. Or take Rte 208 South off of I-84 in Maybrook. 3/4 mi. past Maybrook take a right on Otter Rd and proceed to the course.

Facility Type: Semi-private

Coupon page 200

Club Pro: Ron Reed
Discounts: None
Tee Times: No, good idea to call ahead, though.

Features: Lessons, Showers/Lockers, Driving Range, Practice Area, Pro Shop - Complete, Clubhouse, Restaurant, Bar, Banquet Facilities, Lodging Nearby

Description: A flat to rolling terrain, this course is fairly wide open but deceptively challenging. The best example of this is #15, a 414 yd par 4. It offers a dogleg right with sand left and right and out-of-bounds all along the left. The pear-shaped green is protected by a tree, water and two traps.

Holes	Par	Yards Back Tees	Rating	Slope
18	72	6800	71.6	128

	9 Holes	18 Holes	Hours Mid Season
Weekday:	—	$25.00	7:30 am - Dusk *
Weekend:	—	—	
Cart Fees:	—	$10.00	

Mandatory Cart Rental: No
Club Rental: Yes

Notes: * Open to the public Monday, Tuesday, and Thursday only.

Oyster Bay Golf Course NY 76

Southwoods Rd, Woodbury NY — (516)364-3977

Directions: 495 to Exit 42 North (Seaford-Oyster Bay Expressway) to Rte 25E. At the 3rd light take a left onto Southwoods Rd to the course.

Facility Type: Public

Club Pro: Gene Miller
Discounts: Twilight, Seniors, Juniors
Tee Times: No

Features: Lessons, Showers/Lockers, Driving Range, Practice Area, Pro Shop - Complete, Clubhouse, Restaurant, Bar, Snack Bar, Banquet Facilities

Description: This is an extremely tight and hilly course with undulating greens. It's a Tom Fazio design and was a Golf Digest pick for "Places to Play" in '90 and '91. The course and club house were created from an old estate. The 4th hole is a favorite. It's a 415 yard par 4 and requires very tight shots to an elevated, undulating and well trapped green.

Holes	Par	Yards Back Tees	Rating	Slope
18	70	6351	72.6	129

	9 Holes	18 Holes	Hours Mid Season
Weekday:	—	$40.00	6:30 am - 5:30 pm *
Weekend:	—	$50.00	6:30 am - 5:30 pm
Cart Fees:	—	$40.00	

Mandatory Cart Rental: No
Club Rental: Yes

Notes: * The course is closed on Mondays.

Pehquenakonck Country Club

North Salem NY — (914)669-9380

Directions: Rte 684 North to Exit 8 (Hardscrabble Rd). Turn right onto Harscrabble and go 2 miles to the end. Take a left, go 1/4 mi. and take the 1st right, Bloomer Rd. The course is 1/4 mi. on the left at 2 stone pillars.

Facility Type: Semi-private

Coupon page 201

Club Pro: None
Discounts: Twilight, Juniors
Tee Times: Yes

Features: Pro Shop - Limited, Clubhouse, Snack Bar, Lessons, Showers/Lockers

Description: This course is undergoing constant improvements. The greens are in magnificent shape. The terrain is very hilly, to the point where carts are recommded. It's a short course, but extremely challenging. #4 is a good example. It's a 115 yd par 3, all uphill to a green surrounded by trees and traps.

Holes	Par	Yards Back Tees	Rating	Slope
9dt	66	4458	61.0	95

	9 Holes	18 Holes	Hours Mid Season
Weekday:	—	$15.00	8:00 am - Dusk
Weekend:	—	$19.00	7:00 am - Dusk
Cart Fees:	—	$22.00	

Mandatory Cart Rental: No
Club Rental: Yes

Notes: Memberships are available for very reasonable rates. Call for the weekday special, 8:00 am to 2:00 pm. Ladies day is Wednesday.

Pelham & Split Rock GC

870 Shore Rd, Bronx NY — **Info:** (212)885-1258 **Tee Times:** 718 225 GOLF

Directions: I-95 (New England Thruway) to Exit 8B (Orchard Beach/City Island). Take Pelham Pkwy East to the traffic circle. Or take the Hutchinson River Parkway to the City Island Exit and proceed to the traffic circle. From the traffic circle take Shore Rd North to the course on the left. There are signs for the course at the circle.

Facility Type: Public

Coupon page 201

Club Pro: Tim Trelease
Discounts: Twilight
Tee Times: Yes, 7 days for weekdays, 10 days for weekends. There is a $2 charge for reservations.

Features: Lessons, Showers/Lockers, Practice Area, Pro Shop - Complete, Clubhouse, Snack Bar, VISA/MC, Lodging Nearby

Description: The Pelham course is fairly wide open, but a good test of golf. The Split Rock course is tighter and harder. The 15th, 16th and 17th on Split Rock have been nicknamed "Amen Corner". Both courses are well maintained.

Holes	Par	Yards Back Tees	Rating	Slope
18	70	6405	69.1	113
18	70	6585	70.0	115

	9 Holes	18 Holes	Hours Mid Season
Weekday:	—	$13.50	Dawn - Dusk
Weekend:	—	$15.50	Dawn - Dusk
Cart Fees:	—	$21.00	

Mandatory Cart Rental: No
Club Rental: Yes

Notes: Inquire about tournament packages.

Peninsula Golf Course

50 Nassau Rd, Massepequa NY — (516)798-9776

Directions: Southern State Pkwy to Exit 30. Go South on Broadway. Make a left on Merrick Rd and right on Unqua Rd to the circle and course.

Facility Type: Semi-private

Club Pro: George Tavalaro
Discounts: Twilight
Tee Times: No
Features: Lessons, Practice Area, Pro Shop - Complete, Clubhouse, Restaurant, Bar, Snack Bar, Banquet Facilities, Lodging Nearby

Description: This is a flat and wide-open course that plays long. The course looks easy, but it's deceptive. The greens are in great shape. A club favorite is the #5, a 410 yard par 4 that hits to a narrow approach and a 2-tiered green that slopes up from the back. The 2nd hole is a favorite challenge of the pro. It's a 440 yard par 4.

Holes	Par	Yards Back Tees	Rating	Slope
9	37	3272	71.5	123

	9 Holes	18 Holes	Hours Mid Season
Weekday:	—	$14.00	6:00 am - 6:30 pm
Weekend:	—	$16.00	6:00 am - 6:30 pm *
Cart Fees:	—	$20.00	

Mandatory Cart Rental: No
Club Rental: Yes

Notes: * Closed to non-members Sunday before 12 pm. Cart rental is for 2. Twilight at 5 midseason.

Philip J Rotella Municipal GC

Theills-Mt Ivy Rd, Thiells NY —   **Tee Times:** (914)354-1616

Directions: Palisades Parkway North to Exit 13. Go left onto Thiells-Mt Ivy Rd and 1 mile to the course on the left. Going South on the Parkway exit at Rte 202. Take a left at the exit and another left at the light onto Thiellls/Mt Ivy Rd. The course is 1 mile on the left.

Facility Type: Public

Club Pro: Howard Pierson
Discounts: Twilight
Tee Times: Yes, Wednesday before for weekends

Features: Lessons, Showers/Lockers, Driving Range, Practice Area, Pro Shop - Complete, Restaurant, Bar, Snack Bar

Description: The front 9 is tough, with a little water. #2 is a good example. It's a 604 yard par 5 that tees off out of a chute to a fairway that is out-of-bounds left and right and has two slight doglegs to a two-tiered green. The back 9 softens a bit.

Holes	Par	Yards Back Tees	Rating	Slope
18	72	6502	71.4	126

	9 Holes	18 Holes	Hours Mid Season
Weekday:	$11.00	$18.00	6:30 am - Dusk
Weekend:	$15.00	$25.00	6:00 am - Dusk
Cart Fees:	$12.00	$18.00	

Mandatory Cart Rental: No
Club Rental: Yes

Pine Hills Country Club NY 81

162 Wading River Rd, Manorville NY — Tee Times: (516)878-4343

Directions: 495 to Exit 69. The course is 1 mi. South on Wading River Rd on the right.

Holes	Par	Yards Back Tees	Rating	Slope
18	72	6899	72.2	121

Facility Type: Public

Club Pro: Jimmi Conway
Discounts: None
Tee Times: Yes, $20 for the season. 24 hr tee time $5 in addition to green fees. Otherwise first come.

	9 Holes	18 Holes	Hours Mid Season
Weekday:	$12.00	$18.00	6:00 am - 7:00 pm
Weekend:	$14.00	$22.00	6:00 am - 7:00 pm
Cart Fees:	$14.00	$24.00	

Mandatory Cart Rental: No
Club Rental: No

Features: Lessons, Showers/Lockers, Driving Range, Practice Area, Pro Shop - Complete, Clubhouse, Restaurant, Bar, Snack Bar, Lodging Nearby

Notes: Saturday until 2 and Sunday until 1 is reserved for members. 9 hole play only after 1 pm.

Description: This is a fun course. It appears easy but subtle breaks make it harder. The 4th is a good example. It's a 402 yd par 4 dogleg left with 2 fairway bunkers, ob left and 2 green side bunkers. It's a well-maintained and irrigated course.

Pines Hotel Golf Course NY 82

South Fallsburg NY — Tee Times: (914)434-6000 ext 1584

Directions: Rte 17 to Exit 107 to Rte 42 North into Fallsburg. Follow signs to the hotel.

Holes	Par	Yards Back Tees	Rating	Slope
9	32	2330	30.1	—

Facility Type: Resort

Coupon page 201

Club Pro: Tom DuPlessis
Discounts: Twilight
Tee Times: Yes, 3 days ahead for any day.

	9 Holes	18 Holes	Hours Mid Season
Weekday:	—	$8.00	7:00 am - 6:00 pm
Weekend:	—	$11.00	7:00 am - 6:00 pm
Cart Fees:	$10.00	$20.00	

Mandatory Cart Rental: No
Club Rental: Yes

Features: Lessons, Practice Area, Pro Shop - Complete, Restaurant, Bar, VISA/MC, Driving Range, Showers/Lockers, Banquet Facilities, Lodging Nearby

Notes: The driving range is a practice area hitting into net. Memberships are available.

Description: A Robert Trent Jones design, it offers a challenge for the experienced player, but won't overwhelm the novice. The most challenging hole, number 6 is a par 4, 375 yard dogleg left where the player must hit an accurate tee shot to a sloping fairway, leaving an 8 or 9 iron shot to a well-bunkered green.

Pound Ridge Country Club

Pound Ridge NY — (914)764-5771

Directions: Merritt Pkwy to Exit 35 (High Ridge Rd). Go North 5 miles to the course.

Holes	Par	Yards Back Tees	Rating	Slope
9	35	3000	66.9	112

Facility Type: Semi-private

Club Pro: Mike DiBuono
Discounts: None
Tee Times: No

	9 Holes	18 Holes	Hours Mid Season
Weekday:	$12.00	$20.00	8:00 am - Dusk
Weekend:	$15.00	$29.00	2:00 pm - 6:00 pm *
Cart Fees:	$12.00	$22.00	

Features: Lessons, Driving Range, Practice Area, Pro Shop - Complete, Clubhouse

Mandatory Cart Rental: No
Club Rental: Yes

Description: This course is in good shape. It's well-bunkered, features some side-of-hill lies, and has small elevated greens.

Notes: Closed to non-members weekends before 2 pm.

Poxabogue Golf Course

Wainscott NY — (516)537-0025

Directions: Montauk Highway (Rte 27) in Bridge-hampton.

Holes	Par	Yards Back Tees	Rating	Slope
9	30	1706	—	—

Facility Type: Public

Club Pro: Bob Vishno
Discounts: None
Tee Times: No

	9 Holes	18 Holes	Hours Mid Season
Weekday:	$7.00	$10.50	7:00 am - 6:00 pm
Weekend:	$ 9.00	$13.50	7:00 am - 6:00 pm
Cart Fees:	—	—	
Club Rental:	Yes		

Features: Lessons, Driving Range, Pro Shop - Limited, Restaurant

Notes: Weekend rates apply on Friday. There is a complete driving range at this facility.

Description: This is a well attended course and good for beginners and those just catching up.

Putnam Golf Club

Hill Street, Mahopac NY — Tee Times: (914)628-3451

Directions: Taconic Pkwy to Rte 6, Mahopac-Shrub Oak Exit. Make a right at the light and stay on Rte 6 to 6N. Go left on 6N and approx 3.3 mi. turn left onto Hill Street. Go 1/2 mi. to the club on the left.

Facility Type: Public

Club Pro: Frank Misarti
Discounts: Juniors, Seniors
Tee Times: Yes, 1 week in advance for weekends/holidays only.

Features: Lessons, Showers/Lockers, Practice Area, Pro Shop - Complete, Clubhouse, Snack Bar, Banquet Facilities, Restaurant, Bar

Description: This is a rolling and fairly forgiving course. It is well-maintained with excellent greens.

Holes	Par	Yards Back Tees	Rating	Slope
18	71	6774	72.1	131

	9 Holes	18 Holes	Hours Mid Season
Weekday:	—	—	7:30 am - Dusk
Weekend:	—	—	5:30 am - Dusk
Cart Fees:	—	—	

Mandatory Cart Rental: No
Club Rental: Yes

Notes: Call for green and cart fees. 9 hole play weekdays only after 4.

Red Hook Golf Club

Red Hook NY — Tee Times: (914)758-8652

Directions: Taconic Pkwy, take the Exit for Red Hook. Take Rte 199 West 3 mi. to the light and bear right. This is still Rte 199. The course is 1/2 mi. on the left.

Facility Type: Semi-private

Club Pro: None
Discounts: None
Tee Times: Yes, 1 day for weekends

Features: Showers/Lockers, Practice Area, Pro Shop - Complete, Clubhouse, Restaurant, Bar, Banquet Facilities, Lodging Nearby

Description: This is one of the nicest courses in the Hudson Valley. It has a rolling terrain with wide fairways and room for recovery, but it also offers some challenges. One is the #7, 418 yard par 4. It's a drive into an opening in the trees on an undulating fairway to an elevated green trapped on 2 sides. Drainage on this course is excellent and the condition of the course is always superb.

Holes	Par	Yards Back Tees	Rating	Slope
9dt	70	5529	67.0	121

	9 Holes	18 Holes	Hours Mid Season
Weekday:	$10.00	$16.00	8:00 am - Dusk *
Weekend:	$12.00	$20.00	2:00 pm - Dusk *
Cart Fees:	$10.00	$20.00	

Mandatory Cart Rental: No
Club Rental: No

Notes: * Closed to non-members Monday before 12 pm and weekends before 2 pm. The management is actively pursuing plans to add another 18. Memberships are available.

Robt Moses Golf Course

Babylon NY — (516)669-0449

Directions: Southern State Pkwy to Exit 40. Go south and follow signs to Field #2 in Park.

Holes	Par	Yards Back Tees	Rating	Slope
18	56	—	—	—

Facility Type: Pitch & Putt

	9 Holes	18 Holes	Hours Mid Season
Weekday:	—	$3.00	7:00 am - 5:00 pm
Weekend:	—	$3.00	7:00 am - 5:00 pm
Cart Fees:	—	—	

Club Pro: None
Discounts: Seniors
Tee Times:

Rock Hill Golf Course

105 Clancy Rd, Manorville NY — **Tee Times:** (516)878-2250

Directions: 495 to Exit 70 South to the 1st light. Take a right onto Chapman Blvd. Go1.5 mi. to Clancy Rd and take a left to the course.

Holes	Par	Yards Back Tees	Rating	Slope
18	72	7050	73.7	128

Facility Type: Semi-private

	9 Holes	18 Holes	Hours Mid Season
Weekday:	—	$18.00	6:30 am - Dusk
Weekend:	—	$23.00	11:00 am - Dusk*
Cart Fees:	—	$25.00	

Club Pro: George Cosgrove
Discounts: Seniors, Twilight
Tee Times: Yes, 1 week ahead. Memberships available for weekend mornings.

Mandatory Cart Rental: See notes.
Club Rental: Yes

Features: Lessons, Driving Range, Practice Area, Pro Shop - Complete, Clubhouse, Restaurant, Bar

Notes: * Closed to non-members before 11 am on weekends. Carts mandatory only with tee times and only on weekends.

Description: This is a hilly course. The 8th hole is the highest spot on Long Island. It is also pretty, with tree-lined fairways and water on 4 holes. The greens are of average size and in great shape. #18 is a tough finishing hole. The course was designed by Frank Duanne.

Rockland St Pk Golf Course

Congers NY — Tee Times: (914)268-7275

Directions: Palisades Pkwy going north to Exit 4. At the 1st light take a left onto 9w and go 12 mi. to course on the right.

Facility Type: Public

Club Pro: Billy Osetek
Discounts: Seniors
Tee Times: Yes, Thursday before 12 for weekends

Features: Lessons, Showers/Lockers, Driving Range, Practice Area, Pro Shop - Complete, Snack Bar

Description: The North is a championship course - very challenging. It is long, hilly and tree-lined, easier in the summer when fairways are drier. The South is an executive course.

Holes	Par	Yards Back Tees	Rating	Slope
18	54	2780	—	—
18	72	6864	72.0	125

	9 Holes	18 Holes	Hours Mid Season
Weekday:	$8.00	$14.00	7:00 am - 8:00 pm
Weekend:	$9.00	$16.00	6:00 am - 8:00 pm
Cart Fees:	$11.00	$20.00	

Mandatory Cart Rental: No
Club Rental: Yes

Notes: Prices for the South course are $5 and $6 for 9 and $8 and $10 for 18. Cart fees for the South are $10 and $15.

Rondout Country Club

Accord NY — (914)626-2513

Directions: NY Thruway to Exit 19 (Kingston). Take Rte 28 West to Rte 209 South. Travel approximately 20 minutes, and the course is on the right.

Facility Type: Semi-private

Coupon page 202

Club Pro: John Deforest
Discounts: None
Tee Times: No, suggested to call ahead. Members have preference.

Features: Lessons, Showers/Lockers, Driving Range, Practice Area, Pro Shop - Complete, Clubhouse, Restaurant, Bar, Banquet Facilities, American Express, VISA/MC, Lodging Nearby

Description: This is a scenic and rolling course nestled in a valley. It offers a decent challenge for any golfer. The grass is always in good shape. #4 is the signature, a 554 yd par 5. It's a dogleg left with a bunker right as the fairway slopes off on both sides into water. More water challenges the 3rd shot right and left and the green is long and narrow with trees overhanging.

Holes	Par	Yards Back Tees	Rating	Slope
18	72	6468	72.0	128

	9 Holes	18 Holes	Hours Mid Season
Weekday:	$12.00	$22.00	7:00 am - 7:00 pm
Weekend:	$14.00	$24.00	7:00 am - 7:00 pm
Cart Fees:	—	—	

Mandatory Cart Rental: Yes
Club Rental: Yes

Notes: Cart fees are included. Tennis courts also on the facility. Memberships are available.

Sag Harbor Golf Course

Golf Club Rd, Sag Harbor NY — (516)725-9739

Directions: South of Sag Harbor on Rte 114. Look for Dept Of Environmental Conservation sign.

Holes	Par	Yards Back Tees	Rating	Slope
9	36	3012	—	—

Facility Type: Public

	9 Holes	18 Holes	Hours Mid Season
Weekday:	—	$5.00	8:30 am - 4:30 pm
Weekend:	—	$10.00	8:30 am - 4:30 pm
Cart Fees:	—	—	
Club Rental:	No		

Club Pro: Bill Boeklen
Discounts: None
Tee Times: No

Features: Pro Shop - Limited, Snack Bar

Notes: Memberships are available.

Description: The course is on a nature preserve. The bugs have been known to carry balls away. This is a good course for beginners and the weekend hacker. Sand greens were upgraded to grass.

Sandy Pond Golf Course

Roanoke Ave, Riverhead NY — (516)727-0909

Directions: Take the last Exit on 495. Go to the traffic circle 2 mi. from the end of 495 and go North from circle. The course is 1/2 mile on the left.

Holes	Par	Yards Back Tees	Rating	Slope
9	27	1120	—	—

Facility Type: Executive

	9 Holes	18 Holes	Hours Mid Season
Weekday:	$4.00	—	Dawn - Dusk
Weekend:	$5.00	—	Dawn - Dusk
Cart Fees:	$1.00	—	
Club Rental:	Yes		

Club Pro: None
Discounts: Seniors
Tee Times: No

Features: Practice Area, Pro Shop - Limited, Lessons

Saxon Woods Golf Course

Old Mamaroneck Rd, Scarsdale NY — (914)725-3814

Directions: Hutchinson River Pkwy to Exit 22. The course is directly off the exit.

Facility Type: Public

Club Pro: Anthony Masciolo
Discounts: Twilight
Tee Times: Yes, in person 1 week prior

Features: Lessons, Showers/Lockers, Practice Area, Pro Shop - Complete, Clubhouse, Restaurant, Bar, Snack Bar

Description: This claims to be the toughest public course in Westchester. It was designed by Tillinghast, who designed Bethpage among others, in 1933. The course is wooded, tight with tree-lined fairways and has small greens. It demands accuracy. The fairways are watered, and the course is in good condition.

Holes	Par	Yards Back Tees	Rating	Slope
18	71	6485	70.2	119

	9 Holes	18 Holes	Hours Mid Season
Weekday:	—	$35.00	7:00 am - Dusk
Weekend:	—	$40.00	Dawn - Dusk
Cart Fees:	—	$20.00	

Mandatory Cart Rental: No
Club Rental: No

Notes: County residents pay $11 weekdays and $14 weekends for 18.

Scotts Corners Golf Course

Montgomery NY — (914)457-9141

Directions: I-84 to Exit 5. Go North on 208. The course is 2.5 mi. on the left.

Coupon page 202

Facility Type: Public

Club Pro: None
Discounts: Seniors, Juniors, Twilight
Tee Times: No

Features: Lessons, Practice Area, Pro Shop - Complete, Snack Bar, VISA/MC

Description: Flat and wide, this course is especially good for seniors. The course has the only swing training machine in the county.

Holes	Par	Yards Back Tees	Rating	Slope
9dt	72	6079	67.6	105

	9 Holes	18 Holes	Hours Mid Season
Weekday:	—	$10.00	7:00 am - Dusk
Weekend:	—	$13.00	6:00 am - Dusk
Cart Fees:	$10.00	$18.00	

Mandatory Cart Rental: No
Club Rental: Yes

Notes: This is a double tee course.

Shawangunk Country Club

Ellenville NY — Tee Times: (914)647-6090

Directions: Rte 17 to Exit 113. North on 209 to Ellenville. Follow signs to club.

Holes	Par	Yards Back Tees	Rating	Slope
9dt	68	5621	67.1	118

Facility Type: Semi-private

	9 Holes	18 Holes	Hours Mid Season
Weekday:	$8.00	$12.00	8:00 am - Dusk
Weekend:	$10.00	$15.00	7:00 am- Dusk
Cart Fees:	$12.00	$21.00	

Club Pro: John Durcan
Discounts: Twilight
Tee Times: Yes, 24 hours ahead for non-members

Mandatory Cart Rental: No
Club Rental: Yes

Features: Lessons, Showers/Lockers, Practice Area, Pro Shop - Complete, Clubhouse, Restaurant, Bar, Snack Bar, Banquet Facilities, Lodging Nearby

Description: A picturesque course, always a shallenge and always in good shape with tee to green irrigation. The course is slightly hilly.

Shelter Island Country Club

Sunnyside Ave, Shelter Island Hieghts NY — (516)749-0416 T

Directions: Rte 114 North on Shelter Island to the Mobil Station. Continue on Chase, up the hill, make a left at the top and follow the signs.

Holes	Par	Yards Back Tees	Rating	Slope
9	33	2512	63.8	107

Facility Type: Public

	9 Holes	18 Holes	Hours Mid Season
Weekday:	$10.00	$16.00	7:00 am - Dusk
Weekend:	$10.00	$16.00	7:00 am - Dusk
Cart Fees:	$10.00	$16.00	

Club Pro: None
Discounts: Juniors
Tee Times: No

Mandatory Cart Rental: No
Club Rental: Yes

Features: Pro Shop - Limited, Practice Area, Snack Bar

Description: A hilly and challenging little course with great views from the club house.

Silver Lake Golf Course

915 Victory Blvd, Staten Island NY — Info: (718)447-5686   Tee Times: 718 225 GOLF

Directions: Verranzano Bridge to the Staten Island Expressway. Exit at Clove Road. Take the service road to the 3rd light (Clove Rd) and go right. Turn right at the 3rd light, Victory Blvd, and the course is on left. From NJ, take the Richmond Rd Exit from the Staten Isl Expressway. Take a left at the1st light, Clove Rd. Take a right at the 4th light, Victory Blvd, to the course.

Facility Type: Public

Club Pro: None
Discounts: Twilight
Tee Times: Yes, 7 days for weekdays and 10 days for weekends. There is a $2 reservation charge.

Features: Lessons, Showers/Lockers, Practice Area, Pro Shop - Complete, Clubhouse, Restaurant, VISA/MC

Description: This is a fun course with something for every golfer. #3 is a favorite. It's a par 3, 233 yd shot off an elevated tee over a gorge.

Holes	Par	Yards Back Tees	Rating	Slope
18	69	6050	66.7	114

	9 Holes	18 Holes	Hours Mid Season
Weekday:	—	$13.50	Dawn - Dusk
Weekend:	—	$15.50	Dawn - Dusk
Cart Fees:	—	$21.00	

Mandatory Cart Rental: No
Club Rental: Yes

Notes: Inquire about tournament packages.

Coupon page 202

Smithtown Landing GC

495 Landing Ave, Smithtown NY — (516)360-7618

Directions: 495 to Exit 53 North, Sunken Meadow Parkway. Take it to Exit 4 East, Pulaski Road. Take Pulaski to the end and a right on Main St. Go 1.5 miles to a Gulf Station on left. Road forks. Go straight onto Rose Street. At the end of Rose make a left to the course.

Facility Type: Semi-private

Club Pro: Rick Nielson
Discounts: None
Tee Times: No

Features: Lessons, Driving Range, Practice Area, Pro Shop - Complete, Clubhouse, Bar, Snack Bar, Banquet Facilities, Lodging Nearby

Description: This is a scenic course with a private club atmosphere. It is hilly, tight, well-bunkered and has small greens. The accent is on accuracy. The course is well maintained. The club has an additional 9 hole executive coarse and a driving range.

Holes	Par	Yards Back Tees	Rating	Slope
9	27	1143	—	—
18	72	6786	72.9	129

	9 Holes	18 Holes	Hours Mid Season
Weekday:	$9.00	$18.00	6:30 am - 6:00 pm *
Weekend:	—	—	
Cart Fees:	$12.00	$22.00	

Mandatory Cart Rental: No
Club Rental: No

Notes: * The course is closed on Mondays, and closed to non-residents on weekends. The above rates are for non-residents of Smithtown. Weekend play is reserved for residents only.

South Shore Golf Course   NY 99

200 Huguenot Ave, Staten Island NY — Info: (718)984-0101   Tee Times: 718 225 GOLF

Directions: Staten Island Expressway to the West Shore Expressway. Exit at #4 (Arthur Kill) to a full stop. Go left onto Arthur Kill under the highway and right on Huguenot. The course is on the right.

Coupon page 203

Facility Type: Public

Club Pro: Mario Rapaglia
Discounts: Seniors, Juniors, Twilight
Tee Times: Yes, recommended up to two weeks for weekends.

Features: Lessons, Showers/Lockers, Practice Area, Pro Shop - Complete, Clubhouse, Restaurant, Bar, Snack Bar, Banquet Facilities, VISA/MC, Lodging Nearby

Description: This is a semi-rolling course. It is tight, challenging and pretty. #16 might be called the signature. It's a 388 yd par 4 all up hill drive over a knoll to an elevated green with deep-faced bunkers.

Holes	Par	Yards Back Tees	Rating	Slope
18	72	6317	68.6	113

	9 Holes	18 Holes	Hours Mid Season
Weekday:	—	$13.50	Dawn - Dusk
Weekend:	—	$15.50	Dawn - Dusk
Cart Fees:	—	$21.00	

Mandatory Cart Rental: No
Club Rental: Yes

Notes: Inquire about tournament packages.

Spook Rock Golf Course   NY 100

59 Campbell Ave, Suffern NY —   Tee Times: (914)357-6466

Directions: NY Thruway to Exit 14B. Take a right onto Airmont Rd if going North on Thruway, left if going South. Go 1.5 mi. to Spook Rock Rd. Take a left and go 3/4 mi. to the course.

Facility Type: Public

Club Pro: Martin Bohen
Discounts: None
Tee Times: Yes, for Mon-Thurs, call Sunday 6 pm. For weekends (Fri-Sun) call Thurs 7 am.

Features: Lessons, Showers/Lockers, Driving Range, Practice Area, Pro Shop - Complete, Clubhouse, Restaurant, Bar, Banquet Facilities, Lodging Nearby, Snack Bar

Description: This course was a "Places to Play" pick by Golf Digest in '90 and '91. It was designed by Frank Duane. It has always been among the top picks for public courses in the country. It's wooded and fairly flat. Water is a factor on several holes. The course will challenge the better player.

Holes	Par	Yards Back Tees	Rating	Slope
18	72	6791	73.3	130

	9 Holes	18 Holes	Hours Mid Season
Weekday:	—	$30.00	7:00 am - Dusk
Weekend:	$18.00	$40.00	6:00 am - Dusk
Cart Fees:	$12.00	$22.00	

Mandatory Cart Rental: No
Club Rental: Yes

Notes: Green fees listed are for non-residents. Cart fees are for two people. Renovations are planned for completion in '92.

Sprain Lake Golf Course

NY 101

290 E Grassy Sprain Rd, Yonkers NY — Info: (914)779-9827

Directions: Sprain Brook Pkwy going North, Exit at Jackson Ave. Take a right on East Grassy Sprain Rd and the course is 1/4 mi.

Facility Type: Public

Club Pro: Tom Avezzano
Discounts: Twilight, Seniors
Tee Times: Yes, 1 week ahead in person

Features: Lessons, Showers/Lockers, Practice Area, Pro Shop - Complete, Clubhouse, Restaurant, Bar, Snack Bar

Description: A pretty and hilly course. A resevoir plays into 8 holes. It's a hard course to just eat up.

Holes	Par	Yards Back Tees	Rating	Slope
18	70	6100	68	114

	9 Holes	18 Holes	Hours Mid Season
Weekday:	—	$11.00	7:00 am - 7:00 pm
Weekend:	—	$14.00	6:00 am - 7:00 pm
Cart Fees:	$11.00	$18.00	

Mandatory Cart Rental: No
Club Rental: Yes

Notes: Twilight starts at 5 midseason.

Spring Lake Golf Course

NY 102

Bartlett Rd, Middle Island NY — (516)924-5115

Directions: 495 to Exit 64. Go North on Rte 112 to Rte 25 and East approx 3 mi. to course.

Facility Type: Public

Club Pro: Loring Hawkins
Discounts: Twilight
Tee Times: No

Features: Lessons, Showers/Lockers, Driving Range, Practice Area, Pro Shop - Complete, Restaurant, Bar, Snack Bar, Banquet Facilities, Lodging Near-by

Description: The 18 hole "Thunderbird" is a very long and challenging championship course that has hosted the Metro Public Links Tourney. It is flat and open with large greens. It was one of Golf Digest's "Places to Play" in '90 and '91. The 9 hole "Sandpiper" course is more interesting and demands more careful management.

Holes	Par	Yards Back Tees	Rating	Slope
9	36	3250	—	—
18	72	7048	73.7	125

	9 Holes	18 Holes	Hours Mid Season
Weekday:	$11.00	$22.00	6:00 am - Dusk
Weekend:	$12.50	$25.00	5:00 am - Dusk
Cart Fees:	$12.50	$25.00	

Mandatory Cart Rental: No
Club Rental: Yes

Stone Dock Golf & CC

High Falls NY — (914)687-9944

Directions: NY Thruway to the Kingston Exit. Take 209 South to 213 East. Go 1.5 mi. to Berme Rd and take a right to course.

Facility Type: Semi-private

Club Pro: None
Discounts: None
Tee Times: No

Features: Lessons, Practice Area, Pro Shop - Complete, Clubhouse, Restaurant, Bar, VISA/MC, Banquet Facilities, Lodging Nearby

Description: This is a fairly flat and somewhat narrow course that demands control shots. Water comes into play quite a bit. A good example of this, and a favorite hole, is the 4th, a par 4, 320 yard shot to a 90 degree dogleg left over water. The second shot is over water again to a green that is surrounded by woods and out-of-bounds. A creek runs behind the green.

Holes	Par	Yards Back Tees	Rating	Slope
9	36	3275	69.3	—

	9 Holes	18 Holes	Hours Mid Season
Weekday:	$8.25	$12.50	Dawn - Dusk
Weekend:	$9.75	$15.00	Dawn - Dusk
Cart Fees:	$10.75	$20.00	

Mandatory Cart Rental: No
Club Rental: Yes

Stony Ford Golf Course

550 Rte 416, Montgomery NY — **Tee Times:** (914)457-3000

Directions: I-84 to Exit 5 (Maybrook). Go left off the exit going West and right off exit going East to the light. Go right at the light and follow the road 3 miles to Rte 416. Go left on 416 and the course is 1 mile on the right.

Facility Type: Public

Club Pro: Bob Palmieri
Discounts: Twilight
Tee Times: Yes, 1 week for weekday. For weekends/holidays, 1 week before in person or Wed before after 12 noon by phone.

Features: Lessons, Showers/Lockers, Driving Range, Practice Area, Pro Shop - Complete, Clubhouse, Restaurant, Bar, Banquet Facilities, Lodging Nearby

Description: A Hal Purdy designed course, it is hilly but forgiving - good fun for the competitive and the average golfer. The course is sprinkled and well maintained.

Holes	Par	Yards Back Tees	Rating	Slope
18	72	6651	72.4	128

	9 Holes	18 Holes	Hours Mid Season
Weekday:	—	$20.00	5:30 am - Dusk
Weekend:	—	$24.00	5:30 am - Dusk
Cart Fees:	$11.00	$18.00	

Mandatory Cart Rental: No
Club Rental: Yes

Notes: Green fees listed are for non members.

Sullivan County Golf & CC

NY 105

Rte 52, Liberty NY — (914)292-9584

Directions: Take Rte 17 to Rte 52 West toward Liberty. Take a left on Chestnut in Liberty and the course is 1.5 mi.

Facility Type: Semi-private

Coupon page 203

Club Pro: Earle Soules
Discounts: Twilight
Tee Times: No

Features: Lessons, Showers/Lockers, Practice Area, Pro Shop - Complete, Clubhouse, Bar, Banquet Facilities, Restaurant, Lodging Nearby

Description: Like an old English course, this rolls and undulates a lot. It's not long but has tricky side hill lies. The signature hole is the 515 yard, par 5 #12 that plays across the side of a hill.

Holes	Par	Yards Back Tees	Rating	Slope
9dt	72	6300	69.9	121

	9 Holes	18 Holes	Hours Mid Season
Weekday:	$12.00	$12.00	8:00 am - Dusk
Weekend:	$18.00	$18.00	8:00 am - Dusk
Cart Fees:	$11.00	$17.00	

Mandatory Cart Rental: No
Club Rental: Yes

Sunken Meadow Golf Course

NY 106

Babylon NY — (516)269-3838

Directions: 495 to Exit 53N onto the Sunken Meadow Pkwy to the course.

Facility Type: Public

Club Pro: Francis Zeray
Discounts: Seniors
Tee Times: No

Features: Driving Range, Pro Shop - Complete, Restaurant, Lessons, Clubhouse, Snack Bar

Description: Red is hilly and straightforward. Blue is moderately hilly with a lot of doglegs. And green is flat and wide open.

Holes	Par	Yards Back Tees	Rating	Slope
9	35	3060	34.5	—
9	36	3040	34.2	—
9	36	3125	34.6	—

	9 Holes	18 Holes	Hours Mid Season
Weekday:	$7.00	—	6:30 am - Dusk *
Weekend:	$8.00	—	6:00 am - Dusk
Cart Fees:	—	—	
Club Rental:	Yes		

Notes: * The course is closed on Mondays. There are only pull carts.

Swan Lake Golf Club

388 River Road, Manorville NY — Tee Times: (516)369-1818

Directions: 495 to Exit 69. Go North and follow the signs to the course.

Facility Type: Public

Club Pro: None
Discounts: Twilight
Tee Times: Yes, 1 week ahead at a charge of $25 per party.

Features: Showers/Lockers, Practice Area, Pro Shop - Complete, Clubhouse, Restaurant, Bar, Banquet Facilities

Description: This is a picturesque course with large greens, wide fairways and some water. The course is in good shape and has been a choice of Golf Digest for "Places to Play" for the last two years. The 12th hole was rated one of the 18 toughest on Long Island public courses. It's a 431 yd par 4 that funnels to a narrow approach and a green sorrounded by traps.

Holes	Par	Yards Back Tees	Rating	Slope
18	72	7011	74.4	126

	9 Holes	18 Holes	Hours Mid Season
Weekday:	$12.00	$22.00	6:00 am - Dusk
Weekend:	$14.00	$25.00	Dawn - Dusk
Cart Fees:	—	$25.00	

Mandatory Cart Rental: No
Club Rental: Yes

Swan Lake Golf & CC

Swan Lake NY — Tee Times: (914)292-0748

Directions: Rte 17 to Exit 101 onto Rte 55 West. Go past the Imperial Hotel to Mt Hope Rd and take a right to the course.

Facility Type: Semi-private

Coupon page 203

Club Pro: None
Discounts: Twilight
Tee Times: Yes, 1 week ahead for weekends

Features: Lessons, Driving Range, Practice Area, Pro Shop - Complete, Clubhouse, Restaurant, Bar, Snack Bar, Banquet Facilities, VISA/MC, Lodging Nearby

Description: Ted Robinson designed this well-laid out and well-maintained course. The hills are moderate and the greens are challenging. Approach shots are tough. Golf Digest called #13 one of the hardest holes in the area. It's a 420 yd par 4 dogleg left up a hill to a sloped green that is tough from any angle.

Holes	Par	Yards Back Tees	Rating	Slope
18	71	6800	71.8	132

	9 Holes	18 Holes	Hours Mid Season
Weekday:	$10.00	$15.00	7:00 am - 5:30 pm
Weekend:	$13.00	$20.00	6:45 pm - 5:30 pm
Cart Fees:	$15.00	$25.00	

Mandatory Cart Rental: No
Club Rental: Yes

Tall Tree Golf Course   NY 109

181 Rte 25 A, Rocky Point NY —   Tee Times: (516)744-3200

Directions: 495 to Exit 63. Go North to Rte 25A and turn right heading East. The course is 3 mi. on left.

Holes	Par	Yards Back Tees	Rating	Slope
18	65	4715	62.9	110

Facility Type: Public

	9 Holes	18 Holes	Hours Mid Season
Weekday:	—	$15.00	Dawn - Dusk
Weekend:	—	$17.00	Dawn - Dusk
Cart Fees:	—	—	
Club Rental: No			

Club Pro: Jim Gilbert
Discounts: Twilight
Tee Times: Yes, call ahead for weekends.

Notes: Yearly passes for seniors available.

Features: Lessons, Practice Area, Pro Shop - Complete, Restaurant, Bar, Snack Bar, Banquet Facilities

Description: This is a short course with tight, tree-lined fairways and small tricky greens.

Tamarack Lodge Golf Course   NY 110

Greenfield Park, NY — (914)647-7000

Directions: Rte 17 to Exit 113. Take Rte 209 North and left onto Rte 52. The hotel is 6 miles past Ellenville.

Holes	Par	Yards Back Tees	Rating	Slope
9	30	—	—	—

Facility Type: Resort

	9 Holes	18 Holes	Hours Mid Season
Weekday:	$4.00	—	10:00 am - 5:00 pm
Weekend:	$4.00	—	10:00 am - 5:00 pm
Cart Fees:	—	—	
Club Rental: Yes			

Club Pro: None
Discounts: None
Tee Times: No

Features: Restaurant, Bar, Lodging Nearby

Description: This course is a "pitch & putt".

Tarry Brae Golf Course NY 111

Pleasant Valley Rd, South Fallsburg NY — Tee Times: (914)434-2620

Directions: Rte 17 to Exit 107. Bear right off the exit toward Fallsburg. Go 6 mi. to 1st stop and turn right. Go just 100 ft and turn left. At the 2nd stop, take another left, and the course is 1/2 mi. on the left.

Facility Type: Public

Club Pro: Jay Golden
Discounts: Twilight
Tee Times: Yes, 1st come 1st serve for play before 11 am. Call 5 days ahead for play after 11.

Features: Lessons, Driving Range, Practice Area, Pro Shop - Complete, Snack Bar, Bar, Lodging Nearby

Description: This is a rolling and heavily wooded course that offers a good challenge. It's well-maintained, and the views are panoramic over Echo Lake. The course was a Golf Digest pick for "Places to Play" in '90 and '91. The most talked about hole is 1# that features a red periscope at the tee.

Holes	Par	Yards Back Tees	Rating	Slope
18	72	6890	73.1	128

	9 Holes	18 Holes	Hours Mid Season
Weekday:	$12.00	$20.00	7:30 am - 6:30 pm
Weekend:	$12.00	$20.00	7:00 am - 6:30 pm
Cart Fees:	$7.00	$11.00	

Mandatory Cart Rental: No
Club Rental: Yes

Notes: Cart fee is per person.

Tennanah Lake Golf & CC NY 112

Roscoe NY — Tee Times: (914)794-2900

Directions: Rte 17 to Exit 94. Go back through town if going West on 17, or go right off exit if heading East. Follow the signs approx 4 miles to the motel and golf course.

Facility Type: Semi-private

Club Pro: Gregory Scott Smith
Discounts: Seniors, Twilight
Tee Times: Yes, As far ahead as you can from the opening of the season in May.

Features: Lessons, Practice Area, Pro Shop - Limited, Snack Bar, Lodging Nearby, American Express, VISA/MC

Description: Sam Snead designed this course that features the 2nd highest point in Sullivan Co. You can see CT on a clear day. It is a scenic course with a lot of variation in grading and width. Woods separate the holes and clear streams amble throughout. It is also the trout fishing mecca of the East.

Holes	Par	Yards Back Tees	Rating	Slope
18	72	6854	71.2	119

	9 Holes	18 Holes	Hours Mid Season
Weekday:	$10.00	$18.00	8:00 am - 6:00 pm *
Weekend:	$12.00	$22.00	8:00 am - 6:00 pm
Cart Fees:	$14.00	$22.00	

Mandatory Cart Rental: No
Club Rental: Yes

Notes: * The course is closed on Mondays. Discounts on golf for guests of the motel.

Thomas Carvel Country Club   NY 113

Ferris Rd, Pine Plains NY — (518)398-7101

Directions: Take Exit D25 off the Taconic onto Ferris Rd East to the course.

Facility Type: Public

Club Pro: Sal Molella
Discounts: None
Tee Times: No

Features: Lessons, Showers/Lockers, Driving Range, Practice Area, Pro Shop - Limited, Clubhouse, Restaurant, Bar, Snack Bar, Banquet Facilities

Description: This course was designed by William Mitchell, architect of over 200 courses in Florida. It's a scenic course that sits between the Berkshires and Catskills. It is open, hilly and challenging. #7 is the signature, a par 3, 225 yd shot down a tree-lined fairway to a green with water on the back.

Holes	Par	Yards Back Tees	Rating	Slope
18	72	7300	72.8	141

	9 Holes	18 Holes	Hours Mid Season
Weekday:	$17.00	$27.00	7:30 am - 3:30 pm *
Weekend:	$21.00	$32.00	6:30 am - 3:30 pm *
Cart Fees:	—	—	

Mandatory Cart Rental: Yes
Club Rental: Yes

Notes: Green fee includes cart. * The course closes for 18 hole play at 2 pm and for 9 hole play at 3:30.

Timber Point Golf Course   NY 114

Great River Rd, Great River NY — Info: (516)581-2401   Tee Times: 516 224 PARK

Directions: Southern St Pkwy to Exit 45 E. Go 1 light to Great River Rd and take a right to the end and the course.

Facility Type: Public

Club Pro: Lenney Peters
Discounts: Seniors, Twilight
Tee Times: Yes, up to 1 week and as late as 24 hours only on a touch tone phone and only with a Green Key Card.

Features: Lessons, Showers/Lockers, Driving Range, Practice Area, Pro Shop - Complete, Clubhouse, Restaurant, Bar, Snack Bar, Banquet Facilities

Description: The blue is the longest and white the shortest. Rating/slope figures are Red/Blue - 72.9/121, White/Red - 70.6/116, and Blue White - 71.9/116. The Red/Blue course was private and one of Golf Digests Top 100. It's more of a links-type course. The signature hole is "Gibral-ter", the 240 yd par 3 #5, right on the Great South Bay. It shoots uphill to an island green with absolutely no bail-out.

Holes	Par	Yards Back Tees	Rating	Slope
9	36	3279	—	—
9	36	3162	—	—
9	36	3363	—	—

	9 Holes	18 Holes	Hours Mid Season
Weekday:	—	$27.00	7:00 am - 6:00 pm
Weekend:	—	$31.00	6:00 am - 6:00 pm
Cart Fees:	—	$22.00	

Mandatory Cart Rental: No
Club Rental: Yes

Notes: Rates listed are for non-residents. Residents pay $13 and $15. Twilight begins at 4 pm midseason. Non-residents or those without Green Key Cards may walk on and be matched with a Card holder.

Twin Village Golf Course

Rockland Rd, Roscoe NY — (607)498-9983

Directions: Rte 17 to Exit 94. Go left at the light if heading West and through the 2nd light where the road becomes Rockland Rd. Go 1/2 mi. to the course. If going East, take a left off the exit to the end of the street. Take a left and go 1/2 mi. to the course.

Holes	Par	Yards Back Tees	Rating	Slope
9	32	2100	—	—

	9 Holes	18 Holes	Hours Mid Season
Weekday:	—	$10.00	8:00 am - Dusk
Weekend:	—	$15.00	8:00 am - Dusk
Cart Fees:	—	$8.00	

Mandatory Cart Rental: No
Club Rental: Yes

Facility Type: Executive

Club Pro: None
Discounts: Twilight
Tee Times: No

Features: Snack Bar

Vails Grove Golf Course

Peach Lake, Brewster NY — (914)669-9333

Directions: I -84 to Exit 21. Take Rte 121 South 1.5 mi. to the course in right.

Holes	Par	Yards Back Tees	Rating	Slope
9dt	66	4489	61.5	95

Facility Type: Semi-private

Club Pro: None
Discounts: Twilight
Tee Times: No

Coupon page 204

	9 Holes	18 Holes	Hours Mid Season
Weekday:	—	$15.00	6:00 am - Dusk
Weekend:	—	$15.00	2:00 pm - Dusk *
Cart Fees:	—	$18.00	

Mandatory Cart Rental: No
Club Rental: Yes

Notes: * Weekend play before 2 pm reserved for members only.

Features: Practice Area, Pro Shop - Complete, Clubhouse, Snack Bar, Lodging Nearby

Description: This 65 year old course rolls a little. It is narrow and walkable, challenging and picturesque. Everyone talks about the 9th. It's 465 yards and a par 4 on the 1st 9 and par 5 the 2nd. You'll realize only half way through this hole that you are going up hill.

Van Cortlandt Park GC

Van Cortlandt Park, Bronx — Info: (212)543-4595 Tee Times: (212)543-4585

Directions: Major Deegan South to the Van Cortlandt Exit. Make left at the light off exit. At next intersection, (Van Cortlandt West) get into Deegan North approach. Stay left and go back under highway to course. Deegan North exit at 230th. Take right at light and quick left onto Bailey Ave North to Van Cortlandt West and to Deegan north approach. For NYC residents take the #1 or #9 train to 242nd street stop.

Facility Type: Public

Club Pro: Bill Costner
Discounts: Seniors, Twilight, Juniors
Tee Times: Yes, 1 week for non members, reserve with Visa or Master Card.

Features: Lessons, Showers/Lockers, Pro Shop - Complete, Clubhouse, Snack Bar, VISA/MC

Coupon page 204

Holes	Par	Yards Back Tees	Rating	Slope
18	70	6052	67.6	110

	9 Holes	18 Holes	Hours Mid Season
Weekday:	—	$13.50	Dawn - Dusk
Weekend:	—	$15.50	Dawn - Dusk
Cart Fees:	—	$21.00	

Mandatory Cart Rental: No
Club Rental: Yes

Notes: Twilight starts at 4 pm midseason. Memberships are available for a USGA handicap, periodicals and tee-times 10 days ahead.

Description: Van Cortlandt lays claim to being the oldest course in the country and from the pictures in the museum-like clubhouse, we believe it.. It is wide open and forgiving. The last four holes are hilly and there are several long holes; #2 is 620, and #12 is 607. The 13th is a par 3 over water, which is unusual for a city course. You'll find a bit of everything here and it's open all year round.

Vassar Golf Course

4 Gary, Hyde Park NY — Tee Times: (914)473-1550

Directions: Rte 9 to Rte 44-55 East. Right on Raymond Ave to Vassar College on the left. Ask for the course at the gate.

Facility Type: Semi-private

Club Pro: Harry Vinall
Discounts: Seniors, Juniors
Tee Times: Yes, For foursome only. 1 day advance for weekdays by phone. In person for weekend.

Features: Practice Area, Pro Shop - Complete, Snack Bar

Description: Built in 1928, this is a shotmakers course. It is tight with small greens. It's walkable and in good condition.

Holes	Par	Yards Back Tees	Rating	Slope
9	34	2790	—	—

	9 Holes	18 Holes	Hours Mid Season
Weekday:	$6.00	$10.50	8:00 am - Dusk *
Weekend:	$7.00	$13.00	7:00 am - Dusk
Cart Fees:	$10.00	$17.00	

Mandatory Cart Rental: Yes
Club Rental: No

Notes: * Tuesdays 10 am - Dusk.

Villa Roma Resort & CC

Villa Roma Rd, Callicoon NY — (914)887-5097

Directions: Rte 17 Exit 104 (Monticello). Take 17B west approx 18 mi. to signs for the resort.

Holes	Par	Yards Back Tees	Rating	Slope
18	71	6231	70.6	125

Facility Type: Resort

Club Pro: Matt Kleiner
Discounts: Twilight
Tee Times: No

	9 Holes	18 Holes	Hours Mid Season
Weekday:	—	$22.00	7:30 am - 5:30 pm
Weekend:	—	$22.00	7:30 am - 5:30 pm
Cart Fees:	—	$25.00	

Mandatory Cart Rental: Yes
Club Rental: Yes

Features: Lessons, Showers/Lockers, Driving Range, Practice Area, Pro Shop - Complete, Restaurant, Bar, Snack Bar, Banquet Facilities, Lodging Nearby, American Express, VISA/MC

Description: Designed by David Postlewaite, this course made Golf Digest's "Places to Play" in '91 It is scenic and in excellent condition. It's watered and has bent grass tee to green. #18 is a nice finish. It's a 339 yd par 4. The drive must be 210 to carry over a lake, usually against the wind. The well-trapped and undulating green is guarded on one side by a tree and the other by rough. It's also very pretty!

Walker Valley Golf Course

Rte 52, Walker Valley NY 12588 — (914)744-3105

Directions: Rte 17 to Exit 119. Take Rte 302 East to the end and left onto Rte 52. Go 5 mi. to course.

Holes	Par	Yards Back Tees	Rating	Slope
9	32	1659	—	—

Facility Type: Executive

Club Pro: None
Discounts: Seniors
Tee Times: No

	9 Holes	18 Holes	Hours Mid Season
Weekday:	—	$6.00	6:30 am - 7:00 pm
Weekend:	—	$8.00	6:30 am - 7:00 pm
Cart Fees:	—	—	
Club Rental:	Yes		

Features: Pro Shop - Complete, Restaurant, Bar, Banquet Facilities

Description: A flat course, it is a good walk and a good practice course.

West Point Golf Course

US Military Acadamy, West Point NY —   Tee Times: (914)938-2327

Directions: On 9W in Highland Falls.

Holes	Par	Yards Back Tees	Rating	Slope
18	70	6007	69.0	120

Facility Type: Semi-private

Club Pro: None
Discounts: None
Tee Times: Yes, call ahead for weekends

	9 Holes	18 Holes	Hours Mid Season
Weekday:	—	$17.00	7:30 am - 8:00 pm
Weekend:	—	$17.00	7:00 am - 8:00 pm
Cart Fees:	—	$10.00	

Features: Lessons, Showers/Lockers, Practice Area, Pro Shop - Complete, Snack Bar, VISA/MC

Mandatory Cart Rental: No
Club Rental: Yes

Description: A very pretty course. It is hilly and short and has elevated greens and a good mix of holes. It's a vigorous walk.

Notes: Restricted to all active or retired military personel and active reservists. Green fees are from $8 to $17, depending on rank.

West Sayville Golf Course

Montauk Highway, West Sayville NY — **Info:** (516)567-1704 **Tee Times:** 516 244 PARK

Directions: 495 to Sagtikos Pkwy South to Southern State Pkwy East to the Montauk Highway. The course is right past LaSalle Military Acadamy.

Holes	Par	Yards Back Tees	Rating	Slope
18	72	6700	72.5	124

Facility Type: Public

Club Pro: Fred Gipp
Discounts: Seniors, Twilight
Tee Times: Yes, Up to 1 week and as late as 24 hrs only on a touch tone phone and only with Green Key Card.

	9 Holes	18 Holes	Hours Mid Season
Weekday:	—	$27.00	7:00 am - 6:00 pm
Weekend:	—	$31.00	6:00 am - 6:00 pm
Cart Fees:	—	$22.00	

Mandatory Cart Rental: No
Club Rental: Yes

Features: Lessons, Showers/Lockers, Driving Range, Practice Area, Pro Shop - Complete, Clubhouse, Restaurant, Bar, Snack Bar, Banquet Facilities

Notes: County residents pay $13 and $15. Driving range open until 10 PM. Non-residents or those without Green Key Cards can walk on and be paired with Card holder.

Description: This course is the site of the Sun Rise Pro Am. It is normally windy and a real good test from the back tees. It features a lot of water.

Windy Wes Golf Club,

Circleville, NY — Info: (914)692-5811

Directions: Rte 17 to Rte 302 South in Walkill. Take Old Rte 17 West to your first right, Sands Road. The course is a 1/2 mile.

Holes	Par	Yards Back Tees	Rating	Slope
18	72	6500	—	—

Facility Type: Public

Club Pro: None
Discounts: Seniors, Juniors, Twilight
Tee Times: Yes

Features: Showers/Lockers, Driving Range, Practice Area, Pro Shop - Complete, Clubhouse, Restaurant, Bar, Banquet Facilities, Lodging Nearby

	9 Holes	18 Holes	Hours Mid Season
Weekday:	—	—	7:00 am - Dusk
Weekend:	—	—	7:00 am - Dusk
Cart Fees:	—	—	

Mandatory Cart Rental: No

Notes: Rates will be competitive with other public courses in the area.

Description: This is a new course owned and operated by the Town of Walkill to be opening for the 1992 season. It will be rolling terrain carved out of the woods, and we hear it will be scenic. The course will be well-bunkered and water will come into play on 11 holes. The 13th is a favorite of the architect, Steve Espisito. It's a 330 yard, par 4 with the 2nd shot to an island green.

Woodpark Golf Course

Mt Airy Rd New Windsor NY — (914)564-9913

Directions: Rte 84 to Exit 6 onto 17 K. Go 2 mi. to Union Ave and make a right. Go right onto 207. Go past the main gate of Stewart Airport and make a left onto Mt Airy Rd. Them course is approximately 1 mi.

Holes	Par	Yards Back Tees	Rating	Slope
18	56	850	—	—

Facility Type: Pitch & Putt

Club Pro: None
Discounts: None
Tee Times: No

	9 Holes	18 Holes	Hours Mid Season
Weekday:	$5.00	$8.00	9:00 am - Dusk
Weekend:	$5.00	$8.00	9:00 am - Dusk
Cart Fees:	—	—	

Features: Practice Area, Clubhouse

Description: This is a well-kept facility, good for all ages, particularly beginners.

NY 9   **Greene**

CATSKILL GOLF CLUB
27 Brooks Lane, Catskill NY
(518)943-0302

Enjoy a round of golf in the most enjoyable and best maintained course in the area. Excellent restaurant for after golf relaxation

You are invited to play a COMPLI-MENTARY 9 or 18 round of golf when accompanied with one fully paid round of equal value one time during the 1992 season.

Valid Mon thru Fri (except holidays) from 8 am to 5 pm and on weekends and holidays after 2 pm

Must call ahead for tee times.

POWER CART RENTAL REQUIRED

❏ Validation

PLEASE READ VALIDATION RESTRICTIONS CAREFULLY.

NY 12   **Orange**

CENTRAL VALLEY GOLF CLUB
210 Smith Clove Rd, Central Valley NY
(914)928-6924

Come enjoy 18 holes of challenging golf at scenic Central Valley. Specializing in golf outings. Restaurant. Lounge. Fully-stocked pro shop. Memberships available.

You are invited to play a COMPLI-MENTARY 9 or 18 hole round of golf when accompanied with one fully paid round of equal value one time during the 1992 season.

Valid anytime Mon thru Fri prior to Memorial Day and after Labor Day.

Must call ahead for tee times.

POWER CART RENTAL IS RE-QUIRED

❏ Validation

OFFER IS NOT VALID IF DETACHED FROM BOOK.

NY 14   **Queens**

CLEARVIEW GOLF COURSE
202-12 Willets Point Blvd, Queens
(718)225 GOLF

You are invited to play a COMPLI-MENTARY 9 or 18 hole round of golf when accompanied with one fully paid round of equal value one time during the 1992 season

Valid Mon thru Thurs (except holidays) only after 1 pm.

Must call for assured tee times.

POWER CART RENTAL IS RE-QUIRED

❏ Validation

You are invited to play a COMPLIMENTARY 9 or 18 hole round of golf when accompanied with a fully paid round of equal value two times during the 1992 season.

Valid anytime.

Call ahead for assured tee times

POWER CART RENTAL IS REQUIRED

❏ 1st Time Validation

❏ 2nd Time Validation

NY 21   **Dutchess**

DUTCHER GOLF COURSE
135 E Main, Pawling NY
(914)855-9845

Come play maybe the oldest public golf course in America, established 1890. Located in the historic town of Pawling. Full selection pro shop. Ask about lessons.

OFFER IS NOT VALID IF DETACHED FROM BOOK.

You are invited to play a COMPLIMENTARY 9 or 18 hole round of golf when accompanied with one fully paid round of equal value one time during the 1992 season.

Valid Mon thru Thurs (except holidays) only after 1 pm.

Must call for assured tee times.

POWER CART RENTAL IS REQUIRED

❏ Validation

NY 22   **Kings**

DYKER BEACH GOLF COURSE
86th St & 7th Ave, Brooklyn, NY
(718)225-GOLF

COUPONS ARE NOT VALID FOR LEAGUE PLAY, SPECIAL EVENTS, OR OUTINGS.

You are invited to play a COMPLIMENTARY 9 or 18 hole round of golf when accompanied with a fully paid round of equal value one time during the 1992 season.

Valid anytime April 15 to Oct 30.

Must call ahead for tee times.

POWER CART RENTAL IS REQUIRED

❏ Validation

NY 32   **Ulster**

GRANIT HOTEL & GOLF COURSE
Kerhonkson NY
(914)626-3141

Come enjoy 18 holes of golf in a relaxing mountain atmosphere. Available for groups and 1 day outings. Overnight accommodations available. Banquet facilities.

NY 34   **Orange**

GREEN RIDGE GOLF CLUB
Gregory Rd, Johnson, NY
(914)355-1317

Come enjoy 9 holes of interesting golf in a very friendly atmosphere.

You are invited to play a COMPLIMENTARY 9 or 18 hole round of golf when accompanied with a fully paid round of equal value one time during the 1992 season.

Valid Mon thru Fri (except holidays) until 1:00 pm.

Call ahead for assured tee times.

❑ Validation

PLEASE READ VALIDATION RESTRICTIONS CAREFULLY.

NY 47   **Sullivan**

HUFF HOUSE GOLF COURSE
Roscoe, NY
(607)498-9953

Sharpen up your short game. Enjoy our 9 hole par 3 mountainside course. Restaurant, lounge, lodging available by reservation.

You are invited to play a COMPLIMENTARY 9 or 18 hole round of golf when accompanied with a fully paid round of equal value one time during the 1992 season.

Valid anytime.

Call ahead for assured tee times.

❑ Validation

OFFER IS NOT VALID IF DETACHED FROM BOOK.

NY 50   **Sullivan**

ISLAND GLEN COUNTRY CLUB
Bethel, NY
(914)583-9898

You are invited to play a COMPLIMENTARY 9 or 18 round of golf when accompanied with a fully paid round of equal value 2 times during the 1992 season.

Valid anytime Mon thru Fri (except holidays) only.

Call ahead for assured tee times.

POWER CART RENTAL IS REQUIRED

❑ 1st Time Validation

❑ 2nd Time Validation

You are invited to play a COMPLI-MENTARY 9 or 18 hole round of golf when accompanied with a fully paid round of equal value one time during the 1992 season.

Valid Mon thru Thurs (except holidays) only after 1:00 pm.

Must call for tee times.

POWER CART RENTAL IS REQUIRED.

❑ Validation

NY 57   **Richmond**

LATOURETTE PARK GOLF COURSE
1001 Richmond Hill Rd, Staten Island, NY
(718)225 GOLF

OFFER IS NOT VALID IF DETACHED FROM BOOK.

You are invited to play a COMPLI-MENTARY 9 or 18 hole round of golf when acompanied with a fully paid round of equal value two times during the 1992 season.

Valid anytime Mon thru Fri (except holidays) only. Must call ahead for assured tee times.

POWER CART RENTAL IS REQUIRED

❑ 1st Time Validation

❑ 2nd Time Validation

NY 71   **Ulster**

NEVELE GOLF COURSE
Ellenville, NY
(914)647-6000

A 1000 acre year round resort

COUPONS ARE NOT VALID FOR LEAGUE PLAY, SPECIAL EVENTS, OR OUTINGS.

You are invited to play a COMPLI-MENTARY 9 or 18 hole round of golf when accompanied with a fully paid round of equal value 2 times during the 1992 season.

Valid all day on Tuesdays and Thursdays.

Call ahead for assured tee times.

POWER CART RENTAL IS REQUIRED.

❑ 1st Time Validation

❑ 2nd Time Validation

NY 75   **Orange**

OTTERKILL COUNTRY CLUB
Otter Rd, Campbell Hall, NY
(914)427-2301

Come enjoy 18 holes of challenging golf at scenic Otterkill. Watered fairways, Bent grass greens. Specializing in golf outings. Restaurant. Lounge. Memberships available.

NY 77   **Westchester**

PEHQUENAKONCK CC
North Salem, NY
(914)669-9380

Discover Pehquenakonck, the best-kept secret in
Westchester County. 9 challenging holes, double
tees, lightening greens, friendly atmosphere,
refreshments and YOU to complete the picture.
Memberships available.

You are invited to play a COMPLI-
MENTARY 9 or 18 hole round of golf
when accompanied with a fully paid
round of equal value one time during the 1992 season

Valid Mon thru Fri (except holidays)
only from 8:00 am to 2:00 pm and
weekends and holidays after 12:00
noon.

Call ahead for assured tee times.

POWER CART RENTAL IS RE-
QUIRED.

❏ Validation

PLEASE READ VALIDATION RESTRICTIONS CAREFULLY.

NY 78   **Bronx**

PELHAM & SPLIT ROCK GC
870 Shore Rd, Bronx NY
(718)225-GOLF

You are invited to play a COMPLI-
MENTARY 9 or 18 hole round of golf
when accompanied with a fully paid
round of equal value one time during the 1992 season

Valid Mon thru Thurs (except holidays) only after 1:00 pm

Must call ahead for tee times.

POWER CART RENTAL IS RE-
QUIRED

❏ Validation

OFFER IS NOT VALID IF DETACHED FROM BOOK.

NY 82   **Sullivan**

PINES HOTEL GOLF COURSE
South Fallsburg, NY
(914)434-6000

Come enjoy 18 holes of challenging golf at the
Pines Hotel Golf Club. Nestled in the foothills of
the Catskill Mountains. Arrange your next outing
with us.

You are invited to play a COMPLI-
MENTARY 9 or 18 hole round of golf
when accompanied witha fully paid
round of equal value 2 times during
the 1992 season.

Valid Mon thru Fri (except holidays)
only from 11:00 am to 6:00 pm.

Call ahead for assured tee times.

POWER CART RENTAL IS RE-
QUIRED.

❏ Validation

You are invited to play a COMPLI-MENTARY 9 or 18 hole round of golf when accompanied with a fully paid round of equal vlaue 2 times during the 1992 season.

Valid anytime of the day Mon thru Thurs (except holidays).

Call ahead for assured tee times.

POWER CART RENTAL IS RE-QUIRED.

❑ Validation

NY 90 **Ulster**

RONDOUT COUNTRY CLUB
Accord, NY
(914)626-2513

OFFER IS NOT VALID IF DETACHED FROM BOOK.

You are invited to play a COMPLI-MENTARY 9 or 18 hole round of golf when accompanied with a fully paid round of equal value two times dur-ing the 1992 season.

Valid Mon thru Fri (except holidays) only from 7:00 am to dusk.

Call ahead for assured tee times.

POWER CART RENTAL IS RE-QUIRED.

❑ 1st Time Validation

❑ 2nd Time Validation

NY 94 **Orange**

SCOTTS CORNERS GOLF COURSE
Mongomery, NY
(914)457-9141

COUPONS ARE NOT VALID FOR LEAGUE PLAY, SPECIAL EVENTS, OR OUTINGS.

You are invited to play a COMPLI-MENTARY 9 or 18 hole round of golf when accompanied with a fully paid round of equal value one time dur-ing the 1992 season.

Valid Mon thru Thurs (except holi-days) only after 1:00 pm.

Call for assured tee times.

POWER CART RENTAL IS RE-QUIRED

❑ Validation

NY 97 **Richmond**

SILVER LAKE GOLF COURSE
915 Victory Blvd, Staten Island, NY
(718)225 GOLF

NY 99   **Richmond**

SOUTH SHORE GOLF COURSE
200 Huguenot Ave, Staten Island, NY
(718)225 GOLF

You are invited to play a COMPLI-MENTARY 9 or 18 hole round of golf when accompanied with a fully paid round of equal value one time during the 1992 season.

Valid Mon thru Thurs (except holidays) only after 1:00 pm

Call for assured tee times.

POWER CART RENTAL IS RE-QUIRED

❏ Validation

PLEASE READ VALIDATION RESTRICTIONS CAREFULLY.

NY 105   **Sullivan**

SULLIVAN COUNTY GOLF & CC
Rte 52, Liberty, NY
(914)292-9584

Come enjoy golf and dining.
Lunches and dinners are served at the
restaurant and bar. Memberships are available.
Call for information on outings.

You are invited to play a COMPLI-MENTARY 9 or 18 hole round of golf when accompanied with a fully paid round of equal value two times during the 1992 season.

Valid until 5:00 pm Mon thru Fri (except holidays) only.

Call ahead for tee times

POWER CART RENTAL IS RE-QUIRED

❏ 1st Time Validation

❏ 2nd Time Validation

OFFER IS NOT VALID IF DETACHED FROM BOOK.

NY 108   **Sullivan**

# SWAN LAKE GOLF & CC
Swan Lake, NY
(914)292-0748

Come enjoy 18 holes of challenging and exciting
golf in the jewel of the Catskills. Restaurant and
bar. Memberships are available.

You are invited to play a COMPLI-MENTARY 9 or 18 hole round of golf when accompanied with a fully paid round of equal value two times during the 1992 season.

Valid Mon thru Fri (except holidays) from 7:00 am to 5:30 pm and weekends and holidays after 12:00 noon. Must call ahead for tee times.

POWER CART RENTAL IS RE-QUIRED

❏ 1st Time Validation

❏ 2nd Time Validation

NY 116   **Putnam**

VAILS GROVE GOLF COURSE
Peach Lake, Brewster NY
(914)669-9333

You are invited to play a COMPLI-MENTARY round of golf when accompanied with a fully paid round of equal value two times during the 1992 season.

Valid only before Memorial Day and after Labor Day Mon thru Fri from 12:00 noon to 3:00 pm Call ahead for assured tee times

POWER CART RENTAL IS REQUIRED

❏ 1st Time Validation

❏ 2nd Time Validation

OFFER IS NOT VALID IF DETACHED FROM BOOK.

NY 117   **Bronx**

VAN CORTLANDT PARK GC
Van Cortlandt Park, Bronx, NY
(212)543-4585

America's oldest public golf course, built in 1895. This is a fun layout with excellent greens. We cater to outings and to the ladies.

You are invited to play a COMPLI-MENTARY 9 or 18 hole round of golf when accompanied with a fully paid round of equal value 2 times during the 1992 season.

Valid anytime Mon thru Thurs (except holidays) and weekends and holidays after 4:00 pm. Call ahead for assured tee times.

POWER CART RENTAL IS REQUIRED.

❏ 1st Time Validation

❏ 2nd Time Validation

COUPONS ARE NOT VALID FOR LEAGUE PLAY, SPECIAL EVENTS, OR OUTINGS.

NY 119   **Sullivan**

VILLA ROMA RESORT & CC
Villa Roma Rd, Callicoon, NY
(914)887-5097

Group outings available. Golf clubhouse features lounge, grill room, dining room, available for banquet functions.

You are invited to play a COMPLI-MENTARY 9 or 18 hole round of golf when accompanied with a fully paid round of equal value two times during the 1992 season.

Valid Mon thru Thurs (Except holidays) only from 12:00 noon until 4:00 pm. Call ahead for tee times.

POWER CART RENTAL IS REQUIRED

❏ 1st Time Validation

❏ 2nd Time Validation

Pennsylvania

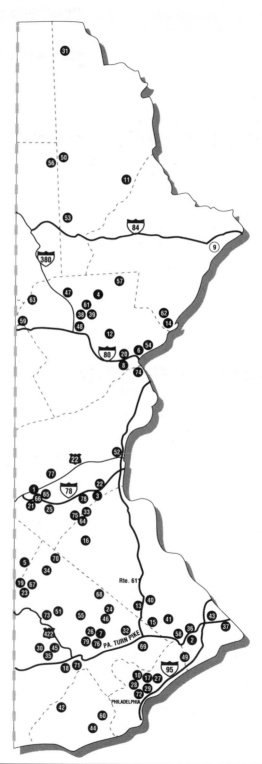

Allentown Municipal GC
PA 1

3400 Tilghman St, Allentown PA — **Tee Times:** (215)395-9926

Directions: Rte 22 to Rte 309 South. Take the Tilghman Street Exit East. The course is 1.5 mi. on the left.

Facility Type: Public

Club Pro: Tom Fenstermacher
Discounts: Twilight
Tee Times: Yes, In person on Sunday or Monday before the following weekend and holiday. Phone reservations start Tuesday.

Features: Lessons, Driving Range, Practice Area, Pro Shop - Complete, Clubhouse, Snack Bar, Lodging Nearby

Description: This is a long and open course with some sand traps. #18 is a favorite, a par 3, 170 yd shot to a green guarded by a deep bunker to the left. The course is generally a good challenge for the average player.

Holes	Par	Yards Back Tees	Rating	Slope
18	73	6590	70.2	123

	9 Holes	18 Holes	Hours Mid Season
Weekday:	—	$10.00	7:00 am - 7:00 pm
Weekend:	—	$13.00	6:30 am - 7:00 pm
Cart Fees:	$10.00	$17.00	

Mandatory Cart Rental: No
Club Rental: Yes

Notes: 9 hole play only after 3 pm - $7.

Bensalem Country Club
PA 2

2000 Brown Ave, Bensalem PA — **Tee Times:** (215)639-5556

Directions: From I-95 in PA, take the Street Road Exit (Rte 132). Go West on Street Rd approximatley 1 mile to Hulmeville Rd and take a left. Make a right at the 1st light, Brown Ave, to the course.

Facility Type: Public

Club Pro: Jim Bogan
Discounts: Seniors, Juniors, Twilight
Tee Times: Yes, 1 week for weekends and holidays

Features: Lessons, Showers/Lockers, Driving Range, Practice Area, Pro Shop - Complete, Clubhouse, Restaurant, Bar, Snack Bar, Banquet Facilities, Lodging Nearby

Description: This rolling course is not necessarily tight, but well placed streams and trees require some very accurate shots. The greens are fairly large and undulate some on this well-kept course. The 14th hole has been called one of the toughest par 3's in the area by touring pros. It's all carry for 200 yards to a pitched green guarded by steep traps.

Holes	Par	Yards Back Tees	Rating	Slope
18	70	6150	68.4	119

	9 Holes	18 Holes	Hours Mid Season
Weekday:	—	$27.00	7:00 am - Dusk
Weekend:	—	$33.00	Dawn - Dusk
Cart Fees:	—	—	

Mandatory Cart Rental: See notes.
Club Rental: No

Notes: Carts are mandatory every day from April 1 to October 1. Twilight is 4 mid-season.

Bethlehem Municipal GC

Ilicks Mill Rd, Bethlehem PA — (215)691-9393

Directions: From Rte 22, take Rte 512 South. This becomes Center Street. After approximately 2 miles look for a large church on the left. After 2 blocks the road forks. Take the right onto Ilicks Mill Road and the course is 1/2 mi.

Facility Type: Public

Coupon page 247

Club Pro:
Discounts: Twilight
Tee Times: Yes, non-residents may reserve weekend tee times in person on Friday for $1.

Features: Lessons, Showers/Lockers, Driving Range, Practice Area, Pro Shop - Complete, Clubhouse, Restaurant, Bar, Banquet Facilities

Description: Arnold Palmer played some of his golf here. It's a well-maintained and heavily played course. The terrain is a mix of flat and hilly. There is no water, the fairways are pretty wide and the large greens are all bunkered.

Holes	Par	Yards Back Tees	Rating	Slope
9	34	2500	—	—
18	71	6830	70.5	112

	9 Holes	18 Holes	Hours Mid Season
Weekday:	—	$11.00	7:00 am - 7:00 pm
Weekend:	—	$13.00	6:00 am - 7:00 pm
Cart Fees:	$10.00	$17.00	

Mandatory Cart Rental: No
Club Rental: Yes

Notes: The 9 hole course is an executive with no carts. Twilight after 3:30 mid-season. Lessons are taught at the driving range.

Buck Hill Golf Club

Golf Drive, Buck Hill Falls PA — Info: (717)595-7511   Tee Times: (717)595-7730

Directions: I-80 to Rte 447 North to 390 South. 1 mi. to course.

Facility Type: Semi-private

Club Pro: None
Discounts: Twilight
Tee Times: Yes, 4 days prior

Features: Lessons, Showers/Lockers, Driving Range, Practice Area, Pro Shop - Complete, Clubhouse, Restaurant, Bar, Banquet Facilities, Lodging Nearby, American Express, VISA/MC

Description: The architect was Donald Ross. This course was a choice of Golf Digest for "Places to Play" in '90 and '91 and offers an excellent mix of holes in a hilly and rolling terrain. A good example is #7 on the blue 9. It's a 180 yd par 3 set on a hillside with a gully between tee and green. The blue/white combination of 9's has a rating of 68.5 and a slope of 122.

Holes	Par	Yards Back Tees	Rating	Slope
9	36	3300	—	—
9	36	3200	—	—
9	34	2900	—	—

	9 Holes	18 Holes	Hours Mid Season
Weekday:	—	$40.00	8:00 am - Dusk
Weekend:	—	$50.00	7:30 am - Dusk
Cart Fees:	—	—	

Mandatory Cart Rental: Yes
Club Rental: Yes

Notes: Preseason green fees for non-members are $25 weekdays and $40 weekends. Cart fees are included in green fees. Group rates are available. Twilight available before Memorial and after Labor Day.

Butter Valley Golf Port PA 5

Bally PA — Tee Times: (215)845-2491

Directions: Rte 422 to Rte 100 North. Turn right on South 7th Street and the course is 1.5 mi.

Holes	Par	Yards Back Tees	Rating	Slope
18	71	6100	—	—

Facility Type: Public

	9 Holes	18 Holes	Hours Mid Season
Weekday:	—	$10.00	7:00 am - Dusk
Weekend:	—	$14.00	Dawn - Dusk
Cart Fees:	$9.00	$15.00	

Club Pro: None

Discounts: Seniors, Twilight

Tee Times: Yes, as far in advance as possible for weekends.

Mandatory Cart Rental: No

Club Rental: Yes

Features: Showers/Lockers, Practice Area, Pro Shop - Complete, Clubhouse, Restaurant, Lodging Nearby, VISA/MC

Notes: 9 hole play only on weekdays. Twilight begins at 3 mid-season.

Description: The course is little hilly. Most people ride the 1st time out. An active airstrip runs right through the middle of the back 9. That's making the most of space! The course is wide open, but small greens make it tougher.

Ceasars Pocono Palace Resort PA 6

Rte 209, Marshall's Creek PA — (717)588-6692

Directions: I-80 to Exit 52. Go North on Rte 209 and the resort is 7.5 miles.

Holes	Par	Yards Back Tees	Rating	Slope
9	35	2950	—	—

Facility Type: Resort

	9 Holes	18 Holes	Hours Mid Season
Weekday:	$12.00	$12.00	8:00 am - 6:00 pm
Weekend:	$15.00	$15.00	7:00 am - 6:00 pm
Cart Fees:	$13.00	$22.00	

Club Pro: Dave Fowler

Discounts: None

Tee Times: No

Mandatory Cart Rental: Yes

Club Rental: See notes.

Features: Lessons, Lodging Nearby, Banquet Facilities, Restaurant, Bar, Driving Range, Practice Area, Pro Shop - Complete, VISA/MC, American Express

Notes: This course is open to the public on availability. Guests have preference. Carts are mandatory on weekends only.

Description: This is a short course, but the fairways are tree-lined, puting a real premium on accuracy. One par 4 tee shot hits to a 10 yard wide landing area. The course is relatively flat and the greens are weel-bunkered and fast.

Center Square Golf Club
Center Square PA — Tee Times: (215)584-4288

Directions: The course is on Rte 73, 2 miles West of Rte 202. If you're coming from the Pa Turnpike, take the Norristown Exit and Germantown Pike North for approximately 5 miles to Rte 202 North.

Facility Type: Semi-private

Club Pro: John Trullinger
Discounts: Seniors
Tee Times: Yes, accepted only on Friday for the same weekend.

Features: Lessons, Practice Area, Pro Shop - Complete, Clubhouse, Restaurant, Bar, Snack Bar, Banquet Facilities, Showers/Lockers

Description: Edmund Ault designed this course. It was the sight of the Women's National Public Links Championship in 1980. The front 9 is flat and the back gets hillier. It's a challenging and popular course.

Holes	Par	Yards Back Tees	Rating	Slope
18	71	6342	69.3	116

	9 Holes	18 Holes	Hours Mid Season
Weekday:	—	$15.50	7:00 am - Dusk
Weekend:	—	$20.00	6:00 am - Dusk
Cart Fees:	$11.00	$22.00	

Mandatory Cart Rental: No
Club Rental: Yes

Notes: Green fee weekends/holidays to walk, $23. Cart fee listed is for two. Senior discount Monday morning only. A limited number of membership are available.

Cherry Valley Golf Course
Stroudsburg, PA — (717)421-1350

Directions: I-80 to Exit 53 (Del Water Gap). Get onto 611 South and take the first right at Cherry Valley Rd to the course.

Facility Type: Public

Club Pro: None
Discounts: Seniors, Twilight
Tee Times: No

Features: Pro Shop - Limited, Snack Bar

Description: This is a hilly course with lots of water. Cherry Creek runs through the middle.

Holes	Par	Yards Back Tees	Rating	Slope
18	71	5785	—	—

	9 Holes	18 Holes	Hours Mid Season
Weekday:	—	$12.00	8:00 am - Dusk
Weekend:	—	$18.00	7:00 am - Dusk
Cart Fees:	—	$22.00	

Mandatory Cart Rental: No
Club Rental: Yes

Notes: Cart rental fee is for a double.

Cliff Park Inn & Golf Course

Milford PA — (717)296-6491

Directions: I-84 to Exit 10. Take Rte 6 South to the Texaco Station and take a right. Take a right at next stop and go 1.5 mi. to course on left.

Facility Type: Resort

Club Pro: Bill Mackel
Discounts: Twilight
Tee Times: No

Coupon page 247

Features: Lessons, Showers/Lockers, Practice Area, Pro Shop - Complete, Restaurant, Bar, Snack Bar, Banquet Facilities, Lodging Nearby, American Express, VISA/MC

Description: This is a difficult course to score on. #3 is a favorite of the pro. It's a par 3, 198 yd shot from an elevated tee to an elevated green. Sounds easier than it is.

Holes	Par	Yards Back Tees	Rating	Slope
9	35	3115	—	—

	9 Holes	18 Holes	Hours Mid Season
Weekday:	$10.00	$10.00	7:00 am - Dusk
Weekend:	$18.00	$18.00	7:00 am - Dusk
Cart Fees:	$12.72	$20.14	

Mandatory Cart Rental: No
Club Rental: Yes

Notes: Green fees listed are for all day play. Bill Mackel runs a 3 day mini golf school that has "The Perfect Swing Trainer".

Cobbs Creek Golf Course

72nd & Lansdowne Ave, Philadelphia PA — **Tee Times:** (215)877-8707

Directions: From Rte 1 turn onto Haverford Ave going East. Turn right (South) onto Lansdowne Ave to the course.

Facility Type: Public

Coupon page 247

Club Pro: Mike Rugg
Discounts: Seniors, Twilight, Juniors
Tee Times: Yes, 1 week prior for any day.

Features: Lessons, Driving Range, Practice Area, Pro Shop - Complete, Clubhouse, Snack Bar, American Express, VISA/MC, Lodging Nearby

Description: Holes play around a creek on the front of this course. The back 9 is lengthy, requiring both distance and accuracy. #10 is a favorite. It's a 447 yard, par 4. It takes an accurate tee-shot on a tree-lined fairway then goes to an elevated and well-bunkered green.

Holes	Par	Yards Back Tees	Rating	Slope
18	71	6660	69.6	116

	9 Holes	18 Holes	Hours Mid Season
Weekday:	—	$15.00	Dawn - Dusk
Weekend:	—	$17.00	Dawn - Dusk
Cart Fees:	—	$19.00	

Mandatory Cart Rental: No
Club Rental: Yes

Notes: Cart fee listed is for 2. $12 for 1

Cricket Hill Golf Club

Hawley PA — Tee Times: (717)226-4366

Directions: Exit 10 off I-84 to Rte 6 North. Course is between Hawley and Honesdale on Rte 6.

Facility Type: Public

Club Pro: Scott Gavin
Discounts: Twilight
Tee Times: Yes, 1 week ahead for weekends

Features: Lessons, Showers/Lockers, Practice Area, Pro Shop - Complete, Clubhouse, Restaurant, Bar, Banquet Facilities, VISA/MC

Description: The course has a rolling terrain and excellent greens. #12 is a favorite. It's a 455 yard par 5. The tee shot is an 8 iron to a quick dogleg, then over a pond to a 2-tiered, figure 8 green. Management is also proud of the personal atmosphere at this course.

Holes	Par	Yards Back Tees	Rating	Slope
18	70	5800	—	—

	9 Holes	18 Holes	Hours Mid Season
Weekday:	$10.00	$16.00	7:00 am - 7:00 pm
Weekend:	$12.00	$18.00	7:00 am - 7:00 pm
Cart Fees:	$11.00	$18.00	

Mandatory Cart Rental: No
Club Rental: No

Evergreen Park GC at Penn Hills

Penn Hills Resort, Analomink PA — (717)421-7721

Directions: I-80 to Exit 52. Take Rte 447 North 4.5 mi. to the town of Analomink. Take a left on Cherry Lane in town to the course.

Facility Type: Resort

Club Pro: Vin Ciarlone
Discounts: Twilight, Seniors
Tee Times: No

Features: Lessons, Practice Area, Pro Shop - Complete, Clubhouse, Bar, Snack Bar, Lodging Nearby, American Express, VISA/MC

Description: This is a flat course with excellent greens. The pins are changed every day. Water comes into play on 4 holes. It's an easy walk

Holes	Par	Yards Back Tees	Rating	Slope
9	35	3150	72.3	—

	9 Holes	18 Holes	Hours Mid Season
Weekday:	$13.00	$13.00	7:00 am - Dusk
Weekend:	$15.00	$15.00	6:30 am - Dusk
Cart Fees:	$15.00	$20.00	

Mandatory Cart Rental: No
Club Rental: Yes

Notes: Call for specials.

Fairways Golf & Country Club

Country Club Lane, Warrington PA — Tee Times: (215)343-9979

Directions: PA Turnpike to the Willow Grove Exit, #27. North on Rte 611 to Rte 132 (Street Rd). Go left (West) to the course.

Facility Type: Public

Club Pro: None
Discounts: Seniors, Twilight
Tee Times: Yes, 1 week ahead for weekends

Features: Practice Area, Clubhouse, Snack Bar

Description: This is a fairly open and rolling course with 2 lakes coming into play and a stream on much of the front 9. #8 is a favorite, a par 4, 400 yd tee-off over a stream to a blind hole, sloped and well-trapped.

Holes	Par	Yards Back Tees	Rating	Slope
18	65	5006	—	—

	9 Holes	18 Holes	Hours Mid Season
Weekday:	—	$14.00	Dawn - Dusk
Weekend:	—	$18.00	Dawn - Dusk
Cart Fees:	—	$20.00	

Mandatory Cart Rental: No
Club Rental: No

Notes: Twilight after 3 pm.

Fernwood Resort & GC

Rte 209, Bushkill PA — Tee Times: (717)588-9500 ext. 4210

Directions: I-80 to Rte 209 North to town of Bushkill. Look for signs.

Facility Type: Resort

Club Pro: Bruce Hooper
Discounts: Twilight
Tee Times: Yes, 1 week prior for any day.

Features: Lessons, Showers/Lockers, Driving Range, Pro Shop - Complete, Clubhouse, Restaurant, Bar, Snack Bar, Banquet Facilities, Lodging Nearby, American Express, VISA/MC

Description: Hilly and green, this course plays much longer than it reads. It was selected by Golf Digest among "Places to Play" in '90 and '91. The favorite hole is the 13th, a 348 yd par 4. The tee shot is straight out 230 yds on a sloped fairway with woods on both sides down to a hidden green.

Holes	Par	Yards Back Tees	Rating	Slope
18	72	6208	68.8	125

	9 Holes	18 Holes	Hours Mid Season
Weekday:	—	$20.00	8:00 am - 6:00 pm
Weekend:	—	$25.00	8:00 am - 6:00 pm
Cart Fees:	—	$13.25.	

Mandatory Cart Rental: Yes
Club Rental: Yes

Notes: Cart fee price per person.

Five Ponds Golf Club PA 15

1225 West Street Rd, Warminster PA — Tee Times: (215)956-9727

Directions: PA Turnpike to the Willow Grove Exit #27. Take Rte 611 North to Rte 132 (Street Rd) and turn right (East). Course is on the left after the 3rd light.

Facility Type: Public

Club Pro: Teaching pros available
Discounts: Seniors, Twilight
Tee Times: Yes, 7 days ahead for weekends.

Features: Lessons, Driving Range, Practice Area, Pro Shop - Complete, Clubhouse, Snack Bar, Bar

Description: Greens are in excellent shape on this rolling course. There are a lot of long par 4's and there is water on 8 holes. Golf Digest picked this for "Places to Play" in '90 and '91.

Holes	Par	Yards Back Tees	Rating	Slope
18	71	6760	71.0	121

	9 Holes	18 Holes	Hours Mid Season
Weekday:	—	$18.00	Dawn - Dusk
Weekend:	—	$22.00	Dawn - Dusk
Cart Fees:	—	$22.00	

Mandatory Cart Rental: See notes.
Club Rental: Yes

Notes: Carts are mandatory on weekends before 11 am. Senior special on Monday and discounts Mon thru Fri. Ladies special on Tuesday.

Fox Hollow Golf Club PA 16

2055 Trumbauersville Rd, Quakertown PA — Tee Times: (215)538-1920

Directions: PA Turnpike to the Quakertown Exit. Go left off the exit onto 663. Go right at the 1st light, Allentown Rd. The 2nd stop sign is the intersection of 5 roads. Take a right on Creamery Rd. Go 1/2 mi. to the end and take a right to the course.

Facility Type: Public

Club Pro: Jack Thompson
Discounts: Seniors, Twilight, Juniors
Tee Times: Yes, as far in advance as possible for weekends. Up to 6 months.

Features: Lessons, Driving Range, Practice Area, Pro Shop - Complete, Clubhouse, Restaurant, Bar, Banquet Facilities, Lodging Nearby, VISA/MC

Description: The front 9 on this course is rolling, the back 9 is hillier. It has new rye grass fairways. The greens are fast and undulating. #15 is known as the "widowmaker." Its a 580 yd par 5 shot down a steep hill to a sharp dogleg, and back over a hill to an elevated and tough green. There's a lot of variety on this course. Water comes into play often. For a public course, this facility is in superb condition.

Holes	Par	Yards Back Tees	Rating	Slope
18	71	6520	68.2	115

	9 Holes	18 Holes	Hours Mid Season
Weekday:	—	$12.00	7:00 am - Dusk
Weekend:	—	$17.00	Dawn - Dusk
Cart Fees:	—	$18.00	

Mandatory Cart Rental: See notes.
Club Rental: Yes

Notes: Carts mandatory only on weekends before 12.

Franklin D. Roosevelt GC PA 17

20th & Patterson, Philadelphia PA — Tee Times: (215)462-8997

Directions: Take the Broad St Exit off I-95. The course is 1/2 mi. from Veterans Stadium at 20th & Patterson.

Facility Type: Public

Coupon page 248

Club Pro: Sean Cooke

Discounts: Seniors, Juniors, Twilight

Tee Times: Yes, 1 week ahead for weekends/holidays

Features: Lessons, Practice Area, Pro Shop - Complete, Clubhouse, Snack Bar, American Express, VISA/MC, Lodging Nearby

Description: This is an open, links-style course with not too many hazards. A good mix of long shots and accuracy is required.

Holes	Par	Yards Back Tees	Rating	Slope
18	70	6443	69.7	109

	9 Holes	18 Holes	Hours Mid Season
Weekday:	$10.00	$14.00	6:00 am - Dusk
Weekend:	$11.00	$16.00	5:30 am - Dusk
Cart Fees:	—	$19.00	

Mandatory Cart Rental:
Club Rental: Yes

Notes: 9 hole play only after 3 on weekends. Cart rental fee listed is for 2. $12 for a single.

General Washington Golf Club PA 18

2750 Egypt Road, Audubon PA — Info: (215)666-7601   Tee Times: (215)666-7602

Directions: Take the PA turnpike to Exit 24. Go South on Rte 202 and immediately take the 422 Bypass West. Get off at Oaks and you will be on Egypt Road. The course is about 1.5 mi.

Facility Type: Public

Club Pro: None

Discounts: Twilight

Tee Times: Yes, 1 week for weekends and holidays.

Features: Practice Area, Pro Shop - Limited, Snack Bar, Restaurant, Banquet Facilities, Bar

Description: The challenge here is on the front 9, which is tighter with trees and has a number of doglegs. The course has a few hills, but is generally a good walk. Changes are being made for the '92 season that will add several strokes to the par.

Holes	Par	Yards Back Tees	Rating	Slope
18	68	5800	66.5	—

	9 Holes	18 Holes	Hours Mid Season
Weekday:	—	$12.00	7:00 am - Dusk
Weekend:	—	$16.00	6:00 am - Dusk
Cart Fees:	$11.00	$19.00	

Mandatory Cart Rental: See notes.
Club Rental: Yes

Notes: Carts are mandatory only on weekends until 12 noon. Twilight begins at 4 mid-season. The restaurant is across the street but caters to those at the course. The Sr discount is for weekdays before 12.

Gilbertsville Golf Club

2944 Lutheran Rd, Gilbertsville PA — **Tee Times:** (215)323-3222

Directions: Rte 100 North to Rte 73 (Boyerstown-Gilbertsville Exit). After the exit take a right at the light and go through Gilbertsville. Stay right at the fork and the road turns into Swamp Rd. Cross Rte 663 and take a left at Lutheran Rd just before the bridge. See signs for the course.

Facility Type: Public

Club Pro: None
Discounts: Seniors, Twilight
Tee Times: Yes, as far in advance as possible for weekends and holidays.

Features: Practice Area, Pro Shop - Limited, Clubhouse, Snack Bar

Description: This is a challenging course for the average player, especially the 8th hole, a 185 yd, par 3 to a 3-tiered green. The greens are generally tough. The fairways are open for the most part, but trees can tighten play up in several areas.

Holes	Par	Yards Back Tees	Rating	Slope
18	71	6458	—	—

	9 Holes	18 Holes	Hours Mid Season
Weekday:	$7.50	$9.50	7:00 am - Dusk
Weekend:	$10.00	$14.00	Dawn - Dusk
Cart Fees:	$10.00	$16.00	

Mandatory Cart Rental: No
Club Rental: Yes

Notes: Twilight rate after 4.

Glen Brook Country Club

Stroudsburg PA — **Tee Times:** (717)421-3680

Directions: I-80 to Exit 49. Take Dreher Ave South 8/10 mi. and bear left at fork to course.

Facility Type: Public

Club Pro: Mike Wells
Discounts: Seniors, Twilight
Tee Times: Yes, as far in advance as possible.

Coupon page 248

Features: Lessons, Showers/Lockers, Practice Area, Pro Shop - Complete, Clubhouse, Restaurant, Bar, Snack Bar, Lodging Nearby, Banquet Facilities

Description: Robert White designed this old, medium hilly, links-type course that wanders through the woods. #7 is referred to as the airplane hole. It plays from one plateau to another.

Holes	Par	Yards Back Tees	Rating	Slope
18	72	6536	71.4	120

	9 Holes	18 Holes	Hours Mid Season
Weekday:	—	$14.00	8:00 am - Dusk
Weekend:	—	$17.00	Dawn - Dusk
Cart Fees:	—	$14.00	

Mandatory Cart Rental: Yes
Club Rental: See notes.

Notes: Cart fee is per person. Carts are mandatory on weekends only.

Golf Club at Shepard Hills

1160 S Krocks Rd, Wescosville PA — **Tee Times:** (215)391-0644

Directions: Rte 22 to Rte 309 South. Take the exit for Rte 222 South. Take a left at the 4th light, Krocks Rd, and the course is 3 blocks on the right.

Facility Type: Semi-private

Coupon page 248

Club Pro: Mike Hersch
Discounts: Seniors, Twilight
Tee Times: Yes, 1 week prior for weekends and holidays. Parties of 8 or more may call any time in advance.

Features: Lessons, Showers/Lockers, Practice Area, Pro Shop - Complete, Clubhouse, Restaurant, Bar, Banquet Facilities, Lodging Nearby, VISA/MC

Description: This course is in good shape and boasts the best-conditioned greens in the Lehigh Valley. It is the site of several Pro-Am events. The course is a little hilly on the front 9 and relatively flat on the back. Several of the fairways are narrow. The 7th is a favorite, and possibly the most interesting. It's a par 3, 170 yard shot down to a green protected by traps all along the front.

Holes	Par	Yards Back Tees	Rating	Slope
18	70	6377	69.9	109

	9 Holes	18 Holes	Hours Mid Season
Weekday:	—	$14.00	7:00 am - Dusk
Weekend:	—	$18.00	6:00 am - Dusk
Cart Fees:	—	$20.00	

Mandatory Cart Rental: See notes.
Club Rental: Yes

Notes: Carts are mandatory on weekend and holiday mornings before 8:30. Twilight discount is after 2 pm.

Green Pond Country Club

3604 Farmersville Rd, Bethlehem PA — **Tee Times:** (215)691-9453

Directions: From I-78 take Rte 22 West to the 25th St Exit in Easton PA. Go left off the exit for 3 lights and take a right on William Penn Hwy. Go 4 mi. and take a right onto Farmersville Rd and 1/2 mi. to the course.

Facility Type: Public

Club Pro: Jim Muschlitz
Discounts: Seniors, Twilight, Juniors
Tee Times: Yes, Monday morning at 7 for following weekend.

Features: Lessons, Showers/Lockers, Driving Range, Practice Area, Pro Shop - Complete, Clubhouse, Restaurant, Bar, Snack Bar, Banquet Facilities, Lodging Nearby

Description: Designed in 1929 by Binder, this is a flat course, well-trapped, with a lot of trees. The par 3 #17 is a tough one and a favorite of the pro. It's a 160 yd downhill shot to a small, narrow green well trapped and ob beyond the green. There is ob on 11 holes, and the fairways are narrow. The course plays longer than it reads. It has been noted for the excellent shape of its greens.

Holes	Par	Yards Back Tees	Rating	Slope
18	71	6531	69.4	126

	9 Holes	18 Holes	Hours Mid Season
Weekday:	—	$13.00	7:00 am - Dusk
Weekend:	—	$15.00	6:30 am - Dusk
Cart Fees:	$10.00	$20.00	

Mandatory Cart Rental: No
Club Rental: Yes

Notes: Open all year weather permitting. Carts are mandatory for outings and tournaments.

Hickory Valley Golf Club PA 23

1921 Ludwig Rd, Gilbertsville PA — Tee Times: (215)754-7733

Directions: Rte 422 West from Philadelphia to Rte 100 North to Rte 73 East. Go approximately 3 miles and turn left on Middlecreek Rd to the course.

Facility Type: Public

Club Pro: Steve Oltman
Discounts: Twilight, Seniors, Juniors
Tee Times: Yes, 1 week for any day.

Features: Lessons, Showers/Lockers, Driving Range, Practice Area, Pro Shop - Complete, Clubhouse, Snack Bar, Banquet Facilities, VISA/MC, Bar, Lodging Nearby

Description: This claims to be the toughest public course in the area. It's flat and tree-lined. Blue and red are narrower. Water comes into play on all three courses, and they are well-bunkered. The challenge is the 9th hole on the blue 9. It's a 620 yard par 5 double-dogleg left with water on the last hundred yards and ob left. The green is small and sloping. Sounds interesting!

Holes	Par	Yards Back Tees	Rating	Slope
9	36	3388	—	—
9	36	3079	—	—
9	36	3338	—	—

	9 Holes	18 Holes	Hours Mid Season
Weekday:	$7.00	$11.00	6:00 am - Dusk
Weekend:	$11.00	$17.00	Dawn - Dusk
Cart Fees:	$14.00	$20.00	

Mandatory Cart Rental: No
Club Rental: Yes

Notes: The red 9 is the longest, the white the shortest. The rating/slope for the red-white is 70.2/114; for red-blue is 71.6/121; and for white/blue is 69.8/114. Cart rental fees listed are for 2. Twilight rate is after 3.

Horsham Valley Golf Club PA 24

500 Babylon Rd, Ambler PA — Tee Times: (215)646-4707

Directions: PA Turnpike Exit for Fort Washington. Take Rte 611 North to 463 West. Turn left, and at 5th traffic light turn left again onto Babylon. The course is 1/8 mi.

Facility Type: Public

Club Pro: Harry Barbin
Discounts: Twilight, Seniors, Juniors
Tee Times: Yes, 1 day for weekday, 1 week for weekends and holidays.

Features: Lessons, Pro Shop - Complete, Clubhouse, Restaurant, Bar, Snack Bar, Banquet Facilities, American Express, VISA/MC, Showers/Lockers, Practice Area, Lodging Nearby

Description: This is a flat course. The #15 par 3 plays to an island green.

Holes	Par	Yards Back Tees	Rating	Slope
18	66	5100	61.7	101

	9 Holes	18 Holes	Hours Mid Season
Weekday:	—	$16.00	7:00 am - Dusk
Weekend:	—	$20.00	Dawn - Dusk
Cart Fees:	$13.78	$22.00	

Mandatory Cart Rental: No
Club Rental: Yes

Notes: Cart price listed is for 2.

Indian Creek Golf Course

1449 Chestnut St, Emmaus PA — Tee Times: (215)965-8486

Directions: I-78 to Cedar Crest Blvd South to Emmaus. Take a right on Chestnut Street (West) to the course.

Coupon page 249

Facility Type: Public

Club Pro: Bill Peet, Frank Stocke
Discounts: Seniors
Tee Times: Yes, Advised to call one day ahead for weekends/holidays, but can sometimes get a time the same afternoon.

Features: Lessons, Practice Area, Pro Shop - Complete, Pro Shop - Limited, Restaurant, Bar

Description: This is a rolling course. It's tight on four holes that play along a stream. #3 is the favorite. It's a par 3, 160 yard hole that tees off a cliff down to an elevated and naturally bunkered green.

Holes	Par	Yards Back Tees	Rating	Slope
9	35	3065	—	—

	9 Holes	18 Holes	Hours Mid Season
Weekday:	$5.00	$9.00	7:00 am - Dusk
Weekend:	$6.00	$10.00	6:30 am - Dusk
Cart Fees:	$7.00	$14.00	

Mandatory Cart Rental: No
Club Rental: Yes

Notes: A new clubhouse is expected for the 1993 season.

Jeffersonville Golf Club

2400 West Main Street, Norristown PA — (215)539-0422

Directions: PA Turnpike to the Valley Forge Exit. Take Rte 202 South and then Rte 422 West. Get off 422 at the Audobon Trooper Exit onto Rte 363 West. Go 6 lights and take a right on Ridge Pike, also called West Main Street. The course is 150 yards.

Facility Type: Public

Club Pro: None
Discounts: Seniors
Tee Times: Yes, Monday for the following weekend and holiday.

Features: Pro Shop - Limited, Clubhouse, Restaurant, Bar, Snack Bar, Banquet Facilities, Lodging Nearby

Description: This is a wide open course and relatively flat with only a few hills. It's a good course for seniors. Fairway and greenside bunkers offer the challenge.

Holes	Par	Yards Back Tees	Rating	Slope
18	72	6279	—	—

	9 Holes	18 Holes	Hours Mid Season
Weekday:	—	$12.00	Dawn - Dusk
Weekend:	—	$15.00	Dawn - Dusk
Cart Fees:	$10.00	$18.00	

Mandatory Cart Rental: No
Club Rental: Yes

John Byrne Golf Club

9500 Leon St, Philadelphia PA — **Tee Times:** (215)632-8666

Directions: I-95, exit at Acadamy Rd. Go West to Frankford Ave and turn right. Go several blocks to Eden St and turn left to the cours

Coupon page 249

Facility Type: Public

Club Pro: Don Beardsley
Discounts: Twilight, Seniors, Juniors
Tee Times: Yes, 1 week for weekends and holidays

Features: Lessons, Pro Shop - Complete, Clubhouse, Snack Bar, American Express, VISA/MC

Description: This is a hilly and tree-lined course with a premium on a solid tee game. #17, a par 4, is the signature hole. Tee off out of a chute with a creek running along the right to a tight landing area. The second shot is a tree-lined dogleg approaching well-bunkered green.

Holes	Par	Yards Back Tees	Rating	Slope
18	67	5234	65	107

	9 Holes	18 Holes	Hours Mid Season
Weekday:	$10.00	$14.00	Dawn - Dusk
Weekend:	—	$16.00	Dawn - Dusk
Cart Fees:	—	$19.00	

Mandatory Cart Rental: No
Club Rental: Yes

Notes: Cart fee listed is for 2. $12 for 1.

Juniata Golf Course

M & Cayuga Streets, Philadelphia PA — **Tee Times:** (215)743-4060

Directions: Rte 1 to Castor Ave East to Cayuga St. Take a right to course.

Coupon page 249

Facility Type: Public

Club Pro: Jim Kealey
Discounts: Seniors, Twilight, Juniors
Tee Times: Yes, 1 week for weekends

Features: Lessons, Practice Area, Pro Shop - Complete, Clubhouse, Snack Bar, Lodging Nearby

Description: This is an easy walking course with small greens. #6 is a favorite It's a par 4, 360 yard uphill shot on a right-sloped fairway to a shallow peanut-shaped green.

Holes	Par	Yards Back Tees	Rating	Slope
18	63	4825	60.7	86

	9 Holes	18 Holes	Hours Mid Season
Weekday:	—	$14.00	Dawn - Dusk
Weekend:	—	$16.00	Dawn - Dusk
Cart Fees:	—	$19.00	

Mandatory Cart Rental: No
Club Rental: Yes

Notes: Cart fee listed is for 2. $12 for a single.

Karakung Golf Course

72nd & Lansdowne Ave, Philadelphia PA — **Tee Times:** (215)877-8707

Directions: Rte 1 to Haverford Ave going East.. Turn right on Lansdowne Ave. to course.

Facility Type: Public

Coupon page 250

Club Pro: Mike Rugg
Discounts: Seniors, Twilight
Tee Times: Yes, 1 week for any day.

Features: Lessons, Practice Area, Driving Range, Pro Shop - Complete, Clubhouse, Snack Bar, American Express, VISA/MC

Description: The course is cut through the trees and features some pretty well-guarded greens. #5 is a good example. It's a par 4, 421 yard long shot to a small bunkered and stream-guarded green. Karakung adjoins Cobbs Creek Golf Course.

Holes	Par	Yards Back Tees	Rating	Slope
18	71	5737	—	—

	9 Holes	18 Holes	Hours Mid Season
Weekday:	—	$14.00	Dawn - Dusk
Weekend:	—	$16.00	Dawn - Dusk
Cart Fees:	—	$19.00	

Mandatory Cart Rental: No
Club Rental: Yes

Notes: Cart fee listed is for 2. $12 for 1.

Kimberton Golf Club

Kimberton PA — **Tee Times:** (215)933-8836

Directions: PA Turnpike to the Valley Forge Exit. Take Rte 23 West approx 1/2 hr, or about 15 miles, to course in Kimberton.

Facility Type: Semi-private

Coupon page 250

Club Pro: Robert Hays
Discounts: Seniors, Twilight
Tee Times: Yes, 1 week for weekends

Features: Lessons, Showers/Lockers, Pro Shop - Complete, Clubhouse, Bar, Snack Bar, Banquet Facilities, Lodging Nearby

Description: The front 9 of this course is flat and a good walk. The course offers some good challenges. The greens are fast. #3 is a par 4 over a pond, an easy one to lose a ball on. This is a George Fazio design.

Holes	Par	Yards Back Tees	Rating	Slope
18	72	6351	69.8	116

	9 Holes	18 Holes	Hours Mid Season
Weekday:	—	$15.00	6:30 am - Dusk
Weekend:	—	$18.00	6:00 am - Dusk
Cart Fees:	$10.00	$18.00	

Mandatory Cart Rental: No
Club Rental: Yes

Lake Lorain Golf Course · PA 31

Pyntelle PA — (717)448-2232

Directions: On Rte 370 in Poyntelle. It's about 15 mi. from Hancock NY.

Facility Type: Public

Club Pro: None
Discounts: Seniors
Tee Times: No

Features: Lessons, Pro Shop - Limited, Clubhouse, Bar, Snack Bar, Banquet Facilities

Description: This is a straightforward course that is walkable. Water comes into play on several holes.

Holes	Par	Yards Back Tees	Rating	Slope
9	35	2900	—	—

	9 Holes	18 Holes	Hours Mid Season
Weekday:	$4.50	—	7:00 am - Dusk
Weekend:	$5.00	—	7:00 am - Dusk
Cart Fees:	$6.00	—	

Mandatory Cart Rental: No
Club Rental: Yes

Limekiln Golf Club · PA 32

1176 Limekiln Pike, Ambler PA — Tee Times: (215)643-0643

Directions: PA Turnpike to the Willow Grove Exit (Rte 611). Go North on Rte 611 to Rte 463 (Horsham Rd) and turn left (West). Take a right on Limekiln Pike (Rte 152) and proceed to the course.

Facility Type: Public

Club Pro: None
Discounts: Seniors
Tee Times: Yes, Monday for the following weekends and holidays.

Features: Showers/Lockers, Driving Range, Practice Area, Pro Shop - Complete, Clubhouse, Bar, Snack Bar

Description: This is a flat and tree-lined course with a good mix of holes. The #1 handicap hole is the 3rd on the blue 9. It's a 398 yd par 4 that plays around a barn and two lakes.

Holes	Par	Yards Back Tees	Rating	Slope
9	35	2987	—	—
9	35	3226	—	—
9	35	3189	—	—

	9 Holes	18 Holes	Hours Mid Season
Weekday:	—	$18.00	6:00 am - Dusk
Weekend:	—	$22.00	6:45 am - Dusk
Cart Fees:	—	$11.00	

Mandatory Cart Rental: See notes.
Club Rental: Yes

Notes: The white 9 is the longest, the red the shortest. The rating and slope for red-white is 67.8/114; for white-blue is 68.9/114; and for red-blue is 67.5/114. Carts are mandatory only on weekends until 4 pm.

Locust Valley Golf Club

5402 Locust Valley Road, Coopersburg PA — Tee Times: (215)282-4711

Directions: From I-78 just East of Allentown go South on Rte 309 approximately 5 miles to Rte 378 and bear right onto Main St. to Pine Brook Junior College and take a right and the course is 1/2 mile.

Facility Type: Public

Club Pro: Richard Garber
Discounts: Seniors, Twilight
Tee Times: Yes, up to 1 week in advance for every day.

Features: Lessons, Showers/Lockers, Practice Area, Pro Shop - Complete, Snack Bar, Banquet Facilities

Description: This used to be a private club. It is a challenging hilly countryside course with a lot of trees and traps. Tee shots are tight and the greens are bunkered on this well-maintained course.

Holes	Par	Yards Back Tees	Rating	Slope
18	72	6451	71.0	132

	9 Holes	18 Holes	Hours Mid Season
Weekday:	—	$13.00	7:00 am - Dusk
Weekend:	—	$18.00	6:00 am - Dusk
Cart Fees:	—	$20.00	

Mandatory Cart Rental: See notes.
Club Rental: Yes

Notes: Carts are mandatory on weekends and holidays up until 10:30 am and for foursomes from May 1 to Oct 10. The cart fee is for 2. Twilight starts at 4:30 mid-season. The course takes tournaments.

Macoby Run Golf Course

McLean Station Rd, Green Lane PA — Tee Times: (215)541-0161

Directions: PA Turnpike to the Lansdale Exit. Take a right off the exit onto Rte 63. After approximately 10 minutes, 63 turns into Rte 29 at a stop. Continue on 29 for 1/2 mi. up hill and turn right at McLean Station Rd (across from elementary school) to the course.

Coupon page 250

Facility Type: Public

Club Pro: Gary Saylor, Teaching Pro
Discounts: Seniors, Juniors, Twilight
Tee Times: Yes, 1 - 2 weeks ahead for weekends and holidays.

Features: Lessons, Driving Range, Practice Area, Pro Shop - Complete, Clubhouse, Restaurant, Bar, Snack Bar, Banquet Facilities, Lodging Nearby

Description: This family run course opened in 1991 and it is continually improving. It is hilly, picturesque and challenging. Water comes into play on several holes. The favorite so far is the 3rd. It's a 490 yard par 5. You must lay up to a creek and then shoot up hill to a 2-tiered green.

Holes	Par	Yards Back Tees	Rating	Slope
18	72	6319	—	—

	9 Holes	18 Holes	Hours Mid Season
Weekday:	$5.00	$9.00	6:00 am - Dusk
Weekend:	$6.00	$11.00	6:00 am - Dusk
Cart Fees:	$5.00	$9.00	

Mandatory Cart Rental: No
Club Rental: Yes

Notes: Open all year, weather permitting.

Meadowbrook Golf Club

Phoenixville PA — Tee Times: (215)933-2929

Directions: Rte 76 to 23 West to Phoenixville. Take 29 South and the course is 1 mi. on right.

Facility Type: Public

Coupon page 251

Club Pro: Ted Campbell
Discounts: Seniors, Twilight
Tee Times: Yes, 1 week for weekends/holidays

Features: Showers/Lockers, Practice Area, Pro Shop - Complete, Clubhouse, Bar, Snack Bar

Description: This is a fairly flat and straightforward course with the challenge coming from small greens.

Holes	Par	Yards Back Tees	Rating	Slope
9dt	72	6380	68.8	111

	9 Holes	18 Holes	Hours Mid Season
Weekday:	$9.00	$9.00	7:00 am - Dusk
Weekend:	$13.00	$13.00	7:00 am - Dusk
Cart Fees:	$10.00	$20.00	

Mandatory Cart Rental: No
Club Rental: Yes

Middletown Country Club

North Bellevue Ave, Langhorne PA — Tee Times: (215)757-6953

Directions: Rte 95 to Rte 1 Exit. Go South on Rte 1 to Rte 413 North to Langhorne. Take a left on Rte 213 (Maple Ave) and go 1 block to Bellevue Ave and turn right to the course.

Facility Type: Public

Club Pro: Scott Matthews
Discounts: Twilight, Seniors, Juniors
Tee Times: Yes, 1 week ahead for any day.

Features: Lessons, Showers/Lockers, Practice Area, Pro Shop - Complete, Clubhouse, Restaurant, Bar, Snack Bar, Banquet Facilities, American Express, VISA/MC, Lodging Nearby

Description: This is a hilly course with many challenging lies and some water. #16 is a 448 yd par 4 requiring a long drive to set up for a 2nd shot over water to a two-tiered green.

Holes	Par	Yards Back Tees	Rating	Slope
18	68	5700	66.7	112

	9 Holes	18 Holes	Hours Mid Season
Weekday:	—	$15.50	6:30 am - Dusk
Weekend:	—	$17.50	6:00 am - Dusk
Cart Fees:	—	$19.50	

Mandatory Cart Rental: No
Club Rental: Yes

Notes: Cart fee listed is for 2. $13 for 1.

Morrisville Golf Farm

Rte 1, Morrisville PA — (215)295-1337

Directions: The facility is on Rte 1 going North just before the New Jersey line.

Holes	Par	Yards Back Tees	Rating	Slope
18	54	1200	—	—

Facility Type: Pitch & Putt

Club Pro: Bill Anderson
Discounts: None
Tee Times: No

	9 Holes	18 Holes	Hours Mid Season
Weekday:	—	$6.00	8:00 am - 11:00 pm
Weekend:	—	$8.00	8:00 am - 11:00 pm
Cart Fees:	—	—	
Club Rental:	Yes		

Features: Lessons, Driving Range, Pro Shop - Complete, Snack Bar

Description: This is a complete golf facility with a "Pitch & Putt", 55 tee driving range and miniature golf. The course is lit in the summer. Price goes up to $8 after 6 on the weekdays.

Mount Pocono Golf Course

10 Pine Hill Rd, Mt Pocono PA — (717)839-6061

Directions: Rte 380 to Rte 940 East. The course is at the intersection of 940 and 611.

Holes	Par	Yards Back Tees	Rating	Slope
9	34	2400	—	—

Facility Type: Public

Club Pro: None
Discounts: Seniors, Twilight
Tee Times: No

	9 Holes	18 Holes	Hours Mid Season
Weekday:	—	$7.00	7:30 am - Dusk
Weekend:	—	$8.00	7:00 am - Dusk
Cart Fees:	$7.00	$13.00	

Mandatory Cart Rental: No
Club Rental: Yes

Features: Pro Shop - Limited, Lodging Nearby

Description: #2 and #3 are a headache on this fairly straightforward course. The course is in the woods with some undulations.

Mt Airy Lodge - "The 18 Best"   PA 39

Mount Pocono PA — Info: (717)839-8811   Tee Times: (800)441-4410

Directions: I-80 Exit 44 (Scotrun) onto 611 North approx 3 mi. to Mt Airy Lodge sign.

Holes	Par	Yards Back Tees	Rating	Slope
18	72	7123	74.3	—

Facility Type: Resort

Club Pro: Harold Diamond
Discounts: None
Tee Times: Yes, call at least 1 - 2 weeks ahead in mid-season.

	9 Holes	18 Holes	Hours Mid Season
Weekday:	—	$35.00	6:00 am - Dusk
Weekend:	—	$45.00	5:00 am - Dusk
Cart Fees:	—	$15.90	

Mandatory Cart Rental: Yes
Club Rental: Yes

Features: Lessons, Driving Range, Practice Area, Pro Shop - Complete, Clubhouse, Restaurant, Bar, Snack Bar, Banquet Facilities, Lodging Nearby, American Express, VISA/MC

Notes: Weekend is Friday - Sunday. Cart fee listed is per person.

Description: This unusual course was designed by Hal Purdy and picked by Golf Digest for "Places to Play" for '90 and '91. You must make up your mind beforehand that every hole is going to call for position shots. It's a very challenging course. And the scenery adds to the experience.

Neshaminy Valley Golf Course   PA 40

Jamison PA —   Tee Times: (215)343-6930

Directions: Rte 263 (York Rd) to Almshouse Rd East. The course is 1 mi. on the right.

Holes	Par	Yards Back Tees	Rating	Slope
18	71	6100	69.0	113

Facility Type: Public

Club Pro: Jim & Nancy Schneider
Discounts: Seniors, Twilight
Tee Times: Yes, call ahead 1 day. Tee times are necessary before 10 on weekdays and before 12 on weekends.

	9 Holes	18 Holes	Hours Mid Season
Weekday:	—	$13.00	6:30 am - Dusk
Weekend:	—	$16.00	Dawn - Dusk
Cart Fees:	—	$10.00	

Mandatory Cart Rental: No
Club Rental: No

Features: Lessons, Practice Area, Snack Bar, Pro Shop - Limited

Notes: Senior specials - $9.50 for 18 plus $8 for cart.

Description: This is a straightforward course in a valley. The Neshaminy Creek comes into play on two holes. It's a good course for seniors. Changes for '92 will toughen things up a little.

Northampton Valley CC

Rte 332, Richboro PA — Tee Times: (215)355-2234

Directions: Take the Newtown Exit off of I-95. Go West on Rte 332 approximately 7 mi. to course.

Facility Type: Semi-private

Club Pro: Tom Borsavage
Discounts: Seniors, Twilight
Tee Times: Yes, tee times for weekends only. Call Monday prior.

Features: Lessons, Showers/Lockers, Practice Area, Pro Shop - Complete, Clubhouse, Restaurant, Bar, Snack Bar, Banquet Facilities

Description: This is a pretty course with a mixed terrain and fairly narrow fairways. A favorite is #5, a par 5, 505 yd shot to a dogleg left, over a creek and around a lake to a protected green.

Holes	Par	Yards Back Tees	Rating	Slope
18	71	6150	68.8	—

	9 Holes	18 Holes	Hours Mid Season
Weekday:	—	$18.00	7:00 am - Dusk
Weekend:	—	$22.00	Dawn - Dusk
Cart Fees:	—	$22.00	

Mandatory Cart Rental: See notes.
Club Rental: No

Notes: Carts are mandatory on weekends until 1 pm.

Olde Masters Golf Club

Newtown Square PA — (215)356-7606

Directions: PA Turnpike to the King of Prussia Exit. Take Rte 202 South to Rte 252 South. At Rte 3 turn right (West) and the course is approxiamately 2 miles.

Facility Type: Public

Club Pro: Bob & Chris Thatcher, Joe Golden, Brian Lee
Discounts: None
Tee Times: No

Features: Lessons, Driving Range, Practice Area, Pro Shop - Complete, Snack Bar, American Express, VISA/MC

Description: This rolling course is tree-lined and tight. The greens are small and well-bunkered. There's call for a lot of accurate shots. Typical is the 2nd hole, a 140 yard par 3. The shot is to a green guarded by a creek in front, bunkers to the sides and ob in back.

Holes	Par	Yards Back Tees	Rating	Slope
9	33	2300	—	—

	9 Holes	18 Holes	Hours Mid Season
Weekday:	$7.00	$10.00	8:00 am - Dusk
Weekend:	$8.00	$11.00	7:00 am - Dusk
Cart Fees:	$11.00	$17.00	

Mandatory Cart Rental: No
Club Rental: Yes

Notes: The driving range has 58 mat tees. The facility also has a miniature golf course.

Oxford Valley Public GC

141 South Oxford Valley Road, Fairless Hills PA — (215)945-8644

Directions: Take the Oxford Valley Exit from Rte 1. Go South on Oxford Valley Road approximately 2 miles to the course.

Facility Type: Public

Club Pro: None
Discounts: None
Tee Times: No

Features: Showers/Lockers, Practice Area, Pro Shop - Limited, Clubhouse, Snack Bar

Description: This is a short course but offers some pretty fair challenges. It's flat, treelined and features some water. There are no fairway bunkers but 75% of the greens are trapped. It's a good course for all levels.

Holes	Par	Yards Back Tees	Rating	Slope
9	31	2025	—	—

	9 Holes	18 Holes	Hours Mid Season
Weekday:	$6.00	$9.00	7:00 am - Dusk
Weekend:	$6.00	$9.00	6:30 am - Dusk
Cart Fees:	—	—	
Club Rental: Yes			

Notes: Inquire about annual greens fee plan. No motorized carts. Closed January and February only.

Paxon Hollow Golf Club

850 Paxon Hollow Road, Media PA — **Tee Times:** (215)353-0220

Directions: From Rte 1, Exit onto 320 North. Go 4 miles and take the 1st left past the Lawrence Park Shopping Center onto Paxon Hollow Road. The course is approximately 2 miles.

Facility Type: Public

Club Pro: John Carson
Discounts: Seniors, Twilight
Tee Times: Yes, 1 week ahead for any day.

Features: Practice Area, Pro Shop - Complete, Snack Bar

Description: This is a short and hilly course that will test your short iron game. The fairways are wide but the elevated greens offer a challenge. There is not too much water and an average number of traps.

Holes	Par	Yards Back Tees	Rating	Slope
18	71	5641	67.4	116

	9 Holes	18 Holes	Hours Mid Season
Weekday:	—	$15.00	7:30 am - Dusk
Weekend:	—	$18.00	7:00 am - Dusk
Cart Fees:	$12.00	$20.00	

Mandatory Cart Rental: See notes.
Club Rental: Yes

Notes: Twilight is after 4 mid-season. A single rider cart is $14. Carts are mandatory only on weekends before 1 pm. Residents of the township take $2 off fees. Sr discounts apply M, W, and F.

Pickering Valley Golf Club

South Whithorse Road, Phoenixville PA — Tee Times: (215)933-2223

Directions: Take the Valley Forge Exit off the PA Turnpike. Go Rte 23 West approximately 5 miles and take a left onto White Horse Rd. The course is 2 miles on the left.

Facility Type: Public

Club Pro: None
Discounts: Seniors
Tee Times: Yes, 1 week for weekends

Features: Lessons, Showers/Lockers, Driving Range, Practice Area, Pro Shop - Complete, Snack Bar, Banquet Facilities

Description: Like other courses in Chester County, this is rolling, and it's scenic. 8 lakes come into play on this, otherwise, wooded and well-trapped course. The front is open and the back a bit tighter. A favorite of management is the par 3, 216 yard 2nd hole. The tee sits 40 ft up and plays over a valley and pond to a narow green, trapped above and below.

Holes	Par	Yards Back Tees	Rating	Slope
18	72	6487	70.3	122

	9 Holes	18 Holes	Hours Mid Season
Weekday:	$10.00	$15.00	Dawn - Dusk
Weekend:	$13.00	$18.00	Dawn - Dusk
Cart Fees:	$9.00	$18.00	

Mandatory Cart Rental: See notes.
Club Rental: Yes

Notes: Carts are mandatory only on weekends and only until 3 pm.

Pinecrest Golf Club

101 Country Club Dr, Lansdale PA — Tee Times: (215)855-6112

Directions: PA Turnpike to Fort Washington Exit (26). 309 North to 202 North., Course is on 202 just North of intersection of 309.

Facility Type: Public

Club Pro: Joe Max
Discounts: Seniors
Tee Times: Yes, 5 days for any day.

Features: Lessons, Showers/Lockers, Practice Area, Pro Shop - Complete, Clubhouse, Restaurant, Bar, Snack Bar, Banquet Facilities, VISA/MC, Lodging Nearby

Description: Ron Prichard designed this course that will remind you of a Florida course - rolling with well-placed bunkers and beautiful greens. #18 is a 434 yd par 4 and a favorite here. It's ob and bunkered right with tree-lined fairway to a well-protected, flat green.

Holes	Par	Yards Back Tees	Rating	Slope
18	70	6331	69.3	122

	9 Holes	18 Holes	Hours Mid Season
Weekday:	$10.00	$18.00	6:00 am - Dusk
Weekend:	$14.00	$25.00	6:00 am - Dusk
Cart Fees:	—	$12.00	

Mandatory Cart Rental: See notes.
Club Rental: Yes

Notes: Cart mandatory until 4 pm on weekends.

Pocono Farms Country Club
PA 47

Lake Rd, Tobyhana PA — **Tee Times:** (717)894-8441

Directions: I-80 to 380 N to the Tobyhana Exit. Take a right to 423 East to 611 South. Go 1 mi. to Cayuga Rd and turn left to course.

Facility Type: Semi-private

Club Pro: Jeff Garner
Discounts: Twilight
Tee Times: Yes, 1 week prior for any day.

Features: Lessons, Driving Range, Practice Area, Pro Shop - Complete, Clubhouse, Restaurant, Bar, Snack Bar, Banquet Facilities, Lodging Nearby

Description: Art Wall designed this course that is cut through the woods. It was a choice by Golf Digest for "Places to Play" in '90 and '91. The signature is #17, a 547 yd par 5. It has water down the whole left side and plays over marsh to a 2-tiered green guarded by water and bunkers.

Holes	Par	Yards Back Tees	Rating	Slope
18	72	6610	70.4	120

	9 Holes	18 Holes	Hours Mid Season
Weekday:	—	$35.00	6:00 am - Dusk
Weekend:	—	$38.00	6:00 am - Dusk
Cart Fees:	—	—	

Mandatory Cart Rental: Yes
Club Rental: No

Notes: Cart fee included in green fees.

Pocono Manor Inn & GC
PA 48

Rte 314, Pocono Manor PA — **Info:** (717)839-7111   **Tee Times:** (800)233-8150

Directions: Rte 380 North from I-80 to Exit 8. Follow the signs. Inn approx 2 miles.

Facility Type: Resort

Club Pro: Greg Wall
Discounts: Twilight
Tee Times: Yes, 1 week prior for non-guests

Features: Lessons, Showers/Lockers, Driving Range, Practice Area, Pro Shop - Complete, Clubhouse, Restaurant, Bar, Snack Bar, Banquet Facilities, Lodging Nearby, American Express, VISA/MC

Description: The "East" course is hilly and shorter, the "West" is long and flat. The signature is #7 on the "East". It's a 77 yd par 3 straight down to a small undulating green guarded by a creek. This was a choice by Golf Digest for "Places to Play" in '90 and '91.

Holes	Par	Yards Back Tees	Rating	Slope
18	72	6480	71.0	—
18	72	6870	72.0	—

	9 Holes	18 Holes	Hours Mid Season
Weekday:	—	$18.00	8:00 am - Dusk
Weekend:	—	$27.00	7:30 am - Dusk
Cart Fees:	—	$13.00	

Mandatory Cart Rental: Yes
Club Rental: Yes

Notes: Cart fee is per person. Home of the Greg Wall Golf School.

Quartette Golf Club

1075 Southampton Road, Phila PA — (215)676-3939

Directions: The course is on Southampton Road approximately 1.25 miles West of US 1 in Philadelphia.

Holes	Par	Yards Back Tees	Rating	Slope
9	27	1089	—	—

	9 Holes	18 Holes	Hours Mid Season
Weekday:	$7.00	$7.00	7:30 am - Dusk
Weekend:	$8.00	$8.00	7:30 am - Dusk
Cart Fees:	—	—	
Club Rental: Yes			

Facility Type: Semi-private

Club Pro: None
Discounts: None
Tee Times: No

Features: Lessons, Practice Area, Pro Shop - Complete, Restaurant, Bar, Banquet Facilities, Lodging Nearby

Description: This is a good course for your iron game and putting. The course slopes down somewhat and a water runs through most of it.

Red Maples Golf Club

Box 106, Waymart PA — (717)937-4543

Directions: The course is on Rte 296, 4 miles South of Rte 6 in South Canaan. Rte 6 can be reached on I-380 North of Scranton or I-84 just West of New Jersey.

Holes	Par	Yards Back Tees	Rating	Slope
9	33	2300	—	—

	9 Holes	18 Holes	Hours Mid Season
Weekday:	$6.00	$9.00	7:00 am - Dusk
Weekend:	$8.00	$11.00	7:00 am - Dusk
Cart Fees:	$8.50	$14.00	

Facility Type: Public

Club Pro: None
Discounts: None
Tee Times: No

Mandatory Cart Rental: No
Club Rental: Yes

Features: Pro Shop - Limited, Snack Bar, Lodging Nearby

Description: This rolling course is short and a relatively easy walk, but not so straightforward. It has trees, water and several hills to mix up your shots. It is considered well-manicured.

Rolling Turf Golf Course

Smith Rd, Schwenksville PA — (215)287-7297

Directions: PA Turnpike to Fort Washington Exit. Take 73 West near the exit into Schwenksville. Turn left onto Centenial Ave. The course is 1 mi. on the left.

Facility Type: Public

Club Pro: None
Discounts: Seniors
Tee Times: No

Features: Practice Area, Pro Shop - Limited, Snack Bar, Clubhouse

Description: There are actually 12 holes on this long executive-like course. The longest hole is 302. There are 2 par 4's and the rest par 3's.

Holes	Par	Yards Back Tees	Rating	Slope
9dt	38	1985	—	—

	9 Holes	18 Holes	Hours Mid Season
Weekday:	$5.50	—	7:00 am - Dusk
Weekend:	$6.00	—	Dawn - Dusk
Cart Fees:	$6.00	—	

Mandatory Cart Rental: No
Club Rental: No

Sawmill Golf Course

5630 Sullivan Trail, Easton PA — (215)759-8200

Directions: The course is 3/4 mi. from Rte 33 on Rte 191 going north.

Coupon page 251

Facility Type: Public

Club Pro: None
Discounts: Seniors, Twilight, Juniors
Tee Times: No

Features: Lessons, Pro Shop - Limited, Clubhouse, Snack Bar

Description: This is a good course for beginners and anyone boning up, but offers a challenge for the experienced golfer. There is no sand or water. There are several challenging side hill lies, however. It is a scenic course and generally very pleasant to play.

Holes	Par	Yards Back Tees	Rating	Slope
9	35	2912	—	—

	9 Holes	18 Holes	Hours Mid Season
Weekday:	$8.00	$8.00	7:00 am - 7:00 pm
Weekend:	$9.00	$9.00	7:00 am - 7:00 pm
Cart Fees:	$9.00	$15.00	

Mandatory Cart Rental: No
Club Rental: Yes

Notes: Twilight rates after 4 pm. Rates are for the day - unlimited play.

Scranton Municipal GC

Lake Ariel PA — Tee Times: (717)689-2686

Directions: Take Exit 4 on I-84. The course is directly off the exit.

Facility Type: Public

Club Pro: Ed Cimoch
Discounts: Seniors
Tee Times: Yes, Wednesday morning at 9 am for the following weekend.

Features: Lessons, Showers/Lockers, Practice Area, Pro Shop - Limited, Snack Bar

Description: There is a good mix of terrain here and a bit of a challenge for every level of golfer. The local press refers to #16 as "The Monster". It's a 318 yard par 4, all up hill.

Holes	Par	Yards Back Tees	Rating	Slope
18	72	6843	71.3	—

	9 Holes	18 Holes	Hours Mid Season
Weekday:	$6.00	$10.00	Dawn - Dusk
Weekend:	$7.00	$12.00	Dawn - Dusk
Cart Fees:	$10.00	$18.00	

Mandatory Cart Rental: No
Club Rental: Yes

Notes: Cart rental price is for 2. The Sr discount is for County residents only. Residents of Scranton with a drivers license receive a discount on green fees.

Shawnee Inn & Country Club

Shawnee-on-Delaware PA — Tee Times: (717)421-1500

Directions: I-80 to Exit 52. Go 1 mi. North on Rte 209 to Buttermilk Falls Rd and take a right to the Inn.

Facility Type: Resort

Coupon page 251

Club Pro: Gordon Neely
Discounts: Twilight
Tee Times: Yes, 1 day for non-guests.

Features: Lessons, Showers/Lockers, Driving Range, Practice Area, Pro Shop - Complete, Restaurant, Bar, Snack Bar, Banquet Facilities, Lodging Nearby, American Express, VISA/MC

Description: Golf Digest selected this course for "Places to Play" in both '90 and '91. The course was designed by WA Tillinghast and re-designed by Fred Waring. It is flat, located on an island in the Delaware River, and with mountains to both sides, it is most scenic. #7 blue is the signature. It's a par 3, 165 yd shot across a river from an elevated tee down to the green. If you don't make the river, that's it.

Holes	Par	Yards Back Tees	Rating	Slope
9	36	3227	—	—
9	36	3438	—	—
9	36	3362	—	—

	9 Holes	18 Holes	Hours Mid Season
Weekday:	—	$30.00	8:00 am - Dusk
Weekend:	—	$53.00	8:00 am - Dusk
Cart Fees:	—	—	

Mandatory Cart Rental: Yes
Club Rental: Yes

Notes: The blue/red has a rating of 72.8 and slope of 129; red/white, 72.2 and 132; and white/blue, 72.4 and 131. Cart fees are included. This is the home of "The Swing's The Thing" golf school, one of the highest rated schools in the country.

Skippack Golf Course

Stump Hall & Cedar Rds, Skippack PA — Tee Times: (215)584-4226

Directions: Outside Skippack, 1/2 mi. off of Rte 73 on Stump Hall Rd. Course is well signed.

Holes	Par	Yards Back Tees	Rating	Slope
18	70	6230	69.9	113

Facility Type: Public

Coupon page 252

Club Pro: None

Discounts: Seniors, Twilight

Tee Times: Yes, 1 week for weekends/holidays for non-members, 2 weeks for members.

	9 Holes	18 Holes	Hours Mid Season
Weekday:	—	$12.00	Dawn - Dusk
Weekend:	—	$18.00	Dawn - Dusk
Cart Fees:	—	$10.00	

Mandatory Cart Rental: See notes.

Club Rental: Yes

Features: Lessons, Driving Range, Practice Area, Pro Shop - Complete, Snack Bar, VISA/MC

Notes: Carts are mandatory on weekends and holidays before 10 am. Memberships are available for preferred tee times.

Description: You will experience every type of terrain on this course. It is well-treed, and water comes into play on 4 holes. The 13th, a par 4, 420 yd hole is the favorite of many who play here. It is a severe drive down hill. The 2nd shot is critical due to a creek 80 yds in front of an elevated and contoured green. The course adjoins Evansburg State Park.

Skyline Golf Course

Carbondale PA — Info: (717)282-5993

Directions: Exit 62 off I-81. Take 107 East for 3 mi. to Rte 247 and go left (North). The course is 1.5 mi.

Holes	Par	Yards Back Tees	Rating	Slope
18	66	4719	—	—

Facility Type: Public

	9 Holes	18 Holes	Hours Mid Season
Weekday:	$4.50	$7.00	Dawn - Dusk
Weekend:	$5.50	$9.00	Dawn - Dusk
Cart Fees:	$8.00	$15.00	

Club Pro: None

Discounts: Seniors

Tee Times: No,

Mandatory Cart Rental: No

Club Rental: Yes

Features: Pro Shop - Limited, Snack Bar

Description: The front 9 is flat and a short and walkable 1915 yards. The back is hillier and may require a cart. This is an old course with big trees and water hazards. There is no sand. The greens are in excellent shape.

Skytop Lodge Golf Course PA 57

1 Skytop, Skytop PA — Tee Times: (717)595-7401

Directions: Heading West on I-80 exit at Marshalls Creek 1 mi. past the toll into Pennsylvania and get onto 447 going North. Take a right onto Rte 390 and the course is approx 3.5 miles on the left.

Facility Type: Semi-private

Club Pro: Reed Gravel
Discounts: None
Tee Times: Yes, weekends and Holidays. Call 1 week before. Guests and members take priority.

Features: Lessons, Showers/Lockers, Practice Area, Pro Shop - Complete, Clubhouse, Restaurant, Bar, Banquet Facilities, Lodging Nearby

Description: This was a Golf Digest selection for "Places to Play" in '90 and '91. It's not hilly but not flat, either. The greens and tees are always in superb condition. #18 is "the gobbler" - it eats a lot of balls. It's a 352 yd par 4, narrow out of the chute to an elevated and sloping green, with a creek in front, a bunker right and a lake on the left.

Holes	Par	Yards Back Tees	Rating	Slope
18	71	6220	69.1	118

	9 Holes	18 Holes	Hours Mid Season
Weekday:	—	$40.00	8:30 am - Dusk
Weekend:	—	$40.00	8:00 am - Dusk
Cart Fees:	—	$30.00	

Mandatory Cart Rental: See notes.
Club Rental: Yes

Notes: This is a resort and semi-private course. Carts are mandatory until 3 pm. Conditions for accepting non-guests for play varies. Important to call ahead.

Somerton Springs PA 58

53 Bustleton Pike, Feasterville PA — (215)355-1776

Directions: The facility is located 1 mile South of Street Rd (Rte 132) on Bustleton Pike.

Facility Type: Executive

Club Pro: Don Cardea
Discounts: Twilight, Seniors
Tee Times: No

Features: Lessons, Driving Range, Pro Shop - Complete, Practice Area, Restaurant, Bar, Banquet Facilities, Lodging Nearby

Description: This is complete golf facility with an 18 hole executive course, a driving range with 10 heated booths and the highly-rated Suburban Golf School and miniature golf. This is a total golf complex.

Holes	Par	Yards Back Tees	Rating	Slope
18	55	2235	—	—

	9 Holes	18 Holes	Hours Mid Season
Weekday:	—	$6.50	8:00 am - Dusk
Weekend:	—	$8.00	8:00 am - Dusk
Cart Fees:	—	—	
Club Rental:	Yes		

Notes: Twilight at 4 pm. The driving range is open until 10:30.

Split Rock Golf Club
PA 59

Blakeslee PA — Tee Times: (717)722-9111

Directions: I-80 to 115 North at the Blakeslee Exit. Go to the light and take a left on Rte 940. The course is 2 mi. on the left.

Facility Type: Public

Coupon page 252

Club Pro: Laura Erskine
Discounts: Twilight
Tee Times: Yes, Call ahead for any day.

Features: Lessons, Driving Range, Practice Area, Pro Shop - Complete, Restaurant, Bar, Banquet Facilities, Lodging Nearby, American Express, VISA/MC

Description: There are plans to open an additional 9 holes late in the summer of '92. The existing 9 is hilly and picturesue. The fairways are fairly narrow. The course is well-maintained with irrigated fairways.

Holes	Par	Yards Back Tees	Rating	Slope
9	35	3000	—	—

	9 Holes	18 Holes	Hours Mid Season
Weekday:	$12.00	$20.00	8:00 am - 6 pm
Weekend:	$14.00	$22.00	7:30 am - 6 pm
Cart Fees:	$6.00	$10.00	

Mandatory Cart Rental: See notes.
Club Rental: Yes

Notes: Cart fees listed are per person. Carts are mandatory until 4 pm. Call for the before-noon midweek special.

Springfield Country Club
PA 60

400 N Sproul Rd, Springfield PA — Tee Times: (215)543-9860

Directions: Rte 1 South from Philadelphia to Rte 320 South and 3/4 mi. to the course.

Facility Type: Public

Club Pro: Bill Erseck
Discounts: Twilight
Tee Times: Yes, Thursday at 8:30 am for weekends/holidays.

Features: Lessons, Showers/Lockers, Practice Area, Pro Shop - Complete, Clubhouse, Restaurant, Bar, Snack Bar, Banquet Facilities

Description: This is a somewhat hilly course with narrow fairways and a lot of traps. The course is in the process of rebuilding all of the greens and adding water.

Holes	Par	Yards Back Tees	Rating	Slope
18	69	5513	62.3	108

	9 Holes	18 Holes	Hours Mid Season
Weekday:	—	$14.00	7:00 am - 7:00 pm
Weekend:	—	$17.00	7:00 am - 7:00 pm
Cart Fees:	—	$20.00	

Mandatory Cart Rental: No
Club Rental: Yes

Notes: Residents of Springfield pay less. Twilight rate after 3 pm.

Strickland's Wiscasset GC   PA 61

Mt Pocono PA — Info: (717)839-7155

Directions: From I-80 take Rte 380 North to the Mt Pocono Exit. Take 940 East to 611 Southand Strickland's Mountain Inn is approximately 1 mile.

Facility Type: Resort

Club Pro: None
Discounts: Twilight
Tee Times: No

Features: Lessons, Pro Shop - Limited, Restaurant, Bar, Banquet Facilities, Lodging Nearby

Description: This is a long executive-type course with par 3's, 4's and a 5. The fairways are tight and it has a good mix of terrain and obstacles. You may find yourself on some side hill lies, but it's a very walkable course. #5 is a favorite. It's a slight dog-leg right to a hidden green.

Holes	Par	Yards Back Tees	Rating	Slope
9	32	2316	—	—

	9 Holes	18 Holes	Hours Mid Season
Weekday:	$7.00	$14.00	7:30 am - Dusk
Weekend:	$8.00	$16.00	7:30 am - Dusk
Cart Fees:	$8.00	$12.00	

Mandatory Cart Rental: No
Club Rental: Yes

Notes: Leesons are referred to the Mt Airy Lodge course, 1/4 mile away.

Tamiment Resort & Conf. Cntr.   PA 62

Tamiment PA — Tee Times: (717)588-6652

Directions: Head North from Stroudsberg on Rte 209 to Bushkill. Go left at the blinking light and 4 mi. to the resort on the left.

Facility Type: Resort

Club Pro: Vince Yanovitch
Discounts: None
Tee Times: Yes, accepted up to two weeks in advance for any day.

Features: Lessons, Showers/Lockers, Practice Area, Pro Shop - Complete, Clubhouse, Restaurant, Bar, Snack Bar, Banquet Facilities, Lodging Nearby

Description: This Robert Trent Jones course was selected by Golf Digest as one of the 200 best in the country. It was also their choice for "Places to Play" in '90 and '91. It plays long, and it's scenic. The most beautiful hole is the 17th, a 580 yard par 5 - a hilly shot to a bunkered green.

Holes	Par	Yards Back Tees	Rating	Slope
18	72	6858	72.7	130

	9 Holes	18 Holes	Hours Mid Season
Weekday:	—	$38.00	8:00 am - 6:00 pm
Weekend:	—	$38.00	8:00 am - 6:00 pm
Cart Fees:	—	—	

Mandatory Cart Rental: Yes
Club Rental: Yes

Notes: Cart fee included with green fee. Guests of the hotel receive reduced green fees.

Thornhurst Country Club PA 63

143 Country Club Estate, Thornhurst PA — (717)472-9521

Directions: I-80 to the Blakslee Exit. Take Rte 115 North approxiamtely 8 miles to River Road and take a right. Go 5 miles and turn left on Bear Lake Rd. The club is 3 mi. on the left.

Facility Type: Executive

Club Pro: None
Discounts: None
Tee Times: No

Features: Pro Shop - Limited, Clubhouse, Restaurant, Bar

Description: This is a flat, well-maintained executive course. There is no water to speak of and no sand, just good practice for your iron game or for beginners.

Holes	Par	Yards Back Tees	Rating	Slope
9	27	1655	—	—

	9 Holes	18 Holes	Hours Mid Season
Weekday:	$10.00	$10.00	8:00 am - 7:00 pm
Weekend:	$10.00	$10.00	8:00 am - 7:00 pm
Cart Fees:	—	—	
Club Rental: No			

Notes: The course caters to outings and has seasonal memberships available for $100.

Tumblebrook Golf Course PA 64

3600 Jacoby Rd, Coopersburg PA — **Tee Times:** (215)282-9021

Directions: Rte 309 to Jacoby Rd East in Coopersburg. The course is 3 miles from 309 on the right.

Facility Type: Public

Coupon page 252

Club Pro: None
Discounts: Seniors
Tee Times: Yes, Call ahead for weekends and holidays.

Features: Practice Area, Pro Shop - Limited, Clubhouse, Snack Bar

Description: This course was designed by Donald Ross. It is hilly and offers a challenge for any level golfer. #7 is an interesting hole - a 235 yd shot over a creek to a somewhat guarded green.

Holes	Par	Yards Back Tees	Rating	Slope
9dt	71	6321	—	—

	9 Holes	18 Holes	Hours Mid Season
Weekday:	$8.00	$8.00	7:00 am - Dusk
Weekend:	$9.00	$9.00	7:00 am - Dusk
Cart Fees:	$10.00	$15.00	

Mandatory Cart Rental: No
Club Rental: Yes

Notes: Twilight rates after 3 pm mid-season.

Twin Lakes Country Club PA 65

Mainland PA — Tee Times: (215)256-9548

Directions: PA Turnpike to Exit 31 (Lansdale). Take a right off the exit and the 1st left onto Old Forty Foot Rd. Go 1/2 mi. to course on right.

Facility Type: Public

Club Pro: None
Discounts: Seniors, Twilight
Tee Times: Yes, 3 weeks ahead for weekends

Features: Practice Area, Pro Shop - Complete, Clubhouse, Bar, Snack Bar, VISA/MC

Description: This is a hilly course with some water. It is fairly tight with trees.

Holes	Par	Yards Back Tees	Rating	Slope
18	70	5540	66.7	117

	9 Holes	18 Holes	Hours Mid Season
Weekday:	—	$16.00	6:30 am - Dusk
Weekend:	—	$19.00	Dawn - Dusk
Cart Fees:	—	$22.00	

Mandatory Cart Rental: See notes.
Club Rental: Yes

Notes: Cart fee listed is for 2. Carts are mandatory on weekends May through Sept.

Twin Lakes Golf Course PA 66

Allentown PA — Tee Times: (215)395-3369

Directions: In the Allentown area 3.5 mi. North of Rte 22 on Cedar Crest Blvd.

Facility Type: Public

Club Pro: None
Discounts: None
Tee Times: Yes, 2 weeks in advance.

Features: Showers/Lockers, Practice Area, Pro Shop - Complete, Clubhouse, Snack Bar

Description: This is an easy walking course, good for seniors. You can't get into too much trouble on this course, but there are a few challenges. Water comes into play on 5 holes.

Holes	Par	Yards Back Tees	Rating	Slope
18	70	6200	—	—

	9 Holes	18 Holes	Hours Mid Season
Weekday:	—	$13.00	6:00 am - 7:00 pm
Weekend:	—	$15.00	Dawn - Dusk
Cart Fees:	—	$20.00	

Mandatory Cart Rental: No
Club Rental: No

Twin Ponds Golf Course PA 67

654 Gilbertsville Road, Gilbertsville PA — Tee Times: (215)369-1901

Directions: From Rte 422, go North on Rte 100 about 9 miles. Go right (East) on Moyer Road, and at the stop, take a left to the course.

Facility Type: Public

Club Pro: None
Discounts: Seniors
Tee Times: Yes, Weekends and holidays, as far in advance as possible.

Features: Practice Area, Pro Shop - Complete, Clubhouse, Restaurant, Bar, Banquet Facilities

Description: This course has a rolling terrain and a lot of trees. The trees are pine so the leaf problem in the fall is minimal. Generally, it's an easy walking course. The fairways are fairly wide, but getting tighter. Water comes into play on 4 holes from 7 ponds. The course is pretty well trapped and the greens are in excellent shape.

Holes	Par	Yards Back Tees	Rating	Slope
18	70	5646	—	—

	9 Holes	18 Holes	Hours Mid Season
Weekday:	—	$9.50	6:00 am - Dusk
Weekend:	—	$13.00	6:00 am - Dusk
Cart Fees:	—	$18.00	

Mandatory Cart Rental: No
Club Rental: Yes

Notes: Cart rental fee is for 2.

Twin Woods Golf Course PA 68

2924 E Orville Rd, Hatfield PA — Tee Times: (215)822-9263

Directions: PA Turnpike to 309 North through Montgomeryville past Zoto's Diner. 1st left is Orville Rd. 1/2 mi. to course.

Facility Type: Public

Club Pro: Bill Carvolth
Discounts: Twilight, Seniors
Tee Times: Yes, reserve for weekends/holidays.

Features: Lessons, Pro Shop - Complete, Snack Bar

Description: This is a flat course good for seniors, but it is not a piece of cake.

Holes	Par	Yards Back Tees	Rating	Slope
9	36	3125	—	—

	9 Holes	18 Holes	Hours Mid Season
Weekday:	$7.50	$7.50	7:00 am - Dusk
Weekend:	$9.00	$9.00	7:00 am - Dusk
Cart Fees:	$9.00	$17.00	

Mandatory Cart Rental: No
Club Rental: Yes

Twining Valley Golf Club PA 69

1400 Twining Rd, Dresher PA — Tee Times: (215)659-9917

Directions: Take the Willow Grove Exit 27 off the PA Turnpike and go South on Rte 611 for 3/4 mi. Take a right on Fitzwater Town Road and another right at the 1st light onto Welsh Rd. Go 2 lights and take a left on Twining Rd and go approximately 1.5 mi. to the course.

Facility Type: Public

Club Pro: Hugh Reilly
Discounts: Seniors, Twilight
Tee Times: Yes, 1 week for any day but especially weekends and holidays.

Features: Lessons, Showers/Lockers, Practice Area, Pro Shop - Complete, Clubhouse, Bar, Banquet Facilities, American Express, VISA/MC, Restaurant

Holes	Par	Yards Back Tees	Rating	Slope
18	71	5762	65.9	114

	9 Holes	18 Holes	Hours Mid Season
Weekday:	—	$18.00	Dawn - Dusk
Weekend:	—	$20.00	Dawn - Dusk
Cart Fees:	—	$22.00	

Mandatory Cart Rental: See notes.
Club Rental: Yes

Notes: Carts are mandatory on weekends only up to 12 noon. Sr discount on Mon and Fri. Twilight starts at 3 pm midseason.

Description: This old-style course was designed by Jock Melville, an old world Scotsman, in 1931. Many people refer to these types as Toomey-Flynn, Donald Ross. The challenge is the up and down play and the side-hill lies you are often left with. Mature trees and fairway bunkers make demands for accuracy. The back nine is more open. The bunkered greens are fair sized.

Upper Perk Golf Course PA 70

Rte 663 and Ott Rd, Pennsburg PA — Tee Times: (215)679-5594

Directions: PA Turnpike to the Quakerstown Exit to Rte 663. Take a right and course is 4 mi. on left.

Facility Type: Public

Club Pro: Jerry Haberle
Discounts: Seniors, Juniors, Twilight
Tee Times: Yes, 2 weeks for weekends.

Features: Lessons, Practice Area, Pro Shop - Limited, Clubhouse, Snack Bar

Description: This is a relatively easy walking course, great for seniors. It's pretty open but getting tighter every year with the planting of new trees.

Holes	Par	Yards Back Tees	Rating	Slope
18	71	6455	70.5	—

	9 Holes	18 Holes	Hours Mid Season
Weekday:	—	$10.00	6:00 am - Dusk
Weekend:	—	$13.00	6:00 am - Dusk
Cart Fees:	—	$18.00	

Mandatory Cart Rental: No
Club Rental: No

Notes: Weekday memberships are available.

Valley Forge Golf Club   PA 71

401 N Gulph Rd, King of Prussia PA — Tee Times: (215)337-1776

Directions: PA Turnpike to Exit 24. The course is directly after the toll.

Holes	Par	Yards Back Tees	Rating	Slope
18	71	6000	68.9	—

Facility Type: Public

	9 Holes	18 Holes	Hours Mid Season
Weekday:	—	$15.00	Dawn - Dusk
Weekend:	—	$19.00	Dawn - Dusk
Cart Fees:	—	$23.00	

Club Pro: Dave Smith
Discounts: Twilight
Tee Times: Yes, Monday for weekends/holidays.

Mandatory Cart Rental: No
Club Rental: Yes

Features: Lessons, Practice Area, Snack Bar, Pro Shop - Limited

Notes: Twilight starts at 4 pm.

Description: This is a relatively flat, open and fairly straightforward course.

Walnut Lane Golf Course   PA 72

800 Walnut Lane, Philadelphia PA — Tee Times: (215)482-3370

Directions: Rte 76 to Rte1/Roosevelt Blvd. Turn at Ridge Ave and go West to the top of the hill and turn right onto Walnut to course at the intersection of Henry Ave and Walnut Lane.

Holes	Par	Yards Back Tees	Rating	Slope
18	62	4500	59.8	91

	9 Holes	18 Holes	Hours Mid Season
Weekday:	—	$14.00	Dawn - Dusk
Weekend:	—	$16.00	Dawn - Dusk
Cart Fees:	—	$19.00	

Facility Type: Public

Coupon page 253

Club Pro: Gary Groff
Discounts: Seniors, Juniors, Twiligh
Tee Times: Yes, 1 week ahead for weekends/holidays.

Mandatory Cart Rental: No
Club Rental: Yes

Features: Lessons, Practice Area, Pro Shop - Complete, Clubhouse, Restaurant, Bar, American Express, VISA/MC, Snack Bar, Lodging Nearby

Notes: Cart fee listed is for 2. $12 for 1.

Description: This is a sporty course, both hilly and tight. The greens are set neatly among the trees of scenic Fairmont Park. You'll use every club in the bag here. It is a good test for a good player.

Waltz Golf Farm

Limerick PA — (215)489-7839

Directions: Rte 422 Bypass West to the Limerick Exit. Turn right to Lewis Rd and go to the end. Take another right to course.

Facility Type: Pitch & Putt

Club Pro: Ted McKenzie
Discounts: None
Tee Times: No

Features: Lessons, Driving Range, Practice Area, Snack Bar

Holes	Par	Yards Back Tees	Rating	Slope
9	27	920	—	—

	9 Holes	18 Holes	Hours Mid Season
Weekday:	$3.00	—	9:00 am - 11:00 pm
Weekend:	$5.00	—	9:00 am - 11:00 pm
Cart Fees:	—	—	
Club Rental: Yes			

Notes: Complete driving range on the facility, as well as miniature golf.

Water Gap Country Club

Delaware Water Gap PA — **Tee Times:** (717)476-0200

Directions: I-80 to Exit 53. Left at light onto 611 South. 3 blocks to Mountain Rd, take right and course is at end.

Facility Type: Semi-private

Club Pro: Bob Luhr
Discounts: Twilight
Tee Times: Yes, 5 days prior for any day.

Features: Lessons, Showers/Lockers, Practice Area, Pro Shop - Complete, Clubhouse, Restaurant, Bar, Snack Bar, Banquet Facilities, Lodging Nearby, American Express, VISA/MC

Description: Built in 1921, this course was designed by Bob White. It was the site of the Eastern Open in 1927. Walter Hagen still owns the record of 64. It's a hilly and well-bunkered course with small greens. #12 is the signature - a par 3, 201 yd narrow shot over a pond to a shallow green with a huge trap.

Holes	Par	Yards Back Tees	Rating	Slope
18	72	6186	70.0	125

	9 Holes	18 Holes	Hours Mid Season
Weekday:	—	$16.00	8:00 am - Dusk
Weekend:	—	$20.00	7:00 am - Dusk
Cart Fees:	—	$28.00	

Mandatory Cart Rental: See notes.
Club Rental: Yes

Notes: Cart fee is for 2 people. The facility has a 22 room hotel.

Wedgewood Golf Course
PA 75

4875 Limeport Pike, Coopersburg PA — **Tee Times:** (215)797-4551

Directions: From Rte 309 go West on Saucon Valley Rd to the end. Take a left onto Limeport Pike and the course is 1/4 mi.

Facility Type: Public

Club Pro: Roger Stern
Discounts: Seniors, Twilight
Tee Times: Yes, Monday before for weekend. Up to 2 weeks before for weekday.

Features: Lessons, Showers/Lockers, Driving Range, Practice Area, Pro Shop - Complete, Clubhouse, Bar, Snack Bar

Description: This is a relatively flat and open course with a few streams. The 17th hole, a par 4, is a favorite. Your shot is over a hill to a dogleg right and around trees to a blind green.

Holes	Par	Yards Back Tees	Rating	Slope
18	71	6162	68.8	122

	9 Holes	18 Holes	Hours Mid Season
Weekday:	$8.00	$13.00	Dawn - Dusk
Weekend:	—	$16.00	Dawn - Dusk
Cart Fees:	$9.00	$18.00	

Mandatory Cart Rental: See notes.
Club Rental: Yes

Notes: Carts are mandatory on weekends before 1 pm. Foursomes only weekends before 11 am. Dress code applies. No tank tops or cut-offs for men or women.

Westover Golf Course
PA 76

401 S Schuylkill Ave, Norristown PA — **Tee Times:** (215)539-4502

Directions: Ridge Pike in Norristown to South Schuylkill Ave going South. The course is 1/2 mi. on the right.

Facility Type: Semi-private

Coupon page 253

Club Pro: Paul Galczyk
Discounts: None
Tee Times: Yes, 5 days ahead for non-members.

Features: Lessons, Showers/Lockers, Practice Area, Pro Shop - Complete, Clubhouse, Restaurant, Bar, Banquet Facilities, VISA/MC

Description: The course is not quite flat, with water coming into play on several holes. #18 is a par 4, 270 yard shot to the other side of water. It's very challenging - you must lay up nearly perfectly to hope for par.

Holes	Par	Yards Back Tees	Rating	Slope
18	70	6437	69.9	116

	9 Holes	18 Holes	Hours Mid Season
Weekday:	—	$29.00	7:00 am - 7:30 pm
Weekend:	—	$32.00	6:30 am - 7:30 pm
Cart Fees:	—	—	

Mandatory Cart Rental: Yes
Club Rental:

Notes: Cart included with green fees.

Willow Brook Golf Course PA 77

Howertown Rd, Catasauqua PA — (215)264-9904

Directions: Rte 22 to the Airport Exit near Allentown. Take 987 North to Race Street and turn left. At the 1st stop take a right (14th St). At the 2nd stop take a left onto Walnut. At the 2nd stop again, turn right onto Howertown Rd, and proceed to the course.

Holes	Par	Yards Back Tees	Rating	Slope
9	35	2950	—	—

	9 Holes	18 Holes	Hours Mid Season
Weekday:	$6.00	$8.00	8:00 am - Dusk
Weekend:	$7.00	$10.00	7:00 am - Dusk
Cart Fees:	$7.00	$14.00	

Facility Type: Public

Mandatory Cart Rental: No
Club Rental: Yes

Club Pro: Steve Chromiak
Discounts: None
Tee Times: No

Features: Lessons, Showers/Lockers, Pro Shop - Limited, Clubhouse, Snack Bar

Description: An easily-walked and straightforward course.

Woodland Hills Country Club PA 78

Hellertown PA —   Tee Times: (215)838-7192

Directions: I-78 to Exit 21 (Hellertown-Bethlehem). Take Rte 412 South only one block and go left on Cherry Lane. Take it to the end and turn left onto Easton Rd. Go approximately 3 mi. and take a left onto Lower Sauken. The course is 1 mi. on left.

Holes	Par	Yards Back Tees	Rating	Slope
18	72	7000	—	—

	9 Holes	18 Holes	Hours Mid Season
Weekday:	—	$14.00	6:30 am - Dusk
Weekend:	—	$17.00	6:30 am - Dusk
Cart Fees:	$12.00	$20.00	

Facility Type: Public

Club Pro: John Long
Discounts: None
Tee Times: Yes, up to 1 week prior to weekends and holidays.

Mandatory Cart Rental: No
Club Rental: Yes

Notes: Memberships are available.

Features: Lessons, Driving Range, Practice Area, Pro Shop - Complete, Clubhouse, Restaurant, Bar, Banquet Facilities, Showers/Lockers, Lodging Nearby, American Express, VISA/MC

Description: This course is undergoing constant improvements under a relatively new owner. 1992 will see two new greens and a longer course. It is rolling terrain with water and bunkers playing a part. A favorite and maybe the hardest is the 3rd, a 415 yd par 4 all up hill. The tee shot is to an area with trees on both sides, and the green is protected by traps right and left.

Woods Golf Center

559 West Germantown Pike, Norristown PA — (215)279-0678

Directions: Rte 202 to Germantown Pike (Old 422) West. The course is approx 2 mi.

Facility Type: Executive

Club Pro: John Lewis
Discounts: Seniors
Tee Times: No

Features: Lessons, Driving Range, Practice Area, Pro Shop - Complete, Clubhouse, Snack Bar

Description: These are an executive course and a "Chip & Putt". The "Chip & Putt" is open until 11 pm midseason. The facility has a complete driving range, as well.

Holes	Par	Yards Back Tees	Rating	Slope
9	27	549	—	—
18	56	3071	—	—

	9 Holes	18 Holes	Hours Mid Season
Weekday:	—	$5.00	Dawn - Dusk
Weekend:	—	$5.50	Dawn - Dusk
Cart Fees:	—	$10.00	

Mandatory Cart Rental: No
Club Rental: Yes

PA 4   **Monroe**

BUCK HILL GOLF CLUB
Golf Drive, Buck Hill Falls, PA
(717)595-7730

A picturesque 27 hole mountain course by
Donald Ross. Pro-shop. Carts. Club rentals.
Driving range. Restaurant and lounge. Golf
packages are available for groups.

You are invited to play a COMPLI-MENTARY 9 or 18 hole round of golf when accompanied with a fully paid round of equal value one time during the 1992 season.

Valid only before June 15 and after Labor Day, Mon thru Fri (except holidays) from 11:00 am to 5:00 pm.

Call ahead for tee times.

POWER CART RENTAL IS RE-QUIRED

❑ Validation

PLEASE READ VALIDATION RESTRICTIONS CAREFULLY.

PA 9   **Pike**

CLIFF PARK INN & GOLF COURSE
Milford, PA
(717)296-6491

Golf one of America's oldest courses
(established in 1913). Complete club house
facilities. Golfer's Grill and Mobil 3 Star
restauraunt for evening dining. Golf instruction.
Club rentals.

You are invited to play a COMPLI-MENTARY 9 or 18 hole round of golf when accompanied with a fully paid round of equal value one time during the 1992 season.

Valid Mon thru Fri (except holidays) only from 8:00 am to 7:00 pm.

Call ahead for tee times.

POWER CART RENTAL IS RE-QUIRED

❑ Validation

OFFER IS NOT VALID IF DETACHED FROM BOOK.

PA 10   **Phila**

COBBS CREEK GOLF COURSE
72nd St & Lansdowne Ave, Phila, PA
(215)877-8707

Front played around stream and trees, the back
lengthens greatly. #10 is a favorite, a par 4, 447
yards. Demanding long straight tee shot and
precise approach to a bunkered, elevated green

You are invited to play a COMPLI-MENTARY 9 or 18 hole round of golf when accompanied with a fully paid round of equal value one time during the 1992 season.

Valid Mon thru Fri (except holidays) from 1:00 pm to 9:00 pm and weekends and holidays after 3:00 pm

Call ahead for tee times.

POWER CART RENTAL IS RE-QUIRED

❑ Validation

You are invited to play a COMPLI-MENTARY 9 or 18 hole round of golf when accompanied with a fully paid round of equal value one time during the 1992 season.

Valid Mon thru Fri (except holidays) from open to close and weekends and holidays after 2:00 pm

Call ahead for tee times

POWER CART RENTAL IS RE-QUIRED

❑ Validation

PA 17   **Phila**

FRANKLIN D ROOSEVELT GC
20th & Patterson, Phila, PA
(215)462-8997

Broad St Exit off 95. 1 mile from Veterans Stadium.

OFFER IS NOT VALID IF DETACHED FROM BOOK.

You are invited to play a COMPLI-MENTARY 9 or 18 hole round of golf when accompanied with a fully paid round of equal value two times dur-ing the 1992 season.

Valid Mon thru Fri (except holidays) from 8:00 am to 6:00 pm and week-ends and holidays after 12:00 noon. Call ahead for tee times.

POWER CART RENTAL IS RE-QUIRED

❑ 1st Time Validation

❑ 2nd Time Validation

PA 20   **Monroe**

GLEN BROOK COUNTRY CLUB
Stroudsburg, PA
(717)421-3680

Colonial John Stroud House Restuarant and Bar - On the Fairway Guest Suites - Championship PGA 18 hole golf course - Pro shop - 80 golf carts.

COUPONS ARE NOT VALID FOR LEAGUE PLAY, SPECIAL EVENTS, OR OUTINGS.

This entitles you to a FREE POWER CART RENTAL with the purchase of two 18 hole green fees 2 times dur-ing the 1992 season.

Valid all day Mon thru Fri (except holidays) and weekends and holi-days after 12:00 noon.

Call ahead for assured tee times.

❑ 1st Time Validation

❑ 2nd Time Validation

PA 21   **Lehigh**

GOLF CLUB AT SHEPERD HILLS
1160 S Krocks Rd, Wescosville, PA
(215)391-0644

Your Public Country Club. Fully stocked pro shop. Group and club outings. PGA Pro, Mike Hersch.

PA 25   **Lehigh**

INDIAN CREEK GOLF COURSE
1449 Chestnut St., Emmaus
(215)965-8486

Enjoy our relaxed, family-oriented atmosphere. 9 holes of varying difficulty on elevated bent grass greens.

You are invited to play a COMPLIMENTARY 9 or 18 hole round of golf when accompanied with a fully paid round of equal value one time during the 1992 season.

Valid Mon thru Fri (except holidays) from 7:00 am to closing and on weekends and holidays after 3:00 pm.

Must call ahead for assured tee times.

❑ Validation

PLEASE READ VALIDATION RESTRICTIONS CAREFULLY.

PA 27   **Phila**

JOHN F. BYRNE GOLF COURSE
9500 Leon St, Phila, PA
(215)632-8666

Come enjoy playing this hilly and tree-lined course. It puts a premium on the solid tee game. A winding creek must be negotiated on 9 of the 18 holes.

You are invited to play a COMPLIMENTARY 9 or 18 hole round of golf when accompanied with a fully paid round of equal value one time during the 1992 season.

Valid Mon thru Fri (except holidays) from 11:00 am to 9:00 pm and weekends and holidays after 3:00 pm.

Call ahead for tee times

POWER CART RENTAL IS REQUIRED.

❑ Validation

OFFER IS NOT VALID IF DETACHED FROM BOOK.

PA 28   **Phila**

JUNIATA GOLF CLUB
M & Cayuga Streets, Phila, PA
(215)743-4060

Rte 1 to Castor Ave East to Cayuga Street. Take a right to the course.

You are invited to play a COMPLIMENTARY 9 or 18 hole round of golf when accompanied with a fully paid round of equal value one time during the 1992 season.

Valid Mon thru Fri (except holidays) from 11:00 am to 2:00 pm and weekends and holidays after 3:00 pm

Call ahead for tee times

POWER CART RENTAL IS REQUIRED

❑ Validation

You are invited to play a COMPLI-
MENTARY 9 or 18 hole round of golf
when accompanied with a fully paid
round of equal value one time during the 1992 season.

Valid Mon thru Fri (except holidays)
from 11:00 am to 9:00 pm and
weekends and holidays after 1:00
pm

Call ahead for tee times

POWER CART RENTAL IS RE-
QUIRED.

❑ Validation

PA 29   **Phila**

KARAKUNG GOLF COURSE
72nd & Lansdowne Ave, Phila, PA
(215)877-8707

Cut through the trees with well-guarded greens.
5 hole is a 421 yard par 4, out-of-bounds left
with long shot to a narrow and bunkered green
with a stream in front.

OFFER IS NOT VALID IF DETACHED FROM BOOK.

You are invited to play a COMPLI-
MENTARY 9 or 18 hole round of golf
when accompanied with a fully paid
round of equal value one time during the 1992 season.

Valid only from Sept. 15 to Dec 31
anytime Mon thru Fri (except holidays).

Call ahead for tee times

POWER CART RENTAL IS RE-
QUIRED

❑ Validation

PA 30   **Chester**

KIMBERTON GOLF CLUB
Kimberton. PA
(215)933-8836

COUPONS ARE NOT VALID FOR LEAGUE PLAY, SPECIAL EVENTS, OR OUTINGS.

You are invited to play a COMPLI-
MENTARY 9 or 18 hole round of golf
when accompanied with a fully paid
round of equal value two times during the 1992 season.

Valid anytime Mon thru Fri (except
holidays) only.

Call ahead for tee times

POWER CART RENTAL IS RE-
QUIRED

❑ 1st Time Validation

❑ 2nd Time Validation

PA 34   **Montgomery**

MACOBY RUN GOLF COURSE
McLean Station Rd, Green Lane PA
(215)541-0161

Scenic and unique new course open to the
public. Golf professional on staff. Wetlands
Restaurant & Bar serving breakfast and light fare.
A friendly family owned and operated course.

PA 36   **Bucks**

MIDDLETOWN COUNTRY CLUB

North Bellevue Ave, Langhorne, PA
(215)757-6953

Come enjoy the best-kept secret in Bucks
County. 18 holes of golf set in a scenic area.
Restaurant, snack bar, carts available.

You are invited to play a COMPLI-
MENTARY 9 or 18 hole round of golf
when accompanied with a fully paid
round of equal value one time during the 1992 season.

Valid Mon thru Fri (except holidays)
only from 12:00 pm to 3:00 pm

Must call ahead for tee times

**POWER CART RENTAL IS RE-
QUIRED**

❏ **Validation**

PLEASE READ VALIDATION RESTRICTIONS CAREFULLY.

PA 52   **Northampton**

SAWMILL GOLF COURSE

5630 Sullivan Trail, Easton, PA
(215)759-8200

At Sawmill, you'll not only enjoy 9 challenging
holes of golf, but also the quiet surroundings and
scenic view of the Blue Mountains.

You are invited to play a COMPLI-
MENTARY 9 or 18 hole round of golf
when accompanied with a fully paid
round of equal value one time during the 1992 season.

Valid Mon thru Fri (except holidays)
from 7 am to 7 pm.

Must call ahead for tee times

❏ **Validation**

OFFER IS NOT VALID IF DETACHED FROM BOOK.

PA 54   **Monroe**

SHAWNEE INN & COUNTRY CLUB

Shawnee-On-Delaware, PA
(717)421-1500

Golfing mecca in the Pocono Mountains. 27 hole
"Delaware River Island Course". Stay & Play
packages feature fine dining and free green fees.

You are invited to play a 9 or 18
hole round of golf for the special
price of $25, cart included, two
times during the 1992 season.

Valid anytime Mon thru Fri (except
holidays) only.

Call ahead for tee times

❏ **1st Time Validation**

❏ **2nd Time Validation**

PA 55　　　　　　　　　　　　　　　　**Montgomery**

SKIPPACK GOLF COURSE

Stump Hall & Cedar Rds, Skippack, PA
(215)584-4226

Enjoy an 18 hole championship and scenic golf course near historic Valley Forge Park. Driving range and snack bar available.

You are invited to play a COMPLIMENTARY 9 or 18 hole round of golf when accompanied with a fully paid round of equal value one time during the 1992 season.

Valid Mon thru Fri (except holidays) from 7:00 am to 4:00 pm and weekends and holidays after 2:00 pm

Call ahead for tee times

POWER CART RENTAL IS REQUIRED

❏ Validation

OFFER IS NOT VALID IF DETACHED FROM BOOK.

PA 59　　　　　　　　　　　　　　　　**Carbon**

SPLIT ROCK GOLF CLUB

Wolf Hollow Rd, Lake Harmony, PA
(717)722-9111

We invite you to play our challenging 9 holes set in the Pocono Mountains. Watered fairways and manicured greens. Golf course lots are available.

You are invited to play a COMPLIMENTARY 9 or 18 hole round of golf when accompanied with a fully paid round of equal value two times during the 1992 season.

Valid Mon thru Fri (except holidays) from 8:00 am to 6:00 pm and weekends and holidays after 1:00 pm Must call ahead for tee times

POWER CART RENTAL IS REQUIRED

❏ 1st Time Validation

❏ 2nd Time Validation

COUPONS ARE NOT VALID FOR LEAGUE PLAY, SPECIAL EVENTS, OR OUTINGS.

PA 64　　　　　　　　　　　　　　　　**Lehigh**

TUMBLEBROOK GOLF COURSE

3600 Jacoby Rd, Coopersburg, PA
(215)282-9021

Come enjoy 9 or 18 holes of challenging golf at Tumblebrook, home of the "Big 9"

You are invited to play a COMPLIMENTARY 9 or 18 hole round of golf when accompanied with a fully paid round of equal value one time during the 1992 season.

Valid anytime Mon thru Fri (except holidays) only from 7:00 am to 6:00 pm

Call ahead for tee times

POWER CART RENTAL IS REQUIRED

❏ Validation

PA 72   **Phila**

WALNUT LANE GOLF COURSE
800 Walnut Lane, Phila, PA
(215)482-3370

Philadelphia's sportiest little course - the course
where everybody learns to love the game of golf.

You are invited to play a COMPLI-
MENTARY 9 or 18 hole round of golf
when accompanied with a fully paid
round of equal value one time during the 1992 season.

Valid any day of the week after
12:00 noon.

Call ahead for tee times

POWER CART RENTAL IS RE-
QUIRED

❑ Validation

PLEASE READ VALIDATION RESTRICTIONS CAREFULLY.

PA 76   **Montgomery**

WESTOVER INN & GOLF CLUB
401 S Schuykill Ave, Norristown, PA
(215)539-4502

Enjoy 18 holes and the Westover Inn. Restaurant
open daily to the public for lunch and dinner.
Area's most flexible meeting and banquet facility.
Parties of 200 - 1400.

You are invited to play a COMPLI-
MENTARY 9 or 18 hole round of golf
when accompanied with a fully paid
round of equal value one time during the 1992 season.

Valid Mon thru Fri (except holidays)
from 7:00 am to 7:30 pm and weekends and holidays after 12:00 noon.

Call ahead for tee times

POWER CART RENTAL IS RE-
QUIRED

❑ Validation

OFFER IS NOT VALID IF DETACHED FROM BOOK.

You are entitled to a *FREE* subscription to the *GOLFERS ADVANTAGE* newsletter, a $7.95 value.

The **GOLFERS ADVANTAGE** newsletter is the perfect complement to your **New York Area Golf Guide**. It keeps you current with course updates, new course openings, notes of interest in the region, public course tournament schedules, new coupons, and other golf travel incentives.

Simply fill in your complete name and address, drop this card in the mail, and look forward to even greater benefits throughout the year.

Name _____

Address _____

City _____ **State** _____ **Zip** _____

We would like to know your handicap, if you have one _____

To order additional copies of the **New York Area Golf Guide**, send $12.95 + $1.50 for shipping and handling to **Powers Golf Guides**, P.O. Box 1961 NYC, NY 10011 or call 1-800-446-8884.

Stand-alone Driving Ranges

The following is a list of driving ranges not associated with a course, as well as some other facilities that offer hitting machines or related services. This is in addition to the majority of courses listed in this guide that do have driving ranges.

Connecticut

Tunxis Fore Driving Range   CT DR1
Location: On Rte 4, 1 mile West of the center of Farmington
Telephone: (203)674-8924
Weekday Hours: 9 am - 9:30 pm
Weekend Hours: 9 am - 9:30 pm
Notes: Open mid-April to mid-October

Prospect Golf Driving Range   CT DR2
Location: On Rte 69 and Hamilton Ave in Prospect
Telephone: (203)758-4121
Weekday Hours: 10 am - 10 pm
Weekend Hours: 10 am - 10 pm
Notes: Open March to the end of October

Pleasantview Golf   CT DR3
Location: On South Rd in Enfield
Telephone: (203)749-5868
Weekday Hours: 9 am - Dark
Weekend Hours: 9 am - 9 pm

Nippy's Field   CT DR4
Location: In Norwich on Rte 12, 3 miles East of I-395
Telephone: (203)886-0865
Weekday Hours: 8 am - 9 pm
Weekend Hours: 8 am - 9 pm
Notes: Open all year

Golf Country   CT DR5
Location: On Rte 80 in North Branford
Telephone: (203)484-2531
Weekday Hours: 10 am - 5:30 pm
Weekend Hours: 9 am - 5:30 pm
Notes: Open end of March to the end of October

CT Golf Center   CT DR6
Location: On Rte 7, 4 miles North of I-84
Telephone: (203)354-0012
Weekday Hours: 9 am - 10 pm
Weekend Hours: 8 am - 10 pm
Notes: Open all year

Mar-Lea Mini Golf   CT DR7
Location: Intersection of Rte 6 and Rte 44 in Bolton
Telephone: (203)649-7023
Weekday Hours: 9 am - 9 pm
Weekend Hours: 9 am - 9 pm
Notes: Open March thru October

Torza's Driving Range   CT DR8
Location: In South Windsor 1/4 mile East of Rte 5
Telephone: (203)289-2278
Weekday Hours: 9 am - 9 pm
Weekend Hours: 9 am - 9 pm
Notes: Open April to the end of October

Belmont's Ridgefield Golf Complex CT DR9
Location: 4 miles East of the Danbury Mall on Rte 7
Telephone: (203)431-8989
Weekday Hours: 9 am - 9 pm
Weekend Hours: 9 am - 9 pm
Notes: Facility is open every month but January. Pro shop.

Danbury Golf Center   CT DR10
Location: 94 Mill Plain Rd in Danbury
Telephone: (203)743-2190

Only Game In Town   CT DR11
Location: 275 Valley Svc Road in New Haven
Telephone: (203)239-9653

Hillside Golf Center   CT DR12
Location: East Hartford CT
Telephone: (203)528-6335

Highland DR   CT DR13
Location: On the corner of Welsh Rd and Rte 229 (West St) in Southington. the range is 1/4 from Pine Valley Golf Course (CT #51)

New Jersey

LT's Golf Center
NJ DR1

Location: Paterson Plank Rd and the Hackensack River near the Meadowlands complex.
Telephone: (201)818-0777
Weekday Hours: 7:30 am - 10 pm
Weekend Hours: 7:30 am - 11 pm
Notes: Open all year. Memberships. Lessons. Chipping and putting area.

Closter DR
NJ DR2

Location: Next to Closter Plaza on Piermont Rd
Telephone: (201)768-0990
Weekday Hours: 7:30 am - 11 pm
Weekend Hours: 7:30 am - 11 pm
Notes: Open all year. Outdoor. Heated booths.

Randolph Golf Center
NJ DR3

Location: 1 mile East of I-80 in Randolph
Telephone: (201)584-1504
Weekday Hours: 9 am - 10 pm
Notes: Open all year.

1srt Tee Indoor Golf Acadamy
NJ DR4

Location: 3/4 mi. North of Pascack Brook Gollf Course (NJ #80) on River Vale Road.
Telephone: (201)358-1660
Weekday Hours: 9 am - 12 am
Weekend Hours: 9 am - 12 am
Notes: Open all year. Lessons. Simulators. Video equipment. Pro shop. Custom Club work.

Golf World
NJ DR5

Location: Just off Rte 23 on Jackson Ave in Pompton Plains
Telephone: (201)831-1148
Weekday Hours: 10 am - 9 pm
Weekend Hours: 9 am - 11 pm
Notes: Heated booths, open all year.

Wayne Golf Center
NJ DR6

Location: On Hamburg Turnpike 2 Miles West of Rte 23.
Telephone: (201)694-7754
Weekday Hours: 9 am - 10 pm
Weekend Hours: 9 am - 10 pm
Notes: Open all year

Sporting Spirit
NJ DR7

Location: On Rte 23 in Stockholm
Telephone: (201)697-3110

Crescent Golf Range
NJ DR8

Location: In Union on Sprinfield Ave, 2 miles West of Rte 78
Telephone: (201)688-9767
Weekday Hours: 9 am - 10 pm
Weekend Hours: 9 am - 10 pm
Notes: Open all year. 60 booths, 37 are heated.

Golf Fanatic
NJ DR9

Location: 4 miles North of Rte 80 on Rte 23 in Pompton Plains
Telephone: (201)839-2930
Weekday Hours: 10 am - 10 pm
Weekend Hours: 10 am - 10 pm
Notes: Open March to November

Darlington
NJ DR10

Location: Campgaw Rd, 3 miles West of Rte 17. See directions for Darlington Golf Course (#25 in NJ)
Telephone: (201)818-0777
Weekday Hours: 6 am - 9 pm
Weekend Hours: 6 am - 9 pm
Notes: Open all year. 22 covered stations.

East Hanover Golf Center
NJ DR11

Location: Highway 10, 2 miles West of Rte 46
Telephone: (201)887-8288
Weekday Hours: 10 am - 10 pm
Weekend Hours: 10 am - 10 pm
Notes: Open all year.

Mount Freedom
NJ DR12

Location: On the Sussex Turnpike, 3 miles South of Rte 10.
Telephone: (201)895-9898
Weekday Hours: 10 am - 10 pm
Weekend Hours: 10 am - 11 pm
Notes: Open all year.

Rocking Ridge DR
NJ DR13

Location: On Rte 624 in Oxford, near Apple Mountain Golf Course (NJ #3).
Telephone: (908)453-3000

Raritan Golf Center
NJ DR14

Location: On Rte 206 in Raritan
Telephone: (908)725-1174
Weekday Hours: 10 am - 10 pm
Weekend Hours: 10 am - 10 pm
Notes: Open all year. Lessons. Complete pro shop.

Bound Brook Golf Range
NJ DR15

Location: On Rte 22, 3 mi. East of Rte 287 in Bridgewater
Telephone: (908)356-9844
Weekday Hours: 11 am - 9 pm
Weekend Hours: 11 am - 9 pm
Notes: 36 mat tees. 7 covered booths. Open all year.

Inman Golf Range
NJ DR17

Location: Inman Ave in Edison 4 miles from the Garden St Pkwy.
Telephone: (908)754-8999
Weekday Hours: 9 am - 11 pm
Weekend Hours: 8 am - 11 pm
Notes: Open all year. Heated booths.

Woodbridge DR
NJ DR18

Location: Rahway Ave in Avenel
Telephone: (908)750-2276
Weekday Hours: 10 am - 10 pm
Weekend Hours: 10 am - 10 pm
Notes: Open March 1 to Dec 15. $500 for a Hole-in-One. Every 7th bucket of balls free.

Lakewood Golf Range
NJ DR19

Location: In Lakewood, 1 mile East of Rte 9
Telephone: (908)364-2190
Weekday Hours: 9 am - 9 pm
Weekend Hours: 9 am - 10 pm
Notes: Open all year. Hours 10 am - 4 pm in the winter.

37 Golf Driving Range
NJ DR20

Location: In Lakehurst on Rte 37, 7 miles West of the Garden State Parkway
Telephone: (908)657-6879
Weekday Hours: 9 am - dusk
Weekend Hours: 12:30 - dusk
Notes: open end of march to the end of October.

Cooper River DR
NJ DR21

Location: Rte 130 South and Park Drive in Pennsauken
Telephone: (609)662-2716
Weekday Hours: 10 am - 7 pm
Weekend Hours: 10 am - 7 pm
Notes: Open all year.

Windsor Greens Golf Center
NJ DR22

Location: On Rte 571, 3 mi. West of Rte 130 in Cranbury
Telephone: (609)799-9854
Weekday Hours: 10 am - 10 pm
Weekend Hours: 10 am - 10 pm
Notes: Open all year. PGA approved. Lessons. Pro shop. Miniature golf.

West Long Branch DR
NJ DR23

Location: On Highway 36 off Exit 105 of the Grdn St Pkwy.
Telephone: (609)544-8787
Weekday Hours: 9 am - 10 pm
Weekend Hours: 8 am - 10 pm
Notes: Open March to the end of Nov.

Ginos DR
NJ DR24

Location: 670 Rte 45 in Mantua
Telephone: (609)468-1643

Ocean View DR
NJ DR25

Location: 145 South Shore Rd in Ocean View
Telephone: (609)624-192

Applegarth Golf Center
NJ DR26

Location: On Applegarth Rd in Cranbury
Telephone: (609)655-3311

Greens at Delran
NJ DR27

Location: In Delran 5 miles North of Rte 73
Telephone: (609)461-6444
Weekday Hours: 8 am - 11 pm
Weekend Hours: 8 am - 11 pm
Notes: Miniature golf. Open all year.

Walsh Golf Center
NJ DR28

Location: In Pennington on Rte 31, 5 miles North of I-95
Telephone: (609)737-2244
Weekday Hours: 10 am - 10 pm
Weekend Hours: 8 am - 10 pm
Notes: Open all year.

New York

Park Avenue Country Club
NY DR1

Location: 635 Ave of the Americas, NYC
Telephone: (212)366-1818
Weekday Hours: 8 am - 4 am
Weekend Hours: 8 am - 4 am
Notes: Restaurant. Golf simulators. Pro shop. Lessons. Seminars. Plans for major expansion.

Richard Metz Golf Studio
NY DR2

Location: 425 Madison Ave, NYC, 3rd Floor
Telephone: (212)759-6940
Weekday Hours: 10 am - 8 pm
Weekend Hours: 10 am - 5 pm
Notes: 4 cages. 3 used for lessons. Video lessons. Pro shop. Closed Sunday. Fridays 10 am - 7 pm.

Turtle Cove Golf Complex
NY DR3

Location: On City Island Rd in City Island
Telephone: (212)885-2646
Weekday Hours: 9 am - 8 pm
Weekend Hours: 8 am - 8 pm
Notes: Open all year. Miniature golf.

Alley Pond Golf Range
NY DR4

Location: 232-01 Northern Blvd in Douglaston, Queens
Telephone: (718)225-9178
Weekday Hours: 7 am - 12 am
Weekend Hours: 7 am - 12 am
Notes: Open all year.

Golf USA
NY DR5

Location: Glen Cove Rd and Voice Rd in Carle Place, LI
Telephone: (516)746-1033
Weekday Hours: 10 am - 8 pm
Weekend Hours: 10 am - 6 pm
Notes: Indoors. Open all year. $15 per 1/2 hour to hit.

Power Play Indoor Golf
NY DR6

Location: Exit 55 off the LIE and go North. 611 Old Willets Path in Hauppauge
Telephone: (516)348-7777
Weekday Hours: 10 am - 10 pm
Weekend Hours: 10 am - 7 pm
Notes: $5 per 1/2 hour. Simulators and nets. Lessons. Pro shop. Indoors. Open all year.

Southhampton Golf Range
NY DR7

Location: On the Montauk Highway in Southampton
Telephone: (516)283-2158
Weekday Hours: 8 am - 10 pm
Weekend Hours: 8 am - 10:30 pm
Notes: Open mid-April to Nov 1.

The Practice Tee
NY DR8

Location: On Rte 303, 3 miles South of the NY Thruway
Telephone: (914)358-5557
Weekday Hours: 8 am - 11 pm
Weekend Hours: 8 am - 11 pm
Notes: Open all year. Heated and covered tees.

Amapro Golf Range
NY DR9

Location: On Rte 52 West, off Exit 100 of Rte 17 in Liberty
Telephone: (914)292-9022
Weekday Hours: 10 am - 10 pm
Weekend Hours: 10 am - 10 pm
Notes: Outdoors. Open March thru October. 25 mat tees, 25 grass. 6 practice bunkers. Pro shop. Miniature golf.

Westchester Golf Range
NY DR10

Location: On Dobbs Ferry Rd West of Sprainbrook Parkway
Telephone: (914)592-6553
Weekday Hours: 8 am - 10 pm
Weekend Hours: 8 am - 10 pm
Notes: Open all year.

Pennsylvania

Golf Hollow
PA DR1

Location: West on Street Rd Exit off 95. 141 Street Rd in Southampton
Telephone: (215)357-6480
Weekday Hours: 9 am - 11 pm
Weekend Hours: 9 am - 11 pm
Notes: Open all year. Miniature Golf. 25 heated booths.

Longknockers DR
PA DR2

Location: In Fairmont Park 2 blocks from the Phila Zoo
Telephone: (215)236-6794
Notes: Open all year. featured in Sports Illustrated. 60 tees on grass.

Golf Sports Inc.
PA DR3

Location: On Rte 23, 2.5 West of Phoenixville
Telephone: (215)935-2201
Notes: Open all year. 120 spots on grass. Complete Pro shop. Clinics. Schools.

US Golf Sports Center
PA DR4

Location: On Rte 1, 3 m West of Rte 76
Telephone: (215)879-3536
Weekday Hours: 9 am - 11 pm
Weekend Hours: 9 am - 11 pm
Notes: Open all year. Complete Pro shop. 8 heated and covered booths.

Burholme Golf
PA DR5

Location: In North East Phila on Cottman Ave 2 mi. West of Roosevelt Blvd
Telephone: (215)742-2380
Weekday Hours: 9 am - 11 pm
Weekend Hours: 9 am - 11 pm
Notes: 50 tee stations. Miniature golf. Open March thru Thanksgiving.

Grand Slam USA
PA DR 6

Location: 2010 Bevin Rd in Allentown
Telephone: (215)965-4487

V - 7 Golf DR
PA DR7

Location: 5218 William Penn Highway in Easton
Telephone: (215)258-2710

Course Reference

Connecticut

New Jersey

New York

Pennsylvania